The Consumer Citizen

The Consumer Citizen

ETHAN PORTER

OXFORD
UNIVERSITY PRESS

OXFORD
UNIVERSITY PRESS

Oxford University Press is a department of the University of Oxford. It furthers
the University's objective of excellence in research, scholarship, and education
by publishing worldwide. Oxford is a registered trade mark of Oxford University
Press in the UK and certain other countries.

Published in the United States of America by Oxford University Press
198 Madison Avenue, New York, NY 10016, United States of America.

Library of Congress Cataloging-in-Publication Data
Names: Porter, Ethan, author.
Title: The consumer citizen / Ethan Porter.
Description: New York, NY : Oxford University Press, [2021] |
Includes bibliographical references and index. |
Identifiers: LCCN 2020025289 (print) | LCCN 2020025290 (ebook) |
ISBN 9780197526781 (hardback) | ISBN 9780197526798 (paperback) |
ISBN 9780197526811 (epub)
Subjects: LCSH: Consumer behavior—United States. |
Consumers—Political activity—United States.
Classification: LCC HF5415.33.U6 P67 2021 (print) |
LCC HF5415.33.U6 (ebook) | DDC 323/.0420973—dc23
LC record available at https://lccn.loc.gov/2020025289
LC ebook record available at https://lccn.loc.gov/2020025290

DOI: 10.1093/oso/9780197526781.001.0001

Hardback printed by Bridgeport National Bindery, Inc., United States of America

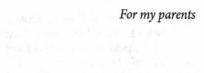

For my parents

I do have a test today, that wasn't bullshit. It's on European socialism.
I mean, really, what's the point? I'm not European. I don't plan on being
European. So who gives a crap if they're socialists? They could be fascist
anarchists, it still doesn't change the fact that I don't own a car.
                                    —*Ferris Bueller's Day Off* (1986)

Men being taken as they are and laws as they might be . . .
                                    —Jean Jacques Rousseau (1762)

CONTENTS

ACKNOWLEDGMENTS

This book would not exist were it not for the wisdom of John Mark Hansen. In endless office meetings, he guided and challenged me, with more patience and thoughtfulness than I deserved. The rest of my dissertation committee was similarly generous. William Howell, Betsy Sinclair, and Eric Oliver were always willing to share their expertise. From afar, Don Green has been an extraordinary mentor and friend. At Chicago, I benefited greatly from John Brehm, Patchen Markell, John McCormick, Sankar Muthu, Martha Nussbaum, Maggie Penn, Jennifer Pitts, Dan Slater, and Richard Thaler. I've been humbled to learn from each of them. My old colleagues at *Democracy Journal*, Kenneth Baer, Andrei Cherny, Clay Risen, and Michael Tomasky, were especially helpful in thinking through the earliest parts of this book.

I am so thankful to the coauthors of various projects discussed. Lucy Barnes, Ryan Buell, Avi Feller, Jake Haselswerdt, Daniel Hemel, and Michael Norton have been sources of inspiration. So too have Don Kinder, Jonathan Ladd, Gabe Lenz, and Liliana Mason, all of whom attended a workshop at George Washington University (GWU) about my book. My GWU colleagues, Sean Aday, Catie Bailard, Robert Entman, Kim Gross, Danny Hayes, Matt Hindman, Dave Karpf, Steve Livingston, Frank Sesno, John Sides, Rebekah Tromble, Chris Warshaw, and Will Youmans, have been inspiring and insightful.

Friends far and wide have also contributed, likely in ways they were not even aware of. Charles Blumenthal, Frank Chi, Alex Coppock, Adam Dean, Elana Dean, Rob Dieringer, Brian Feinstein, Yonah Freemark, Alfredo Gonzalez, Josh Handelman, Allison Harris, Alex Hertel-Fernandez, Morgan Kaplan, Josh Keating, Aaron Keyak, Steven Klein, Allen Linton, Emma Mackinnon, Daniel Nichanian, Dave Szakonyi, Ben Weyl, Vanessa Williamson, and Thomas J. Wood have all made this a much better book. I am also grateful for the support of the National Science Foundation, the Omidyar Network, GWU, and the University of Chicago, which funded many of the studies presented here. Seminars at GWU,

Yale, and the University of Chicago were tremendously helpful. The editors of *Journal of Politics* and *Behavioural Public Policy*, which published early versions of some of this work, deserve thanks too. The anonymous reviewers of this manuscript were excellent, and David McBride, my editor, has been a delight.

My family is the bedrock of my life. I am so lucky to have had so many loving grandparents, aunts, uncles, cousins, and now in-laws. Gideon and Seth Porter have been the best brothers anyone could ask for. I pinch myself every day that I was lucky enough to marry Ronit Zemel. She's the love of my life (and a great editor, too). My parents have always nurtured my curiosities and passions. I love them very much. I dedicate this book to them.

Introduction

In March of 2018, a man from Oklahoma was asked to explain why he supported the teachers' strikes then roiling across his state. The teachers were striking for better pay, increased education funding, and higher taxes. This man identified as a conservative, making his support for the strikes surprising. But as he put it, "You have to pay for nice things." Pointing to his S.U.V., he said he "could have had a cheaper car, but that wouldn't have been as good" (Galchen 2018).

In one sentence, he transformed a debate about government into a commonplace observation about consumer goods. The impulse behind it was not unique to this man. Some seventeen years earlier, President George W. Bush introduced his tax-cut proposal by describing Americans as "overcharged." While campaigning for the bill, Bush proclaimed, "The growing surplus exists because taxes are too high and government is charging more than it needs." And after signing the bill into law, he declared, "I told the American people that our federal government was overcharging them . . . and on your behalf I demanded a refund."[1]

From the Oklahoman, we see a policy position explained by reference to an expensive consumer good. From the forty-third president, we see the government rendered as if it were an ordinary firm, guilty of soaking its customers. An SUV helped the Oklahoman to become an unexpected supporter of tax increases. In describing his tax cuts, President Bush used language that, to an everyday consumer, would sound like simple common sense. What unifies both claims is their appeal to consumer thinking. The Oklahoma man supported tax increases because his experiences as a consumer taught him that quality and cost are intertwined. President Bush, meanwhile, described his tax cuts as repairing an overcharge, a basic breach of consumer norms.

When we think of the consumer's role in American politics, we tend to think of the height of conflict: the dumping of tea into Boston Harbor, the civil rights activists who braved segregated lunch counters. The relationship between the consumer and politics can be traced back even further, to the nation's inception.

The Consumer Citizen. Ethan Porter, Oxford University Press (2021). © Oxford University Press.
DOI: 10.1093/oso/9780197526781.003.0001.

American revolutionaries virtually invented the commercial boycott, refraining from purchasing a wide variety of British goods. A British military leader of the time expressed bewilderment upon encountering the practice: "I never heard of a people, who by general agreement, and without sumptuary laws to force them, that ever denied themselves what their circumstances would afford, and custom and habit prompted them to desire" (Breen 2005, p. xvi).

Yet such moments of grand historic significance are rare. Everyday consumer experiences, however—the minutia of buying, thinking about buying, and being asked to buy—are a constant of our lives. Their ordinariness does not preclude these experiences from having political consequences. On the contrary, their very status as commonplace activities grants them influence on our politics. What we do when we buy things, and how we think about what we buy, is tied up with our political thoughts and behaviors.

To the man in Oklahoma, and to President Bush, basic principles were at stake. Just as the price of a consumer good fluctuates with the perceived value of the good, so too should taxes change with the perceived quality of government. If we want better government, we must tolerate more taxes; but if we have paid more in taxes than we should have, we are entitled to a refund, just like a customer who accidentally paid too much. If we are shopping for groceries, after we pay the cashier, we expect to leave the store with our groceries in hand, and a receipt attesting to our purchase. Similarly, if we are buying a car, we know that higher prices will probably lead to a better-performing vehicle. We have paid for something, and we expect to receive what we paid for in return. We might call this principle, "You get what you pay for," and we mean it quite literally. And if we do not receive what we have paid for, we are angered, and perhaps expect to get our money back.

We learn these lessons far afield from politics, as ordinary purchasers of goods for ourselves and our families. Yet they bleed into our politics, affecting how Americans view politics, policy, and even the government itself. A substantial number of Americans judge government and its services by the standards of a commercial firm. On a nationally representative survey conducted in 2018, about 37% of Americans agreed with the proposition that government "should be run like a business." Of course, government is *not* a business—from far it—but this does not preclude Americans from viewing it like one.

Appeals to consumer decision-making, after all, are ubiquitous. They announce their presence to us loudly during the Super Bowl, and discretely, when we are staring at a menu and deciding what to order for lunch. Americans are asked to buy, and asked to consider to buy, goods of nearly all sizes and all prices, nearly all of the time. Appeals to political decision-making, meanwhile, are much less common. A pollster may call with a survey; a colleague may suggest that we donate to a political campaign; our government periodically asks us to vote. Still, compared to consumer decisions, political decisions rarely intrude on everyday life. For most people, most of the time, politics is a faint echo at best. Consumer decisions, however, are all around us. About 70% of the US gross domestic product (GDP) comes from consumer spending, a figure that dwarfs that of many other prosperous nations (Emmons 2012; US Bureau of Economic Analysis 2020).

But macroeconomic data does not come close to capturing the extent to which consumer decisions have burrowed themselves into our everyday lives. Consider several recent initiatives of Amazon.com. In 2015, the company introduced Dash Buttons, a system for ordering goods through Amazon. Dash depended on users placing branded buttons throughout their homes. There were buttons for products as disparate as Jack Daniels whiskey and Tide detergent. The buttons were meant to be connected to the Internet and placed in strategic locations throughout the home. The Tide button could be placed in the laundry room, the Jack Daniels button in the liquor cabinet. A user who ran out of the good in question could simply press a button. An order would then be transmitted to Amazon, which would refill the supply of the good.

While Dash buttons have been phased out, they marked only the beginning of Amazon's gradual intrusion into Americans' homes. Of late, the company has found success with its "virtual assistant," Echo. Users place their Echo anywhere in their houses, and then issue a variety of voice commands. Echo can play music; Echo can dim the lights. But from Amazon's perspective, the most important feature may be its ability to facilitate orders directly from users back to Amazon. If you notice you're out of detergent, you don't even need to press a button: you can just tell Echo to order some for you. And you don't even need to be home when the goods arrive. Amazon now offers a program, Amazon Key, through which customers can virtually allow company representatives into their homes to drop off packages when they're away. Reports indicate that Amazon will eventually unveil a domestic robot that will follow users around their houses, obediently taking product orders (Gurman and Stone 2018). All of these initiatives, undertaken by one of the world's largest retailers, effectively turn consumer decisions into a kind of home decoration, as familiar as—and perhaps even part of—the furniture.

On the unusual occasions when they are asked to evaluate some aspect of politics or government, citizens may apply the techniques with which they much more frequently evaluate everyday consumer goods. On such occasions, government and politics can become intermingled with consumer goods, so that the former are viewed in terms similar to the latter. Spending much of their time as consumers, citizens squint and convert government into an ordinary firm, politicians into providers of consumer goods, taxes into costs, and government services into benefits.

The paucity of political decisions, and the ubiquity of consumer ones, can lead people to think about politics as if they were still thinking about consumer goods. Indeed, the ways in which they think about consumer goods comes to shape how they think about government, politicians, taxes, and government benefits. The citizen is not just a citizen, but a consumer citizen. Viewing citizens as *consumer* citizens helps make sense of an outstanding political puzzle: How do most people make sense of the political world?

In part, the answer depends on the extent to which everyday people rely on their consumer experiences when they make political decisions. Reliance on such experiences, it turns out, can lead to disappointment. Government usually does not abide by the "You get what you pay for" principle. Government typically extracts money without making clear what is being provided in return. Broadly, government is not designed to accommodate consumer expectations.

Moreover, government doesn't always work like a firm. Often, it hardly resembles even a half-well-functioning one. Some people then come to distrust it, and disengage from it. They don't think they are receiving government benefits that are as valuable as the taxes they are paying, and so they want to pay less. When a company treats a consumer badly, the consumer punishes the company; when government fails to behave as a well-functioning and fair company would, citizens punish the government with the means at their disposal, such as distrusting government, advocating for lower taxes and reduced government spending, and supporting politicians who do the same. All that having been said, reliance on consumer techniques does not *always* lead people toward anti-government outcomes. As I show in later chapters, the use of such techniques can lead people to sign up for health insurance, and such techniques can be leveraged to increase trust in government.

While it may be tempting to believe that, on political matters, citizens set aside the small things that otherwise occupy them and always make thoughtful political decisions, a voluminous literature suggests otherwise (e.g., Converse 1964; Delli Carpini and Keeter 1997; Achen and Bartels 2016). It may be further tempting to decry the encroachment of market-based norms into the political realm, and set sharp boundaries between politics and the market (e.g., Satz 2008; Sandel 2012). Politics, as theorized from Aristotle onward, should be about issues of public concern. The consumer, in contrast, is the consummate private actor. He should be banished from the political world, the world of the public. However well-intentioned, such concerns miss the present empirical reality: the citizen has already become a consumer citizen. To speak of the consumer citizen is to speak of people as they are, not as we might wish them to be.

Robert Dahl (1961) described *Homo Politicus* as the political outgrowth of the apolitical *Homo Civicus*. This book investigates another species: *Homo Emptor*. *Homo Emptor* is neither apolitical nor an Aristotelian political animal. "Political man," Dahl wrote (1961, p. 225), "unlike civic man, deliberately allocates a very sizable share of his resources to the process of gaining and maintaining control over the policies of government." In contrast, *Homo Emptor* devotes a "very sizable share" of his resources, both cognitive and pecuniary, to his consumer life. *Homo Emptor* is, first, a potential buyer of everyday consumer goods, confronted ceaselessly with overtures from private firms peddling their wares, and reacting just as ceaselessly. Norms that guide *Homo Emptor*'s decision-making as a consumer come to be used in the political realm. Politics, for *Homo Emptor*, is at best a secondary domain. His world beckons him to the mall, grocery store, and Internet far more frequently than it does to the voting booth. And when confronted with political decisions, the more familiar consumer environment has left an impression that does not easily wash away.

The recognition of *Homo Emptor* should not be understood as yet another indictment of the American voter. In some cases, *Homo Emptor*'s reliance on what he has learned as a consumer may lead him to make decisions which serve his interests and those of his community. In other cases, this will be less true. I offer evidence of both. As has been pointed out (e.g., Gigerenzer and Todd 2000), not all shortcuts are bad for those who use them. The same is true for reliance on the consumer shortcuts studied here. Rather than castigating citizens for democratic incompetence, this book identifies the consumer realm as an unexpected source of political behavior, and then traces the consequences, for both good and ill.

Perhaps this source should not be as unexpected as it first might seem. As historian Lizabeth Cohen has put it, over the twentieth century "the market relationship" became "the template for the citizen's relationship to government" (Cohen 2003). Today, the number of consumer decisions that a citizen faces, whether measured over a year, a day, or a week, easily surpasses the number of political decisions she faces. The commitment to mass consumption that followed World War II endures from the shopping mall to the voting booth to Amazon.com, and much of the cognitive space in between, with surprising effects on our politics.

The Psychology of the Consumer Citizen

At least since Thorstein Veblen (1899 [1999]) explained how consumer goods can be used as signals of social status, scholars have known that consumer goods are not *just* consumer goods. They convey meanings independent of their use and they leave traces on the social world (Trentman 2016). In political science, however, the consumer has mostly been relegated to the status of metaphor, with the supposition being that we can understand citizens' political decisions better if we think of citizens *as if they were* consumers, or some variation thereof (e.g., Tiebout 1956; MacKuen, Erikson, and Stimson 1992, 2001; Tomz and Sniderman 2005; Grynaviski 2010). Alternatively, consumer behavior has been viewed as wrapped up in political choices, with people shifting their purchasing patterns to correspond with their political views (e.g., Endres and Panagopoulos 2017; Gerber and Huber 2009). In such studies, politics precede consumer decisions. But people *already are* consumers. While political scientists have assumed that politics is the independent variable affecting consumer behavior, the opposite may also be true.

Previous research has shown that consumer decision-making can have profound effects on everyday life. Sendhil Mullanaithan and Eldar Shafir (2013) have written of the ways in which the mere exposure to consumer decision-making can arrest some subjects' capacity for cognition. Across multiple studies, they show that reminding less-well-off subjects about the pressures of consumer life—the bills they owe, the limited funds in their bank account—reduces one's cognitive "bandwidth." Stressful consumer decisions have deleterious psychological effects on the poor in particular, they argue.[2]

Citizens bombarded by appeals to their consumer decision-making will become accustomed to using their consumer decision-making apparatus. When politics contains cues familiar to people from the consumer environment, some people will fall back on those strategies that they are familiar with from the consumer world. Evaluations of many objects often proceed based on rules learned from prior experience (Chaiken 1980; Eagly and Chaiken 1984). Many people learn to evaluate objects in the consumer environment—and then they bring what they have learned into politics.

This claim—that people make decisions about politics in ways initially developed for consumer decisions—is likely to disappoint some readers. Surely, citizens take politics more seriously than that. They understand that forming an attitude about a policy or politician has no relationship to the way in which we form attitudes about consumer goods. People are politically engaged enough, and politically sophisticated enough, to realize that politics is distinct from the countless consumer decisions they make every day.

As a rich literature attests, however, many citizens are disengaged from politics, knowing little about the political system, public policy, and the politicians who ostensibly represent them (e.g., Converse 1964; Achen and Bartels 2016). Though political scientists may spend significant time thinking about politics, and a select group of people may spend an inordinate amount of time debating and deliberating over political matters, most citizens do not. And though philosophical definitions of citizenship may obligate citizens qua citizens to constantly engage with the political world, most people hardly engage at all.

Yet even though citizens may not be what democratic theorists want them to be, they nonetheless have ample tools at their disposal to think about politics. Partisan affiliation offers one such shortcut, having near-religious sway over its adherents and pointing the way on complicated policy matters (e.g., Green, Palmquist and Shickler 2002). Social identities, such as race and religion, can also do the trick, simplifying the messy complications of politics into a more digestible form (Achen and Bartels 2016). Generally, these approaches can be thought of as heuristic strategies, whereby citizens are relying on simple decision rules to make otherwise complex decisions while exerting as little effort as possible.[3] As I show, at least one heuristic that some people use when making political decisions—the *alignability heuristic*—can be located in the consumer realm, with implications for vote choice, social policy uptake, and attitudes toward taxation.

Heuristic strategies stem from the finite resources of the human mind. We are not cognitively equipped to systematically evaluate the sheer amount of information before us (e.g., Chaiken 1980; Taber and Lodge 2013). Druckman and Lupia (2000) write that political preferences arise when citizens "convert information from their environment into evaluations of political objects." But environments change. Some environments are frequented more than others. Most environments are not political at all. One popular model of attitude formation proposes that people make evaluations by summing a set of beliefs about the object in question while attaching different weights to different attributes (e.g., Druckman and Chong 2007).

The argument of this book is premised on the notion that, when asked to evaluate an unfamiliar object, individuals may rely on evaluative techniques developed elsewhere—techniques with which they are more familiar. More precisely, the decision-making tools that citizens rely on in one environment can come to shape their evaluations in another. Citizens learn how to make decisions as consumers, and they take what they have learned and apply it to political decisions. The tools from the consumer environment migrate to the political environment.

Think here of how habits, learned over years with great repetition, ingrain themselves into our lives, affecting our behavior automatically, even in moments when we least expect them (Neal, Wood, and Quinn 2006). Indeed, consumer life is replete with repetitive behaviors that, over time, become habit (Wood and Neal 2009). A story relayed by William James suggests how repeated behavior in one context can come to shape behaviors elsewhere. The story goes that, upon seeing a military veteran walking while carrying food, a "practical joker" yelled, "Attention!" The veteran promptly brought his hands down and dropped his food. Not on any battlefield, the veteran was nonetheless obeying the command that had been issued to him (James 1892 [1985]). A citizen asked to make a political decision is somewhat similar to the soldier, affected in one domain by what he learned in a very different one.[4]

Crucially, this argument does not obviate the utility of other kinds of informational shortcuts. Party affiliation, social identity, and the vast array of other heuristics that scholars have identified as playing a role in the political world have their place. They may stand alongside, or overlap with, the strategies that people take from the consumer world.[5] Sometimes people rely on the consumer world to convey other shortcuts on which they rely. Consider, for example, "racialized economics," which, according to Sides, Tesler, and Vavreck (2018), helps explain support for Donald Trump in the 2016 presidential election. "Racialized economics," the authors wrote, amounted to anxieties about how nonwhite or immigrant groups were undeservedly prospering and benefiting from government programs.

At least in some instances, such anxieties have been expressed in consumer terms. As one white American put it, African Americans were using government programs to buy "gold chains and a Cadillac when I can barely afford a Cavalier" (Gest 2016, p. 95; as quoted in Sides, Tesler, and Vavreck 2018, p. 175). Once again, an everyday person makes reference to an ordinary good to express a political point. Here, unlike the Oklahoman we met earlier, the point is racialized. But the consumer elements of the argument are similar—suggestive of the broad reach that consumer thinking enjoys in American politics.

Consumer experiences come to shape politics for at least three reasons. The first reason is the comparative ubiquity of consumer decisions. We spend far more time, and devote far more cognitive resources, to thinking about consumer choices than we do political ones. Private firms make many more appeals for our support than do political campaigns or parties. Most people spend far more time thinking about, say, how much they're willing to spend on a pair of jeans than what they want tax policy to look like. As has been known at least since Walter Lippmann (1922 [1997]), the amount of time people spend, or don't spend, thinking about politics matters. And as we shall soon see, Americans spend far less time on politics.

The second reason is the surface-level structural similarity of consumer and political decisions. As a consumer, you are often tasked with choosing between discrete items on a menu—do I want to order this item or that one?—just as you are tasked with choosing between candidates, parties, or policies. As a consumer, you are frequently asked to consider the costs and benefits of a particular good. The terms may be different, with costs rendered as taxes and government services rendered as benefits, but politicians often ask us to do the same.[6]

A third and final reason for the influence of the consumer world on politics has to do with the rhetoric of political elites. A long-standing finding in political science holds that, when forming their views, citizens take cues from their co-partisan leaders (e.g., Zaller 1992; Lenz 2012). Political leaders have been unafraid to speak in consumer terms. President George W. Bush sold his tax cuts using consumer language. When the man mentioned earlier castigated African American welfare recipients for buying expensive material goods, he was echoing claims made years before by Ronald Reagan about supposed "welfare queens" who, yes, also drove Cadillacs (Lybarger 2019). Using consumer language when making political claims is not new.

Nor has it been the exclusive provenance of one party. Consider, for example, the Clinton administration's "Reinventing Government" initiative, which sought to provide a new "customer service contract with the American people." The intention was to make government provide services more efficiently, along the lines of the private sector. The initial report of the Clinton administration's initiative, while conceding some inherent differences between government and the private sector, was clear: The federal government needed to treat citizens like customers, and do so in a way that would satisfy private-sector standards. The government must "put customers first," and do so by "injecting the dynamics of the marketplace" (Gore 1993). A similar approach was taken by President Barack Obama, as he described the Affordable Care Act (Obama 2009). When political leaders speak, people—particularly co-partisans—listen. Both parties have long spoken in consumer terms. And the people have listened.

Does the influence of consumer lessons on political behavior help or harm ordinary people? This question echoes a long debate about the virtues of political heuristics, and whether, in the aggregate, they lead to more or less competent voters. (For a review, consult Kuklinski and Quirk [2000]). If consumer citizens are appealed to *as consumer citizens*, their attitudes and behaviors about a wide range of political subjects can change. They can become more trusting of government spending, they can be more likely to sign up for social programs, they can increase their store of political knowledge, and they can trust their government overall much more. But it cuts both ways. The power of consumer thinking can also lead people to prefer candidates who, quite explicitly, make promises against their own interests, and to deepen their animus toward Congress. Ultimately, the answer to this question depends on to what end people use those lessons.

There are two intertwined concepts, previously explored in the behavioral economics and management literatures, that are especially useful for understanding how consumer thinking can manifest itself in political thinking. The first comes under the umbrella of *consumer fairness*. Consumers, it has been found, are attentive to the perceived fairness of a transaction; they will reward vendors who offer them fair deals, and penalize those who do not. They are sensitive to the extent to which fluctuations in the change of a price of a good *align* with the change of a cost. Citizens respond more favorably to price increases when they believe that such increases reflect cost increases borne by the firm (Bolton and Alba 2006).

In short, consumers want the price of a good to align with the costs borne by a firm. This does not mean they oppose firms profiting; indeed, within reason, they are content with firms profiting. Yet when a price increase is not owed to a cost increase—for example, when a hardware store hikes the prices of shovels during a snowstorm—they regard the increase as unfair, and voice their objection. And they do the same when they believe the firm is using a price increase to cross-subsidize some other part of its business—that is, to support an unrelated line of products (Kahneman, Knetsch, and Thaler 1986a).

There is no clear analogue for price in politics. But there are costs and benefits. In the form of taxes, citizens pay political costs—and in the form of government services, politics offers some benefits. These analogies, however imperfect, can help us understand attitudes toward taxes and government spending. As I show, it turns out that some citizens want the costs of government to *align* with the value of services that government provides. Contrary to the canonical take on the public's attitudes toward taxes and government spending (Sears and Citrin 1985), citizens do not crave "something for nothing."

As consumers, people are content to pay for goods, and even for firms to profit when they do. So too are consumer citizens content to pay taxes, *provided they receive some government services in return*. Political scientists often describe citizens as believing there is a trade-off between government spending and taxation: with lower taxes come less government spending, and vice versa.[7] Alignability suggests otherwise. For consumer citizens, the trade-off is not a trade-off at all. Indeed, the inclusion of both government costs and benefits— taxes and government services—can serve as a prerequisite for the former to garner favor.

The second concept, related but distinct, is *operational transparency*. There are, of course, countless advocates of government transparency, and many efforts are ongoing to make government more transparent. These efforts, however, often amount to little more than public data dumps. One assumption of such efforts is that transparency will always elicit positive responses. *Operational transparency* proposes a more nuanced view. Consumers, it has been shown, react positively when they see—when they have visual evidence of—the efforts undertaken on their behalf. They want to see what firms have done for them.

Unfortunately, many governmental efforts at transparency lack this quality. Instead, they provide all available information to all citizens. For example, as of this writing, visitors to the city of Chicago's "data portal" are greeted with a blizzard of options, covering topics ranging from "administrative and finance" to "sanitation" to "historic preservation." Evidently, connecting visitors to specific services they are using, especially those they can *see* as they are being used, is not a priority. *Operational transparency* argues that it should be. The efforts that government undertakes on citizens' behalf should be highlighted—those are what should be made transparent. Recent evidence indicates that, for the most part, citizens are unaware of the services that government provides them. Even beneficiaries of government services have trouble "tracing" those benefits back to government (Arnold 1990; Mettler 2011). Yet naively revealing "the submerged state," by making *all* of government transparent all at once, is unlikely to have much of an effect. Instead, what matters is that the operations of government, including and especially those that pertain to citizens, be made more transparent. As this book shows, doing so can have dramatic effects on people's trust in government.

The ubiquity of consumer decisions, and the consumer-tinged rhetoric of elites, paves the way for consumer thinking to barge into political decisions. Like an uninvited guest dominating a dinner conversation, or a military veteran who still obeys commands long after the battle has ended, *Homo Emptor* can shape politics when and where we least expect it.[8]

The Ubiquity of Consumer Decisions

An old joke, most recently popularized by David Foster Wallace (2009), goes like this:

> There are these two young fish swimming along, and they happen to meet an older fish swimming the other way, who nods at them and says, "Morning, boys, how's the water?" And the two young fish swim on for a bit, and then eventually one of them looks over at the other and goes, "What the hell is water?"

We are so immersed in a world of consumer appeals that we hardly notice them. Consider the following. At the end of 2016, Amazon Prime, the paid-membership program that Amazon offers for free shipping, counted more than 65 million active members (Gustafson 2017). That is, more than 65 million people were paying Amazon more than $100 annually for free shipping and media content. In that same period, about 63 million people voted for Donald Trump, the man who became president. The popularity of the American president or at least the number of Americans who voted for him, is exceeded by the popularity of a subscription program to the nation's largest retailer.

In any given year, an individual will be confronted with far more consumer decisions than political ones. This not only appears intuitively true—the number of times one enters a store to shop surely exceeds the number of times one enters a voting booth—but is supported by available empirical evidence. The contrast between the Consumer Expenditure Survey (CES) and the American National Election Study (ANES) is revealing in this regard. Sponsored by the Bureau of Labor Statistics, the CES is meant to measure the consumer behavior of Americans. In 2012, the average subject reported making about 152 purchases over the course of the year. Meanwhile, ANES data from the same year—a presidential election year no less, when political engagement is presumably at a high-water mark—paint a portrait of an electorate that makes far fewer political decisions than consumer decisions. Only 11% of respondents report donating to a particular candidate's campaign; only 38% report talking to others, informally, about supporting or opposing a candidate or party; less than 6% report going to a political rally, meeting, or speech. When the time horizon is expanded, the picture does not change. When asked about the previous four years, the vast majority of subjects said they had not signed a petition; not given money to a nonreligious organization, such as a civic or political one; and not attended a public meeting of their local government (American National Election Study 2012).

To investigate the disparities between the number of consumer and political decisions, several years ago I conducted a short survey over the Internet. At random, I asked about 250 voting-age Americans about the frequency of their political decisions, while another 250 were asked about the frequency of their consumer decisions. To determine what counted as consumer and political decisions, I relied on the American National Election Study and the Consumer Price Index. Those people asked about the frequency of their political decisions were presented with the types of activities that the ANES records as participation, and then asked to identify how many of those activities they had engaged in over the previous week. Over that time period, had they urged others to support a particular candidate? Had they donated to a political party? Likewise, those people asked about the frequency of their consumer decisions were presented with the types of consumer spending categories that the Bureau of Labor Statistics uses to compile the Consumer Price Index. Over the past week, had they bought food or beverages? What about educational payments or car payments? To make for an even number of consumer and political decisions, several political questions were original and not from the ANES. (For the full list of questions, consult the appendix subsection "Consumer Vs. Political Decisions Survey Questions.")

Not coincidentally, I fielded the survey on Monday, November 10, 2014—one week after the midterm elections. The survey asked about decisions made over the past week, inclusive of the election. Given the likely high level of political activity over this time period, the survey was meant to be an aggressive test of my claim.

The results were unambiguous. People who were asked about their political decisions reported making fewer than one such decision over the previous week. More specifically, the people asked about their political decisions reported making, on average, .87 political decisions. By contrast, the people quizzed about their consumer decisions reported making, on average, 3.05 such decisions over the same time period. In one of the most politically active weeks of the calendar, when we think of America as abuzz with argument and activism, the number of consumer decisions outpaced the number of political decisions by more than a three-to-one ratio.

This is also true for the broader category of civic life. Consider the Time Use Surveys of Americans, studied so profitably by Robert Putnam in *Bowling Alone* (2000). As Putnam observes, the amount of time Americans devote to civic life is vanishingly small. Yet left unexamined by Putnam is the contrast in the amount of time people devote to civic life and the amount they devote to consumer life. In 2016, the American Time Use Survey found that, on average, Americans spend .32 hours a day, or slightly more than twenty minutes, on anything that could be classified as "organizational, civic and religious activity." Over that same period, they spent twice as much time every day on average purchasing goods or services. On weekends, the average amount of time spent purchasing consumer goods rises to 1.87 hours a day. Meanwhile, when religious and spiritual activities are excluded—leaving us only with only civic and organizational activities—the average American spent only about .22 hours each weekend day on civic or organizational activities. In other words, over the weekends, during which they can enjoy the bulk of their free time, Americans spend almost *nine times* the amount of time on consumer activities as civic ones.

Figure 1.1 displays how many hours each day, on average, Americans reported spending on consumer behavior, as well as how much time they reported spending on "organizational, civic and religious activity," between the years 2003 and 2017. Here, I've collapsed the smaller categories and presented data from all the years that the Bureau of Labor Statistics makes available. There are, of course, always limitations to self-reported data. But the data that is self-reported presents an unmistakable pattern. On the weekdays, the difference between consumer and civic behavior has long been enormous, with people spending far more time on the former than the latter. While the difference diminishes on the weekends, it has remained steadily large. The discrepancy almost certainly extends beyond this time series. "Private life in democracy is sometimes so busy, so excited, so full of wishes and of work, that hardly any energy or leisure remains to each individual for public life," observed Alexis de Tocqueville, nearly two centuries ago (Tocqueville 1835 [2001], p. 293).

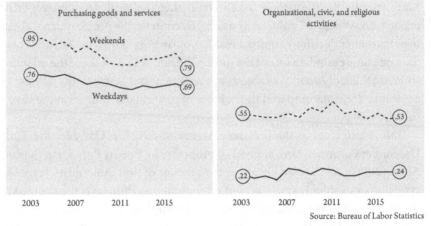

Americans' Time Use, Consumer and Political Behavior (2003–2017)

Figure 1.1 Time use on consumer and civic behavior.

Figure 1.2 shows all categories. As should be clear, these categories are incredibly broad, encompassing all kinds of activities beyond those we could credibly describe as political. Even with these broad categories, however, time devoted to consumer decisions occupies large chunks of many Americans' days.

It would be easy to ascend a soapbox at this point and decry the discrepancy. "Americans should spend more time on politics and less time shopping!" And perhaps they should. Or perhaps the differing amounts are well justified. Should citizens be obligated to spend more of their free time dwelling on the demanding minutia of politics? Ultimately, the answer is beside the point. Whether Americans *should* spend more or less time shopping or not, they *do* spend an inordinate amount of time shopping, particularly in comparison to politics. With all this in mind, my claim is limited to the following: the discrepancy between the amount of time people spend shopping and the amount they spend on politics, not to mention the surface similarities between some consumer and political choices as well as the consumer rhetoric of both political parties, helps make the consumer world a source of political influence.

Who Is the Consumer Citizen?

If you are reading this, you may very well be thinking: "That doesn't sound like me. *I* certainly don't think about politics as a consumer citizen." And you're probably right; you don't. If you are reading this book, you are unusual. You are not only interested in politics cursorily; you are interested enough to read

Americans' Time Use, Consumer and Political Behavior (2003–2017)

Facets report average daily time use, in hours

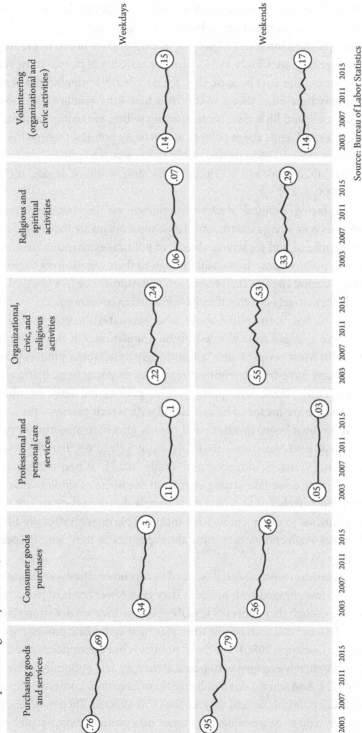

Source: Bureau of Labor Statistics

Figure 1.2 Time use on consumer and civic behavior, with all categories.

hundreds of academic pages about it, without requiring backroom gossip or slogans for your preferred party. Political scientists have long recognized that those people most interested in politics, like the readers of this book, are, well, a little strange (e.g., McClosky 1964). The vast majority of people know very little about politics. This isn't because they are necessarily antipolitical or apathetic. They simply have other things to do. They have jobs, families, and inner lives. And so they spend little time contemplating policy, evaluating candidates, and talking to their friends about political subjects. As political theorist Iris Marion Young once mused, "Most people would rather watch television, read poetry or make love" than think and act in the demanding world of democratic politics (Young 2000, p. 17).

When facing political decisions, reliance on lessons from consumer experiences goes along a continuum. Those most reliant are those for whom politics is peripheral and for whom objects of political evaluations are unfamiliar. For them, politics is not important enough in their regular lives to necessitate sustained mental energy. The presence of a consumer cue in a political context compels them to rely on what they have learned as consumers.

Much ink has been spilled about what separates the most politically informed and engaged from the rest of the population. On this point, there is little doubt: Most people know "astonishingly little" about politics (Converse 1964). Many have trouble connecting policy to party (e.g., Baldassarri and Gelman 2008). Those who participate in politics regularly, or who know which policies are meant to be associated with which parties—the kind who show up to town board meetings and eagerly affix their signature to petitions and perhaps read Vox.com—are likely more well-to-do than the rest of the population (Verba, Schlozman, and Brady 2012). When making political decisions, they often take strong cues from members of similar social groups (Achen and Bartels 2016). What most people do when they are not thinking about politics—in other words, what most people do with virtually all of their waking lives—affects *how* they think about politics on those unusual occasions when they do so.

The Americans who are *best* described as consumer citizens are those who, as a type, are less engaged with politics. They have lower levels of political knowledge, and though they generally lean Republican, they are not strong partisans. Politics does not call such people to engage their systematic processing abilities (Petty and Cacioppo 1986). For them, politics is but a peripheral concern. They are less cognitively engaged with politics; they are less politically aware (Zaller 1992, p. 43). And when a cue familiar to them from their consumer experiences emerges in a political context, they are the most affected. Their preferences, such as they are, tend to be unstable; time series data portrays most people's political preferences as gyrating wildly back and forth over time, with little discernible consistency, particularly among those with less amounts of political information

(Kinder and Kalmoe 2016, p. 40). However, other, better-informed people are not altogether immune. The political beliefs and behaviors of better-informed people can still be affected by cues from their consumer lives.

What the Consumer Citizen Sees

To get a better profile of the consumer citizen, consider the results of a nationally representative survey administered in the summer of 2018. The survey asked a series of questions designed to zoom in on people who generally express views that we might think of as consistent with the consumer citizen perspective. One of the core questions asked respondents to agree with the statement that "Government should be run like a business," with available responses on a 1–5 scale. Respondents could strongly disagree or just disagree with the statement; they could strongly agree or just agree; or they could refrain from offering an opinion.

The sample was nearly split: while 40.2% disagreed, 37% agreed. (The remaining abstained.) Let us refer to the average respondent who agreed as *Homo Emptor*. *Homo Emptor* leans Republican. He (and he is a he) is white. He attended college, but did not finish. *Homo Emptor* is very different from the average person who disagreed with the statement. Compared to this man, whom we can call *Homo Civicus*, *Homo Emptor* is less well-off and less well educated. He participates in politics far less often, and he reports being less interested in politics in general. He also expresses markedly less trust in government spending. (All these differences are significant by conventional standards. Table A.2, located in the appendix, presents demographic profiles of both *Homo Emptor* and *Homo Civicus*.) I return to this survey in Chapter 3.

Should we be so surprised that a person who believes government should be judged as if it were a private company has little faith in government spending? I think not. Even at its best, government provides salient benefits intermittently— benefits that *Homo Emptor* may be entirely unaware of anyways. Costs, meanwhile, come at him fast and furious. He has more trouble ignoring those.[9] And so to him, the government is not just similar to any private company—to him, it is similar to a private company that is giving him a bad deal. Research shows that people attach value to the perceived value of a deal; as the behavioral economists put it, they can get utility out of a transaction (e.g., Thaler 1999). When it comes to government, this man perceives his deal to be a bad one. The government, in his mind, is ripping him off.

To understand *Homo Emptor*'s perspective, think of how he might have responded to George W. Bush's tax cuts. Because of the cuts, the federal government mailed out rebate checks to millions of taxpayers. The checks were for $300 or $600. The actual economic effects of the checks were muted (Shapiro and Slemrod 2003). Yet many Americans were quite pleased with them.

Chris Martin, an air-conditioner repairman, was one such person. "You get taxed enough on so many things already, it's better to get something back," Martin explained to the *New York Times* (Cushman 2001). As a point of fact, unless Martin had immigrated to the United States immediately before speaking to a reporter, he very likely had received "something back" from the government in return for the taxes he'd paid. Maybe that something came in the form of the home mortgage interest deduction; maybe it was a tax credit he'd received while getting his education; maybe it was the roads he drove on.

Yet the memory of all those services eluded him. And understandably so. Consider what Martin's typical weekend might look like. He probably receives a paycheck on Friday. As usual, he notes it is slightly less than he would like, as the government has taken its sizable share. That evening, he takes his wife out to a restaurant. The following day, he brings his children to a playground. He spends Sunday working around the house. He fears he pulled a muscle, so he takes a painkiller. While he spent the weekend aggravated by the costs imposed by government, he took advantage of three complex benefits—healthy food, public parks, and safe drugs. Yet he likely never connected any of them to the government. And on those rare occasions when he does make explicit use of government services—say, by casting a vote or signing up for a government program—he probably has to confront a blizzard of paperwork that leaves him exasperated (Herd and Moynihan 2018).

Given the salience of government's costs, the near-invisibility of its benefits, and the frustrations often associated with using its services, the consumer citizen may come to punish government. In this context, punishment amounts to voicing support for policies and politicians that would diminish government spending. While a consumer can choose to spend less at a vendor that has fallen out of favor, a citizen can only vote for politicians who promise to reduce the cost of government itself. In this person's mind, the government has acted just like an unfair company. He will punish them as he would punish the company: by withholding his support. Exit is cost-prohibitive. He has little inclination to leave his family and friends and move to a place different from the one he is familiar with or where he was raised.[10]

He can, however, voice support for policies that would reduce the amount of money going into and going out of government coffers. He can vote for politicians who would do the same. And, having little confidence that government is spending his money wisely, he can become deeply distrustful of government itself. As Figure 1.3 shows, such attitudes are increasingly common. While there have been ebbs and flows, by and large, trust in government and confidence in how government spends your tax money have plummeted in recent decades.

This book is about describing *Homo Emptor*—what his political beliefs are and what political actions he takes. It is also about how he can be changed.

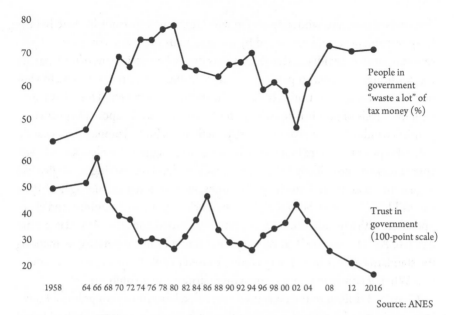

Figure 1.3 ANES Trust in Government Measures. The top panel shows attitudes toward government's use of tax money, while the bottom displays an aggregate measure of trust in government.

Book Outline

The second chapter begins by describing my experiences advocating for and then testing "taxpayer receipts," itemized estimates of how government spends tax money. Before any testing, I wrote in the *Washington Post* and elsewhere that I expected taxpayer receipts to boost trust in government. Naturally, I was thrilled when the Obama administration made such receipts available on the White House website—but crestfallen to test them and learn that they did not affect attitudes as I'd anticipated. This prompted me to take a closer look at research into consumer fairness. Inspired by that literature, I develop the idea of *alignability*, which proposes that people want either (a) the amount they pay government, in the form of taxes, to roughly align with the value of the benefits they receive in return (cost-benefit alignability), or (b) the use of their tax money to align with the source of its collection (source-use alignability). Multiple experiments, conducted online and once in person—at Chicago bus stops—make clear how alignability can affect attitudes toward taxation. Alignability can improve people's attitudes toward taxes in general and earmarked taxes in particular.

In the third chapter, I ask: If consumer fairness can affect attitudes toward taxation, what else can it do? It turns out that a whole host of people's political views are wrapped up in the extent to which they conflate consumer and political decisions. Americans who support Donald Trump are especially likely to believe the government should be judged by the standards of private companies. I present experimental evidence that documents that, when politicians of both parties use consumer rhetoric, co-partisans of those leaders subsequently come to view politics in strikingly consumerist terms. In another experiment, I find that voters with low levels of political knowledge look most positively upon a hypothetical political candidate who promises cost-benefit alignability, compared to a candidate who promises more benefits than costs. This suggests that less knowledgeable voters are more likely to rely on consumer decision-making strategies like alignability than more knowledgeable ones, even if doing so cuts against their ostensible self-interest. Second, I describe a field experiment administered in cooperation with a health insurance cooperative funded under the Affordable Care Act (ACA; "Obamacare"). A message that framed the cooperative as meeting the standards of cost-benefit alignability caused people to enroll in the cooperative. When it comes to politics, consumer fairness can go quite far.

Chapter 4 drills into the consumer citizen's relationship with political knowledge and attitudes toward redistribution. A survey experiment in the United States shows that taxpayer receipts can increase knowledge; evidence from a field experiment conducted in the United Kingdom, about the UK government's nationwide distribution of taxpayer receipts, reaches similar conclusions. Yet the receipt is unable to affect a host of attitudes, including toward redistribution. But the consumer citizen's attitudes toward redistribution can be changed—not just through alignability, as we have learned in previous chapters, but because of the everyday pressures of consumer life. This is illustrated by an experiment inspired by the concept of "scarcity" (Mullanaithan and Shafir 2013), which reveals that reminders of consumer debts can lead people to become more supportive of higher taxes on the rich.

In Chapter 5, I show how approaching the consumer citizen as the consumer citizen can affect trust in government. To do so, I describe the concept of *operational transparency*. Operational transparency refers to the extent to which a company's operations are visible to consumers. Higher levels of operational transparency can make consumers more loyal to and supportive of companies. An experiment conducted with the consumer psychologists who pioneered operational transparency makes clear that a similar dynamic can affect trust in government. When people see a computer simulation of the construction of a generic American town that we dubbed "Anytown" and that we designed to provide an operationally transparent view of government services, their trust in government shoots up. However, as an additional experiment shows, when applied to governmental processes, operational transparency can reduce trust in government.

The concluding chapter returns to the theoretical stakes. If citizens are *consumer citizens*, what does this suggest for the quality of democracy? While the rise of the consumer citizen may trouble some democratic theorists, I argue that, because the consequences of this rise are as yet unfinished, the effects on democracy may not be especially pernicious. As the previous chapters have shown, appealing to people as consumer citizens can increase their political knowledge, increase their trust in government, and lead them to sign up for health insurance. After offering guidance for policymakers, I then describe a new approach to civic education, modeled on the lessons of this book. Ultimately, what the consumer citizen implies for democracy is up to us—the citizens who must balance our obligations as citizens with the ubiquity of consumer life.

The Consumer Citizen
and Consumer Fairness

By now, Americans' lack of trust in their government is an old story. From its apogee in the mid-twentieth century, trust in government has fallen precipitously, more or less ever since. As of this writing, Pew finds that only 18% of Americans trust government to do what is right "always or most of the time"— a long cry from the 77% who did so in 1964, the highest number recorded.[1] Similarly, majorities of Americans have maintained skepticism about government spending. According to the American National Election Study (ANES), since 1970 about two-thirds of U.S. citizens report thinking that the government wastes "a lot" of their tax money. And this is not *just* a question of partisanship, with Republicans growing distrustful as Democrats have remained stable. Rather, members of both parties have become more distrustful.

Political scientists have offered a bevy of explanations for trust in government— and the absence of it. One account, alluring for its parsimony, holds that trust is largely a function of the performance of those in office. If political leaders are befallen by scandal, trust can erode (Bowler and Karp 2004); conversely, if they oversee economic growth, trust can grow (Citrin and Green 1986). Trust is also said to be wrapped up in the relationship between an individual's partisanship and the political party in control (e.g., Keele 2005).

Still others argue that trust is related to fundamental characteristics of American culture. We would prefer not to have to deal with the messy realities of governmental process, and instead want politics to take place outside of view (Hibbing and Theiss-Morse 2002). More broadly, our culture is suffused with the spirit of "Lockean liberalism," which champions the individual and looks skeptically upon the kind of collective actions taken by government (Hartz 1955).

These explanations all have much to offer. None of them are incompatible, however, with a different explanation: that the absence of trust in government is, in part, related to the absence of information about what government actually

The Consumer Citizen. Ethan Porter, Oxford University Press (2021). © Oxford University Press.
DOI: 10.1093/oso/9780197526781.003.0002.

does. I stumbled upon this explanation in my first year out of college, when the experience of paying my taxes had left me stunned. I'd sent the IRS a not-insubstantial check, and I'd received nothing in return—not even an acknowledgment that they'd received what I'd sent them. I only knew they'd received my check because they cashed it. I had successfully discharged my obligation as a taxpaying citizen, but I had no idea what I'd gotten for my money.

This was strange. Most transactions result in a receipt of some kind—an acknowledgment that one has paid, and a summary of what one has paid for. Many cash registers have notes affixed to them telling customers that, if they don't receive a receipt, they are entitled to a refund. Yet when much more money is involved—when one sends tax money to the government—the government sends nothing back. Certainly there is no promise of a refund. I had little reason to trust the way in which my government was spending my money. Who knew what they had done with it? They might as well have dropped it down a well.

And if I wasn't sure how government was using my tax money, there would seem to be little hope for many other people. At the time, I was being paid to work at a journal focused on public policy, a position that afforded me ample time to dwell on the details of American government. Most people don't have that luxury. They know little about what government does or the benefits it provides. Suzanne Mettler (2011) has documented the extent to which many government programs are not recognized as originating from government. For example, 60% of those who claimed the home mortgage interest deduction denied that they had used a government social program.

Even more startling about Mettler's data is the extent to which programs like Medicare, food stamps, and the G.I. Bill—which consist of government providing direct benefits to people—are also not regarded as originating from government. By her measures, 53.3% of student loan recipients, 41.7% of those who receive veterans' benefits, nearly 40% of Medicare beneficiaries, 28% of Medicaid recipients, and about a quarter of food stamp recipients report that they have *not* actually received government benefits. It turns out that the demand for "government to get its hands off my Medicare" is not just the battle cry of an uninformed few, but representative of a broad swath of public opinion.

To close this informational gap—to let people know, in other words, that Medicare *is* a government program—in 2010 and 2011 I wrote a series of articles for the *Washington Post* and elsewhere in which I advocated that the federal government provide all taxpayers with a "taxpayer receipt" (Porter 2010; Kendall and Porter 2011). The idea of a taxpayer receipt is simple. Just like an ordinary receipt, a taxpayer receipt documents what, precisely, your taxes have paid for. It does so by taking the amount of taxes you've paid and then breaking down government spending on a per-capita basis. For example, if you paid $1,287 in federal income taxes one year, and 10% of federal government spending went toward defense, your receipt would show that you'd paid $128.70 toward defense—and so on, for other government spending categories, until every dollar you'd paid in taxes was accounted for.

A taxpayer receipt is a crude tool. It generalizes spending into broad categories, sometimes oversimplifying in the process. Government taxing and spending don't actually work like the receipt implies, with the IRS collecting taxes and then disbursing the appropriate amounts to the appropriate agencies and departments. In reality, the IRS collects money, deposits it into the Treasury, and then Congress and the president wage a routinized battle over how to spend it. Tax money, in reality, is fungible; one dollar taxed could just as easily go to funding roads as paying off the national debt.

A taxpayer receipt may be subtly misleading. But as a tool capable of informing people about the uses of their tax money, it would be hard to beat. With a receipt, I would have less of a reason to think that government was wasting my money. Though I might disagree with how the government had spent it, a receipt would disabuse me—and others—of the sneaking suspicion that all my money had been wasted. I'd have a more precise, personalized idea of what government actually did with my money, and so would many other Americans.

While I championed the receipt publicly, I had little expectation that anything would come of it. Rarely do policy proposals become policy reality. So you can then imagine my enthusiasm when President Barack Obama announced in his 2011 State of the Union address, pictured in Figure 2.1, that his administration would indeed create a taxpayer receipt. "Because you deserve to know exactly how and where your tax dollars are being spent, you'll be able to go to a website and get that information for the very first time in history," he said (Obama 2011). I couldn't have said it better myself.

What followed was more than anything I could have realistically hoped for. Between 2011 and 2014, people could log into a White House website, enter their income over the previous year, and see a breakdown of where their tax money had gone. You can see what it looked like in Figure 2.2. It wasn't exactly a receipt, in that it wasn't given to taxpayers after they had paid their taxes. In fact, their exposure to this receipt depended on their ability to find the website and their willingness to volunteer their time and personal financial details. Contrast this with stores that are so eager to give you a receipt they promise you a full refund if you don't receive one. There was a miles-wide gulf between what the U.S. taxpayer receipt *could* be and what it actually was.

Still, it was something. At the least, it would give people a look inside government, increasing their knowledge about what exactly government does with their money. As economist Alice Rivlin once argued, "Taxes are more acceptable when the taxpayer knows exactly what they are to be used for"

Figure 2.1 President Barack Obama delivering the 2011 State of the Union address, when he announced the U.S. taxpayer receipt.

Online Tax Receipt

Have you ever wondered how much of your own tax dollars actually go to support foreign aid? To support education? Well, now you can find out – and you might be surprised.

In his State of the Union Address, President Obama promised that this year, for the first time ever, American taxpayers would be able to go online and see exactly how their federal tax dollars are spent.

Just enter a few pieces of information about your taxes, and the taxpayer receipt will give you a breakdown of how your tax dollars are spent on priorities like education, veteran's benefits, or health care.

Launch the Federal Taxpayer Receipt

Figure 2.2 The version of the taxpayer receipt that appeared on the White House website.

(Rivlin 1989, p. 116). For most Americans, as Figure 1.3 illustrated, taxes are plainly not acceptable; a taxpayer receipt could, it would seem, change at least that. For his part, President Obama argued that, if nothing else, the receipts would make for a more informed citizenry—and that, in and of itself, would be a worthwhile goal. "As a general principle, my administration's attitude is: the more people know, the more effectively we can govern, and it actually turns out to be good politics too because we think we got the facts on our side in a lot of these debates," he said in a video introducing the receipts. "We think that the more people know, the better they will be able to judge some of the debates which are going to be taking place in Washington with respect to how do we pay down the deficit, how do we reform the tax system, and so forth."[2]

To find out if taxpayer receipts can indeed increase people's trust in government, I fielded an experiment in 2012. U.S.-based participants were recruited over Amazon's Mechanical Turk service, a popular, cost-efficient tool for recruiting survey participants (e.g., Berinsky, Huber, and Lenz 2012). Treatment effects observed on Mechanical Turk tend to mirror those obtained on nationally representative samples (e.g., Mullinx et al. 2015; Nyhan et al. 2017; Coppock and McClellan 2017). For more discussion of Mechanical Turk, consult the appendix subsection "A Note on Methodology."

In my experiment, some participants were randomly exposed to their taxpayer receipt from the past year, based on the White House data available at the time. Some other participants were randomly shown something else: a "Benefits Number." Marrying publicly available data to participants' responses to demographic questions, the Benefits Number presented participants with *only* a monetary estimate of how much they'd benefited from government over the previous year.

The logic behind including a Benefits Number is simple. Maybe instead of wanting to know the details of where their taxpayer money went, people only want to know how they personally have benefited from government. Perhaps people don't need any formats familiar to them from consumer life to make them aware of government benefits they are otherwise neglecting. Perhaps they just need to know that they're benefiting from government in the first place.

The existing scholarly literature on tax attitudes gives us reason to believe this might be the case. As Anthony Downs put it, "If voters are unaware of the potential benefits of certain types of government spending," then the resultant federal budget might be less than what it would be were voters aware of all the benefits that government provides; by implication, making them aware would increase government spending (Downs 1960, p. 546). According to Jack Citrin and David Sears's canonical look at Americans' tax attitudes, people mostly want government to provide them as many benefits as possible, at as little cost as possible. *Tax Revolt: Something for Nothing in California*, written in the aftermath of the California "tax revolt" of the late 1970s, marshals survey data to reach conclusions about how Californians feel about their taxes, and how Americans in general do. As Sears and Citrin wrote,

> Substantial majorities of the California electorate wanted cutbacks in government spending and taxes, and expressed strong preferences for a smaller or less powerful government bureaucracy, while at the same time (and by equally strong majorities) requesting additional services in most areas of government responsibilities. . . . This paradoxical mixture of attitudes prevailed throughout the period of the California tax revolt. And the same mentality is evident in the attitudes of Americans nationwide. (Sears and Citrin 1985, p. 44)

In other words, when it comes to taxes and government spending, people want a free lunch. (Or, as Sears and Citrin memorably described it, people have the following incompatible demands: "Taxes, No! Big Government, No! Services, Yes!") (Sears and Citrin 1985, p. 243). The Benefits Number distills this desire, completely evading the question of costs and focusing on benefits alone. It bears no resemblance to any object in the consumer world. For a moment, it tells people who see it that they have only reaped benefits from government. To take Sears and Citrin seriously is to think that this is the kind of fantasy in which Americans want to indulge.

The inclusion of the Benefits Number made this experiment a test of two competing theories. The taxpayer receipt would test whether informing people about government would enhance their trust in government. Meanwhile, the Benefits Number would allow for a test of a simpler, contrary proposition: that people simply want to know how much they're getting from, or benefiting from, government. Costs be damned; people want their benefits.

The study proceeded as follows. After answering demographic questions, recruited participants were randomly assigned to see either their Taxpayer Receipt, their Benefits Number, a combination of their Benefits Number and their Taxpayer Receipt, or neither. Participants assigned to see their Taxpayer Receipt were shown two slides. The first slide prepared them for what was to come, and the second slide displayed their receipt.[3]

The receipt a person saw next depended on the answer supplied to the household income question. The displayed receipt took the reported income, assumed the lowest possible tax rate according to the federal income tax schedule, and then proportionally divided the estimated tax by the categorical allocations in the federal budget. Respondents were then told how much of their tax money was spent on fourteen budget categories.[4] All data and spending categories came directly from the White House online taxpayer receipt; however, to prevent respondents' feelings about President Obama from influencing their views of the receipts, the data were not identified as such.

People shown their Benefits Number were also shown two successive slides. Again, the first was meant to be neutral and provide context for what follows.[5] After clicking ahead, participants were taken to another slide in which they were presented their Benefits Number, which was described with the following language: "By our estimates, someone like you received [insert variable amount] from the federal government over the past year." The Benefits Number combined general approximations of the value of the federal cash transfers, tax expenditures, and tax deductions that likely redounded to subjects over the previous year. The cash transfers incorporated into the measure are those that flow from the federal government to local governments and those that flow from the federal government to individuals. Five such transfers were included: Social Security benefits, veterans' benefits, federal student aid, Medicare, and the per-pupil federal contribution to local public education. The policies included were chosen because of the broadness of their beneficiary base and their status as items that, according to Mettler (2011), many people might fail to pick up on as originating from the government.[6]

After seeing either their Taxpayer Receipt, their Benefits Number, a combination of both, or neither, all participants answered three workhorse trust questions from the American National Election Study. A general question about trust in government reads, "How much of the time do you think the government in Washington can be trusted to do what is right?" Respondents could answer, "Just about always," "Most of the time," "Some of the time," or "Almost never." A second question, focused on perceptions about the motives of political decision-makers, asks, "Would you say the government is pretty much run by a few big interests looking out for themselves or that it is run for the benefit of all the people?" Respondents could answer, "Few big interests" or "Benefit of all." Finally, another question probes respondents' level of trust in how government uses their tax money: "Do you think that people in the government waste a lot of money we pay in taxes, waste some of it, or don't waste very much of it?" Respondents could select from "A lot," "Some," or "Not very much."[7]

The Taxpayer Receipt, I'd hoped, would let people know that the government was not in fact wasting all of their money—their money had actually been spent on something—and that trust in government would increase as a result. Results appear in the Appendix. Table A.3 in the Appendix shows aggregated responses to the entire battery. Descriptive statistics are available in Appendix Table A.4.

The expectations I'd confidently proclaimed from the mountaintop of the *Washington Post* had not been borne out. The receipt was not some kind of magical elixir. Letting people know what the government was doing on their behalf had not actually caused an uptick in trust in government overall, or even in taxing and spending. While there was some evidence that the receipt had changed attitudes in the direction I'd anticipated, so had the combination of the Taxpayer Receipt and the Benefits Number, as well as the Benefits Number on its own. Another political scientist, John Sides, investigated the taxpayer receipt at around the same time as I did. He too was unable to find the receipt changing people's minds (Sides 2011). If there were effects from the receipt alone on attitudes, they were likely far too small to make much of a difference. And that's a big if.[8]

In thinking about the connection between taxes and attitudes toward government, I'd done two things wrong. First, I'd neglected to think about fairness. More precisely, I'd neglected consumer fairness. Second, I'd cast too broad a net. Rather than investigate the relationship between perceptions of taxes and attitudes toward government in general, I should have focused precisely on the relationship between such perceptions and attitudes toward taxes and government spending in particular. Broader questions about trust in government in general would have to wait.

Taxes and Consumer Fairness

Recall the last time you went out to eat. Were you taking your spouse out for a meal, enjoying a night away from it all? Or were you rushing from meeting to meeting, scooping up a sandwich on the go? Either way, you likely made a decision that reflected, however intuitively, some notion of consumer fairness. Consumer fairness is quite different from the kinds of fairness political scientists and philosophers are used to thinking about in political contexts (e.g., Rawls 1971; Hochschild 1986). It's more anodyne and, by definition, more likely to affect consumer decision-making. But that doesn't mean it can't have political effects.

If, the last time you dined out, you went to a nice restaurant, you were probably willing to pay more than if you were grabbing a quick bite, and vice versa— even if the food were exactly the same (Thaler 1999). Alternatively, if at the end of the meal you were told that an unexpected surcharge would be added to your final bill because the duck you had ordered was an especially rare item, you would likely not be happy (Kahneman, Knetsch, and Thaler 1991). Either way, of course, you would presumably expect to pay *something*. If your waiter at a fancy restaurant or the person behind the counter at a sandwich shop had told you that your food was free, you might have recoiled, assuming that you were being served yesterday's leftovers.

This isn't to say you wouldn't prefer to pay the lowest price possible. Of course you would. But you likely are not a single-minded pursuer of low prices.

Central to consumer fairness is the idea that people are willing to pay more for an item *if* they believe that the costs of producing it are roughly commensurate to the price paid for it. Consumers are even comfortable with profits. But if profits appear excessive or exploitative of a particularly unfortunate, unpredictable situation—as when a store selling snow shovels hikes prices exponentially after a snowstorm—they may be unhappy (Thaler 1999; Kahneman, Knetsch, and Thaler 1986a). Generally, people want price increases (to them) and cost increases (to the firm) to *align* (Bolton and Alba 2006). Consumers neither want nor expect a free lunch. Within certain parameters, they are willing to pay for what they buy, and they are even willing to grant the firm a profit.

Consumer fairness can help explain a number of otherwise puzzling economic phenomena, on the part of firms and consumers. Daniel Kahneman, Jack Knetsch, and Richard Thaler (1986a) argued that concerns about fairness effectively prevented firms from maximizing profits. In one survey, the vast majority of respondents regarded a firm that would raise shovel prices after a snowstorm as engaging in unfair behavior; the same was true for a car dealership that raised prices for a particularly in-demand yet hard-to-come-by automobile. In one vignette, survey respondents were told about a landlord whose rising costs forced him to raise the rent on a poor tenant, even though the increase might force the tenant to move. Seventy-five percent of respondents found the action to be unfair. While consumers do not begrudge firms a profit motive, they do not like profits to come at the expense of people. Respondents viewed salary cuts undertaken by a struggling company as fair, but unfair when imposed by a profitable company. Ultimately, consumer fairness flows from a *dual entitlement principle* that binds both buyers and sellers. Buyers—consumers—believe they are entitled to a purchase price roughly comparable to a "reference transaction," or a transaction that recently occurred within both the firm's and its customers' community or frame of reference. Sellers, meanwhile, are entitled to a profit "within the limits of the reference transaction" (Kahneman, Knetsch, and Thaler 1986a; 1986b).

Consumer fairness isn't just an airy-fairy, abstract concept. People's perceptions of fairness have real consequences. Consumers weigh the fairness of a particular good's price when deciding whether to purchase it (Martins and Monroe 1994). When they feel that a vendor is not being fair, consumers are more likely to be dissatisfied with the good sold, if not outright angry (Oliver and Swann 1989). They are also likely to tell other consumers about the perceived unfairness, leading to negative costs for the vendor (Zeelenberg and Pieters 2004).

For their part, vendors are acutely aware of consumers' perceptions about unfairness. Examples testifying to vendors' concerns with fairness are all around us. Why, for example, do events such as concerts and sporting events sell out well before all the demand has been captured and reflected in higher possible prices (Kahneman, Knetsch, and Thaler 1986a)? Why do most popular restaurants not engage in "dynamic pricing" and charge extra for reservations during peak hours? In many cases, firms willfully leave excess demand—and thus profits—on the table. The likely explanation is that firms anticipate that such actions would generate accusations of unfairness, sowing the seeds of resentment and diminishing future profits. Indeed, recent experimental work has found that consumers do regard dynamic pricing as an unfair practice (Haws and Bearden 2006).

The role of fairness in consumer decision-making can be thought of as an extension of the role that fairness has been found to play in broader economic contexts. The "ultimatum game," a popular tool in behavioral and experimental economics, offers strong experimental evidence that fairness concerns have real material consequences. In the game, one player unilaterally proposes how to divide a pot of money between himself and another player. If the second player does not accept the first player's proposal, then neither player receives the money. If fairness did not matter—that is, if players were just maximizing all that they could—then the other player should accept any amount the proposer offers. Any amount of money would seem to be better than no amount of money (Camerer 2003). And yet, despite theoretical predictions, this sort of behavior is almost never observed (Thaler 1988). Proposers rarely offer the minimal amount possible, and when they do, that offer is usually rejected (Guth, Schmittberger, and Schwarze 1982; Guth and Teitz 1990). Indeed, even when analysts think that the role of fairness has been overstated, they nonetheless concede that players voluntarily give up a "nontrivial" portion of their money (Forsythe et al. 1994).

The contours of consumer fairness have recently been mapped out by Bolton and Alba (2006), who find over the course of four experiments that, when forming perceptions of fairness, consumers consider the *alignability* of price increases with cost increases. To them, aligned costs are those that directly relate to the item being sold, while nonaligned costs "are legitimate costs incurred by the vendor that do not have a self-evident association with a specific vendor offering, such as rent" (Bolton and Alba 2006, p. 259). Generally, if people believe that a price increase has occurred due to an increase in a firm's alignable costs, the price increase will be regarded as fair; if the price increase cannot be explained by an alignable cost increase, people will regard it as unfair.

Consumer fairness broadly implies that people are sensitive to perceptions of both the costs they've paid *and* the value of what they received in return. When they go shopping, they are neither monomaniacal seekers of low costs, nor do they frown whenever a firm profits. And if you ask them, they're perfectly happy to tell you that, all else being equal, they'd prefer the value of their government benefits to approximate the taxes they've paid. Consider a short survey I fielded over Mechanical Turk in June 2014, of about 100 Americans. After a brief discussion of what constitutes government costs and government benefits, participants were asked to use a slider to indicate what cost-to-benefit ratio they wanted government to provide. The scale went from 0 to 100, with 0 representing all cost and no benefits, and 100 representing all benefits and no costs.[9]

Participants were then presented with a slider and told, "Responses near 0 indicate that you'd like to pay more than you receive in benefits, while responses near 100 indicate that you'd like to receive more in benefits than you pay." The classical story would have expected the average answer to be 100, or close to it. More is better than less.

Or so we're often told. The mean response was actually 64.3. In fact, only 10.7% of participants moved the slider all the way to 100. After they'd answered my questions, I asked people if they had any thoughts. "Kind of a no-brainer," said one participant who'd responded with a 100. "Yes, I would like maximum benefits for minimum cost." His views were less common than he (and, at that point, I) assumed they would be. More representative was another comment, offered by someone who'd chosen 50: "I don't think I should get more than I pay."

Was this just cheap talk? Or something more? To find out, I had to conduct a new experiment.

The Cost-Benefit Alignability Experiment

In the first Taxpayer Receipt experiment, I had spent lots of time trying to give people accurate or semiaccurate depictions of where their tax money had gone and how much money they'd received in government benefits. While I was happy to do my subjects a favor by sharing this information with them, my commitment to realism was also limiting. To test whether such sensitivity extends to political attitudes, I would need to manipulate the stuff of which people's perceptions are made.

And so, in this new experiment, I presented people with artificial estimates of both the amount of taxes they'd paid the previous year and the amount of benefits they'd received over the previous year. If people do indeed prefer for their costs and benefits to align, they should view their taxes most favorably when they are told that is the case. Conversely, if people just want a free lunch, they should be happiest when they are told that's what they're getting. The experiment was designed to put both perspectives to the test.

In September 2016, after collecting participants' demographic information, I showed them a slide offering some basic explanatory details about government costs and benefits.[10] Then I randomly assigned people to conditions in which they were told that their costs exceeded their benefits, their benefits exceeded their costs, or the two were roughly aligned. I worried about people's well-documented troubles with numbers (e.g., Ansolabehere, Meredith, and Snowberg 2013; Merola and Hitt 2016), and so I did not mention specific numbers. I also told respondents that the estimates were based on their previous answers (a claim I disabused them of in a postexperiment debrief).

The language for each condition read as follows:

- *Benefits Condition:* "Based on your previous answers, you have likely received government benefits that are larger in value than the costs you have paid. In other words, you got back more than you paid."
- *Costs Condition:* "Based on your previous answers, you have likely received government benefits that are smaller in value than the costs you have paid. In other words, you paid more than you got back."
- *Alignbaility Condition:* "Based on your previous answers, you have likely received government benefits roughly equal in value to the costs you have paid. In other words, you got back about the same amount as you paid."

Everyone then answered three questions. They answered first the question from the ANES about trust in government spending used in the previous experiment; a "feeling thermometer" question, in which they were asked to express their feelings about taxes with a 0–100 feeling thermometer, with higher numbers denoting warmer feelings; and a question from John Mark Hansen's paper "Individuals, Institutions and Public Preferences over Public Finance" (1998) that probes support for greater government spending, even if greater spending necessitates higher taxes. This question reads, "Do you favor increases in the taxes paid by ordinary Americans in order to increase spending on domestic programs like Medicare, education, and highways?" Responses are recorded on a 1–5 scale, with higher numbers corresponding to more support for increases. The virtue of this question is that it forces respondents to confront the trade-off between higher taxes and higher spending. As Ellis and Stimson (2012) note, there is reason to think that Americans do not consider trade-offs when asked to respond to a question related to taxing and spending.

Results appear in Table 2.1. This is a standard Ordinary Least Squares (OLS) regression, in which the "cost" condition is excluded.[11] Unsurprisingly, telling people that they'd paid more into government than they received in return, as I did in the *Cost* condition, provoked a sharp, negative reaction across all measures. The table should make two things clear. The first is that being told that one's government costs and benefits are roughly aligned in value spurs one to be more trusting of how the government uses one's tax money. The same conclusion can be drawn from the feeling thermometer results; seeing the *Alignability* condition

Table 2.1 **2016 Alignability Results**

	Dependent Variable					
	Trust in Government Spending		Support for Tax Increases		Taxes FT	
	(1)	(2)	(3)	(4)	(5)	(6)
Aligned	0.106**	0.098**	0.171*	0.162*	8.655***	8.595***
	(0.046)	(0.045)	(0.091)	(0.084)	(2.103)	(2.078)
Benefits	0.110**	0.100**	0.129	0.120	8.453***	8.228***
	(0.046)	(0.045)	(0.092)	(0.085)	(2.106)	(2.083)
Constant	1.419***	1.261***	2.839***	4.002***	36.687***	32.680***
	(0.032)	(0.208)	(0.065)	(0.392)	(1.487)	(9.658)
Covariates?	No	Yes	No	Yes	No	Yes
Observations	928	926	928	926	928	926
R^2	0.008	0.147	0.004	0.242	0.023	0.148
Adjusted R^2	0.006	0.089	0.002	0.190	0.021	0.090
Residual Std. Error	0.569	0.543	1.138	1.026	26.181	25.248
	(df = 925)	(df = 866)	(df = 925)	(df = 866)	(df = 925)	(df = 866)
F Statistic	3.732**	2.527***	1.897	4.686***	11.024***	2.550***
	(df = 2; 925)	(df = 59; 866)	(df = 2; 925)	(df = 59; 866)	(df = 2; 925)	(df = 59; 866)

Note: *$p < 0.1$; **$p < 0.05$; ***$p < 0.01$

Covariate details: Models with covariates include variables for age, education, race, sex, household income, party ID, ideology, and U.S. state.

Covariate details: Further variable details can be found in the Appendix subsection "Mechanical Turk Demographic Questions."

increased how people feel about their taxes by about 8.5 percentage points. And as the third and fourth columns of Table 2.1 show, there is also some evidence that the *Alignability* condition made people more supportive of higher government spending, even at the cost of additional taxes. Descriptive statistics appear in Appendix Table A.6.

To be sure, it's not as if Americans don't want a good deal. The *Benefits* condition also moved people to think more positively about their taxes. But, so far as this evidence shows, the effects of the *Alignability* condition and the *Benefits* condition are virtually indistinguishable. In both cases, people were told that they're getting a good deal with their taxes; and in both cases, this led to a surge in support for taxes. Furthermore, while the *Alignability* condition was able to increase people's support for increased government spending and taxes, the *Benefits* condition effect on the same outcome was not statistically significant by conventional standards.

This result is surprising. When it comes to taxes, Americans have been described as wanting "something for nothing," or a free lunch (e.g., Sears and Citrin 1985). Some people surely do want a free lunch. *But the allure of free lunch is no greater than the allure of cost-benefit alignability.* When they evaluate their taxes, people bring a version of consumer fairness with them. When it comes to their taxes, Americans do not *only* want a free lunch. As the saying goes, there's no such thing. As consumers, they're willing to pay more when the cost of producing a good are made salient, or when a price increase appears commensurate to perceived costs to the firm (Kahneman, Knetsch, and Thaler 1986b; Thaler 1999).[12] Similarly, when people are led to believe that government costs approximate the value of benefits that government provides, they respond by viewing their taxes more favorably than they would otherwise.[13]

In either case, people are perceiving positive value from the deal itself. Richard Thaler (1999) has dubbed this "transaction utility": that is, people attach utility to the value of the "deal" they perceive themselves to be receiving. This is true when the good itself in question remains constant. When it comes to government, they appreciate the deal they get when they believe they are getting more in value than what they paid in. But they also appreciate getting about the same amount in return as what they paid in. The only thing they don't like is getting less than what they paid for. That's a bad deal. Nobody likes those.

Homo Emptor at Chicago Bus Stops

One experimental result, on its own, is never enough. In this case, perhaps the finding described above is an artifact of the stylized experimental setting. Perhaps people did not take seriously the estimates provided. In general, it's possible that online survey takers are adept at figuring out the hypotheses of the people administering surveys, and adjust their responses to try and please the people paying them. These are called "demand effects."[14] With these concerns in mind, I looked for a site of "real-world" cost-benefit alignability, where the per-capita cost of an actual government service mirrored the per-capita price of that service.

Fortunately, bus service in the city of Chicago is just such a service. According to the federally funded National Transit Database (2013), the Chicago government spends about $2.55 on each passenger for each ride. Meanwhile, the listed fare is $2.25: that's what most riders spend each time they ride. Chicago bus stops represent an appealing test of the effects of cost-benefit alignability precisely because the per-capita benefit of each bus ride, understood as the amount of money spent by the city on each bus rider, roughly aligns with the listed price of a single bus fare. One might even say that bus riders are earning a "profit" from the city for each ride they take; thirty cents is not a king's ransom, but especially for everyday riders, it adds up.

On a sweltering July day in 2015, a team of undergraduate research assistants and I fanned out over bus stops in the affluent Lincoln Park neighborhood.[15] At each bus stop, the mobile app Randomizer, available (at the time) free of charge at the Apple store, was used to randomly assign people to one of the four conditions. Each of the following randomly assigned conditions were read aloud to would-be bus riders.

- *Alignability Condition:* "First, as you may know, the city spends about $2.55 on each passenger per trip, and the listed fare is $2.25. It spends about as much on each passenger as each passenger spends on each ride."
- *Cost Condition:* "First, as you may know, the listed fare is $2.25—that's what it costs you."
- *Benefit Condition:* "First, as you may know, the city spends about $2.55 on each passenger per trip—money the city spends on you."
- *Control:* No information presented.

Randomization was done with the app on a person-by-person basis. My students and I would walk up to riders waiting at the bus stop, smile, and ask each person if they wanted to take part in an academic study. Those who agreed to participate—and virtually everyone did—were then read the text corresponding to their condition and subsequently asked questions, including, "On a scale from 1 to 100, how do you feel about paying taxes for government services? 100 means you feel very warm and positive about paying taxes for government services, and 1 means you feel very cold and negative toward paying taxes for government services." Ideally, we would have asked more questions—but the incoming buses severely limited the time we had for each survey.[16] Descriptive statistics appear in Appendix Table A.8.

The bus stop results mirrored the Mechanical Turk results from the previous study. Once again, just being told that the cost of government—understood here as the money required to ride the bus—was roughly equivalent to the value of the service received in return for that cost—understood as the money the city had put into the ride—had significant, positive effects on peoples' attitudes toward taxes. As measured by the feeling thermometer, the effects generated by this condition were larger in size than the effects yielded by the other conditions, including the condition in which people were just told about the per-capita value of the benefit they were going to receive when they were on the bus.

As Figure 2.3 shows, people assigned to the *Alignability* condition reported a mean response of 65.6 on the feeling thermometer; people in the benefit condition reported a 58.5 mean response on the same question. When feelings toward taxes are regressed on the *Alignability, Benefit,* and *Control* conditions, the alignability coefficient is positive, significant at conventional levels, and the largest-sized effect. Meanwhile, exposure to the *Cost* condition deflated attitudes toward taxes. This makes intuitive sense and lends the results additional plausibility. People do not like being reminded about the costs they are about to pay.

All this doesn't mean Americans will rebuff a free lunch, or an inexpensive one, when they are offered one. What it does mean is that being told that the per-capita costs and benefits of a government program are roughly alignable yields just as powerful a positive effect on attitudes toward taxes (compared to costs) as being told just about the value of the per-capita benefit provided by the same program. Alignability—which, by design, brings costs that otherwise wouldn't be there into the picture—can actually increase positive feelings toward taxes.

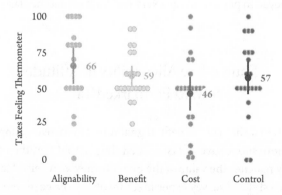

Figure 2.3 Bus stop results: Feeling thermometer results by condition, with mean and 95% confidence intervals.

This is an important, albeit subtle point: alignability increases warmth toward taxes compared to costs alone, despite the explicit invocation of costs. From a free-lunch perspective, this is surprising. Americans are *not* opposed to mentions of costs, but they are opposed to mentions of costs that do not reflect cost-benefit alignability. These results further underscore the depth of opposition to costs—but costs *alone*, when not paired with alignable benefits.

I present regression results in Table A.7, located in the Appendix. First, I model just the effects of the *Alignability* condition on feelings toward taxes, while the model column replicates the specification of the prior alignability experiment. The third model adds in the *Control* condition, while continuing to exclude the *Cost* condition. Again, being told that the cost of a government service is commensurate with the value of the service makes one more likely to view taxes more positively.

In addition, as Figure 2.3 makes clear, the *Control* condition does reasonably well. While the effects are substantially larger for alignability than control, the difference is not statistically significant. However, the difference between alignability and costs is significant, as is the difference between costs and control. Americans dislike costs most of all; they like cost-benefit alignability more. But at least in this case, they were comparably content with just using the service, sans any information about costs and benefits.[17]

The central point remains. The combined presentation of per-capita benefits *and* per-capita costs—when both are close in value to each other—has a positive impact on attitudes. This, in turn, can be understood as a manifestation of Americans' reliance on consumer fairness norms in political contexts. Americans are not only accepting of costs when alignability is met, but the placement of costs *adjacent to benefits* can even make them more positive about taxes and government spending. This is true, regardless of whether Americans are surveyed online about hypothetical taxes and government spending, or if they are surveyed in person, about a very real (and sometimes fast-approaching) city bus.

Source-Use Alignability in Attitudes toward Earmarked Taxes

So far, I've shown that cost-benefit alignability can increase support for taxes. People are more supportive of taxes when they're told that the cost of government roughly matches the value of the benefits they've received in return—and this is true in a stylized survey experiment involving the costs and benefits of all federal government programs, as well as in the field, concerning a specific public service.

In their early seminal work on consumer fairness, Kahneman, Knetsch, and Thaler (1986a; 1986b) realized that people react negatively to situations where firms make changes to one part of their business because of how another part of their business is doing. For example, consumers regard price hikes on one set of rental apartments unfair if the hikes are owed to a landlord's concerns about another set of rental apartments. On the other hand, if a landlord charges higher rents on otherwise identical apartments because the higher-priced apartment was more expensive to build, that decision is regarded favorably. As the authors put it, "A firm is only allowed to protect itself at the transactor's expense against losses that pertain directly to the transaction at hand" (Kahneman, Knetsch, and Thaler 1986b, p. 733).

In the consumer's mind, costs are assigned to specific goods. Government taxing and spending, however, generally do not work this way. We pay our taxes at least once a year and perhaps every other week, and benefits are distributed gradually over time, and often with no discernible connection to the payment of taxes. There is one notable exception: earmarked taxes. Earmarked taxes can pinpoint both the source of the tax collected and the purpose for which the tax money is used. Here, then, the power of alignability should be especially powerful.

Every U.S. state uses earmarked taxes. In 2005, 24% of all state tax revenues were the product of earmarked taxes, and in some states the figure was far greater. In some cases, such as when fuel taxes are earmarked for highways, taxes are used for expenditures that benefit the people who pay the tax. In other cases, taxes are earmarked for expenditures that help solve a problem generated by the item or activity being taxed. Tobacco taxes are sometimes earmarked for cancer research and treatment, while alcohol taxes are sometimes earmarked for substance abuse prevention and treatment.

Scholars have offered several explanations for the popularity of earmarking. Prominent among them is a version of the theory that motivated my initial confidence in the taxpayer receipt: earmarks are popular because they make clear where one's tax money is going. Alice Rivlin argued that, in the absence of earmarking, "taxpayers may have no clear idea of what the money is spent for, they may believe that the money is spent wastefully or even fraudulently, or that a substantial part of it goes for services of which they disapprove" (Rivlin 1989, p. 114). That having been said, earmarking might not increase support for taxation if voters oppose the program for which revenues are earmarked. Earmarking increases the "salience" of goods financed through taxation. If those public goods are desired by voters, then earmarking will increase support for the tax in question (Listokin and Schizer 2013).

The explanation that Rivlin (1989) articulated asserts that earmarking should lead to higher support for taxes when the designated expenditure is one that voters support. This explanation, however, does not offer any explanation for the phenomenon of *source-use alignability*—that is, the popularity of earmarked taxes in which the use of the tax money is closely linked to the source of its collection. If public spending on cancer research is popular, then this theory might predict that politicians would garner support for a tax by earmarking revenues for cancer research. But the theory does not explain why we might expect to see tobacco taxes earmarked for cancer research as opposed to, say, watercraft taxes earmarked for cancer research.

Appreciating the role that consumer fairness plays in Americans' attitudes toward taxes suggests a coherent account of source-use alignability. As we know, consumers respond more favorably to increases in the prices of goods and services when those increases are aligned with changes in the costs of inputs that go into the good or service that the consumer is purchasing. At the same time, consumers tend to react negatively to price increases when they believe that they are cross-subsidizing the provision of other goods or services by the same vendor, or otherwise merely enriching the vendor.

If consumer fairness norms can influence attitudes toward taxation, then we might expect to see a preference for alignability when it comes to earmarked taxes. In the previous two experiments, I've shown that cost-benefit alignability can increase support for taxes and government spending. Here, I test whether source-use alignability can do the same. While Rivlin directs our attention to the popularity of the designated expenditure, source-use alignability focuses on the fit between the tax and the expenditure for which revenues are earmarked.

To test this idea, law professor Daniel Hemel and I presented an Internet-based sample with descriptions of hypothetical taxes. We looked at two kinds of common earmarked taxes. First, we studied taxes that follow the basic rule of "you get what you pay for": that is, taxes on an activity that are used to fund a service benefiting participants in that activity. Second, we also studied taxes that conform to the so-called Pottery Barn rule of "you break it, you buy it": taxes on an activity that are used to fund efforts mitigating negative consequences generated by that activity.

In both studies, some participants were randomly assigned to see a version of the tax that met the source-use alignability criterion. Other participants were randomly assigned to see a *misaligned* version of the tax, in which the funds were spent on a distant use. And still other participants, a *Control* condition, saw only a description of the tax, with no details about its use.

For the "you get what you pay for" taxes, we presented subjects with hypothetical taxes on gasoline and jet fuel. Specifically, participants were randomly assigned to one of six conditions—two versions of aligned, two versions of misaligned, and two versions of no-use. The conditions read:

- *Aligned:* "Some people think we should have a new tax on gasoline, the kind used in automobiles. The money generated from this tax would be used to fund highways."; OR "Some people think we should have a new tax on jet fuel, the kind used in airplanes. The money generated from this tax would be used to fund airports."
- *Misaligned:* "Some people think we should have a new tax on gasoline, the kind used in automobiles. The money generated from this tax would be used to fund airports."; OR "Some people think we should have a new tax on jet fuel, the kind used in airplanes. The money generated from this tax would be used to fund highways."
- *No-Use:* "Some people think we should have a new tax on gasoline, the kind used in automobiles."; OR "Some people think we should have a new tax on jet fuel, the kind used in airplanes."

Similarly, to study "you break it, you buy it" taxes, we tested hypothetical earmarked taxes on plastic bags and alcohol. Again, both are common earmarked taxes. And again, participants were randomly assigned to one of six conditions. If they were assigned to an *Aligned* condition, they were told either about a tax on plastic bags that would go to enforcement or antilittering laws, or to a tax on alcohol that would go to enforcement of anti–drunk driving laws. Again, to create the misaligned conditions, we transposed source and use. Some people were told about a tax that would be collected on alcohol and go toward antilittering, while others were told about a tax on plastic bags that would fund the enforcement of anti–drunk driving laws. Participants in the no-use conditions were told about taxes on either alcohol or plastic bags, with no use specified.

Below the description of their assigned tax, participants were asked to evaluate their attitudes toward the tax with a 0–100 feeling thermometer. Unlike the previous two studies in this chapter, however, we also managed to add a question about preferred magnitude for the tax rate in question, this time providing participants with a $0–$1.00 slider to answer.[18] People were then reminded of the purpose of the tax. Exposure to treatment and measurement of the dependent variable occurred after collection of standard demographic data.[19] Participants were recruited via Lucid, a provider of national survey data tied to Census benchmarks.[20] Descriptive statistics for both studies appear in the Appendix, in Tables A.10 and A.12.

When the earmark satisfies the source-use alignability criterion, we found that earmarking has a strong, positive effect on people's attitudes toward a hypothetical tax. Appendix Table A.9 displays feeling thermometer results for the "you get what you pay for" study. Table A.11 repeats the same analysis for the "you break it, you buy it" taxes. For both kinds of taxes, no matter how we model it, the conclusion is the same: source-use alignability enhances people's attitudes toward earmarked taxes. By contrast, earmarking a tax for a misaligned use has a much weaker impact on attitudes, one that falls short of conventional levels of statistical significance. And people generally don't like not being told about the use of a tax. So, Rivlin (1989) was right—but only to an extent. People prefer having more information than less, but they like having information about source-use alignability most of all.

When participants were asked to report the preferred rate of tax rather than just their warmth toward the tax, results were broadly similar. Located in the Appendix, Table A.13 shows results for the "you get what you pay for" taxes; also located in the Appendix, Table A.14 shows the same for "you break it, you buy it" taxes. With "you get what you pay for" taxes, earmarking a tax for an aligned use causes participants to support a higher tax rate. The effect is more muted when the tax is earmarked for a misaligned use. With "you break it, you buy it" taxes, the effect of earmarking on rate preferences when the tax and use are aligned remains positive and significant, while the effect of earmarking when tax and use are misaligned does not make yield a statistically discernible effect.[21]

An alternative way to present the same results is to focus on the gap between the responses of the aligned and misaligned groups only. Table 2.2 reports the differences between alignment and misalignment groups across both kinds of taxes and across outcome variables. Row 2 shows the difference between the feeling thermometer outcomes across the aligned and misaligned conditions for hypothetical "you get what you pay for" earmarked taxes. While the differences between the alignment and misalignment groups elsewhere fall short of statistical significance, the consistency with which aligned earmarks outperform misaligned earmarks provides more support for the source-use alignment hypothesis. Perhaps the most powerful evidence, however, comes from the final row of Table 2.2, where we compare how all aligned responses once again differ

Table 2.2 **Differences between Aligned and Misaligned**

Quantity	Difference	95% Confidence Interval
Study 1 Aligned FT - Study 1 Misaligned FT	3.97***	1.20 – 6.74
Study 2 Aligned FT - Study 2 Misaligned FT	2.45	–.82 – 5.7
Study 1 Aligned Rate - Study 1 Misaligned Rate	2.00	–.43 – 4.44
Study 2 Aligned Rate - Study 2 Misaligned Rate	.53	–2.12 – 3.19
All Aligned Rate - All Misaligned Rate	1.27	–.54 – 3.07
All Aligned FT - All Misaligned FT	3.18***	1.04 – 5.34

Note: ***p < 0.01

from all misaligned responses. As the 3.18-percentage-point difference between the two quantities makes clear, across a wide range of hypothetical taxes, aligned earmarked taxes are viewed more favorably than misaligned earmarked taxes.

If people's preference for source-use alignability is consistent with consumer fairness, so too is their opposition to not having *any* information about where their tax money is going. In these experiments, the no-use condition puts respondents in a position analogous to walking into a store, paying a price—a tax—for an item, without being sure what, specifically, they are purchasing. It is no wonder that this condition diminishes feelings about taxes.

Conclusion

I believed that a taxpayer receipt would increase trust in government. I was wrong. Though receipts provide people with more information about where their tax money is going, à la Rivlin (1989), they don't actually make people feel better about the government, or even about their taxes. But by appealing to consumer fairness norms, people's attitudes about their taxes, specifically, can change. Two experiments make clear that, when citizens are told that the costs of government, as borne by them, align with the monetary value of the services they receive, their feelings toward taxes become increasingly positive—and, at the least, this increase roughly matches the increase witnessed when people are just told about the value of the services they receive. This is *cost-benefit alignability*. Furthermore, as the final two experiments in this chapter make clear, *source-use alignability* also matters to people. When taxes are described in ways that achieve this kind of alignability, where the source of the tax matches the use of the tax, not only do people feel better about the tax, but they're somewhat willing to tolerate higher tax rates.

From the perspective of *Homo Emptor*, all of this is no surprise. The vast majority of decisions that he makes involve responding to a combination of costs and benefits. Of course, he is happy to pay as little as possible, and get as much as possible in return. Yet he is also pleased when the amount he has paid roughly accords with the value of what he receives in return. Conversely, he punishes vendors when they give him less than what he paid for, and, all else being equal, he would prefer not to cross-subsidize other activities. In the political realm, this means that he does not like to think that he paid more in taxes than he received back in benefits, or that a tax collected for one specific purpose is being used for another purpose altogether.

Maxims from consumer life—"There is no such thing as a free lunch"—have traction in the political realm. For good reason, *Homo Emptor* has little expectation of receiving free lunches from government. After all, he has little expectation of receiving them elsewhere. Counterintuitive though it may sound, presenting costs and benefits together can have just as powerful effects on attitudes toward taxes as presenting the value of the benefits alone. Sometimes, the effects can be even more powerful.

In her magisterial survey of Americans' attitudes about taxes, Vanessa Williamson (2017, p. 26) interviewed a man named Daniel, a self-professed political independent, who told her that he "think[s] of taxes as the cost of running the country." Taxes, in other words, are a cost we bear to receive the services that the country provides. Or, as another one of Williamson's interview participants—a Democrat named Denise—bluntly put it, "You get the service, you pay for it" (Williamson 2017, p. 36). Not everyone shares this view, of course. In a 2018 nationally representative survey, I found that Republicans are starkly more likely to believe it than Democrats. (More on this in the next chapter.) But as the experiments presented in this chapter demonstrate, the average American is nonetheless moved to become more supportive of government spending—and may even be willing to tolerate higher tax rates—when this maxim is met.

3

The Consumer Citizen, Politicians, and Policy

How far does all this go? Consumer fairness can upend some of our under-standing about Americans' attitudes toward taxes and government spending. Can it also affect the politicians for whom citizens vote, and the public policies for which they choose to sign up?

One way to think of Americans' reliance on consumer fairness norms in polit-ical contexts is as a manifestation of their underlying attitudes toward capitalism. Scholars who've looked for the roots of Americans' political behavior have often turned their attention to the citizens' commitment to elements of capitalism, such as free (or at least less regulated) enterprise and economic individualism. And with good reason: a rich literature has found that support for capitalism has not only endured across the centuries but continues to serve as the bedrock for a constellation of other political attitudes (e.g., McClosky and Zaller 1984; Feldman 1988; Feldman and Zaller 1992; Lipset 1996). In the evocative con-struction of McClosky and Zaller (1984), "capitalist values" are "deeply etched into the national consciousness."[1]

This commitment, it has been argued, also extends into the electoral arena. Beliefs in economic individualism color candidate evaluations (Feldman 1986). As Hofstadter (1948, [1989], xxxvi) put it, "The range of vision embraced by the primary contestants in the major parties has always been bound by the horizons of property and free enterprise." Political journalists regularly claim, sometimes with evidence, that voters prefer politicians who have "business experience." Candidates from both parties trumpet their business acumen while campaigning, describing it as a de facto qualification for public office. On occasion, they even wish to make it de jure: in 2012, Republican presidential nominee Mitt Romney suggested adding a constitutional amendment mandating that only people with prior business experience be eligible for the nation's highest office (Ho 2012).

The Consumer Citizen. Ethan Porter, Oxford University Press (2021). © Oxford University Press.
DOI: 10.1093/oso/9780197526781.003.0003.

Presidential contender Donald Trump made use of such clichés during his campaign, as have countless candidates for everything from Congress to town council. One way to understand Americans' penchant for business experience is to view it as consistent with their general aversion to politics, and their comparatively greater respect for business. Small businesses in particular are trusted by far more people than are the major government institutions. As of 2017, while 40% of Americans said they trusted the Supreme Court, 32% trusted the presidency, and 12% trusted Congress, 70% reported trusting small business (Newport 2017). With this in mind, politicians who boast of their business experience are probably making a wise choice.

Successful U.S. politicians are more likely to hail from business backgrounds than not (Carnes 2013). Yet there is little evidence that business success, or even business experience, in and of themselves wins elections. As the long list of business leaders–turned–failed politicians can attest, elections turn on a great deal of other factors. Ground was never struck on the Perot or Bloomberg presidential libraries.

Americans may not carry a special brief for business leaders turned politicians. But when politicians speak in consumer terms, making allusions to alignability and consumer fairness, people listen. Indeed, they become more attached to consumer citizenship, expressing stronger levels of agreement with its precepts. With the language they use, political leaders can contribute to the development of consumer citizens. As we'll soon see, while Americans do not wish for their politicians to *be* businesspeople, they are responsive when their political leaders use consumer language. In some instances, Americans even prefer that their politicians describe policies in ways familiar to them from their consumer lives. In this manner, capitalist values affect vote choice in the contemporary United States—not at the level of foundational philosophy, but by offering voters a suite of lessons from their consumer lives that they can and do draw upon when evaluating political candidates.

Those who've described Americans' electoral choices as reflective of their fundamental commitment to capitalism are correct. In this chapter I drill down into the specifics of how that commitment plays out. Broadly, Americans view their politicians more favorably when those politicians describe their policies as meeting standards of consumer fairness. They also become more attached to the tenets of consumer citizenship when their political leaders speak in consumer terms.

The influence of consumer fairness norms on vote choice has surprising implications. Typically, when it comes to political candidates, we might think that voters would prefer the one who is promising them the most benefits. From this perspective, voters reward candidates for offering as much as they can possibly offer. This is an elaboration of the free-lunch understanding of Americans' attitudes toward taxes, whereby citizens are understood to want as much as possible, which in turn incentivizes politicians and political aspirants to offer voters as much as possible. Politicians distribute "particularized" benefits, because doing so enhances their chances of reelection (Mayhew 1974). By one measure, an additional $100 in per-capita government spending can increase votes cast in favor of an incumbent by 0.4 to 2 percentage points (Levitt and Snyder 1997). What politicians offer voters usually differs along predictable partisan lines. A Democrat may offer a surge in social programs, while a Republican may offer more in tax cuts. In different ways, both parties offer to put as much as they possibly can in voters' pockets.

But this perspective has its limits. Resources are finite. Candidates for elected office know this, or at least they appear to. In their campaign book, *Putting People First*, Bill Clinton and Al Gore were clear: "We can no longer afford to pay more for— and get less from—our government" (1992, p. 23). What people put into government is related to what they get out. Republican candidates, even when they assert that Americans should be able to keep all of the money they earn, rarely call for the abolition of taxation altogether. For an exception to prove the rule, consider the Republican presidential primary debate held the night of September 22, 2011. At one point, candidate Michele Bachmann, congresswoman from Minnesota, insisted that, indeed, every American should be able to keep every penny that they earn. Yet when pressed by the moderator, she also insisted that every American should pay some kind of tax—even $10 a year, or, as she puts it, about the cost of two Happy Meals at McDonald's.[2]

No one should pay taxes, but everyone should pay taxes: the immediate incoherence of this position prevents it from being routinely uttered aloud. Similarly, though they often strive for more generous social programs, Democrats never pledge to, say, divide up all the money in the government's coffers and divide it equally among the voters. V. O. Key (1966) was right: The voters are not fools. There are limits to what they expect politicians to offer them.

Politicians are not fools either. The limits that politicians seem to stick to when describing policy map onto the limits outlined by consumer fairness. Over the course of this chapter, I'll show that voters sometimes prefer candidates who offer them *fewer* government benefits, particularly when those benefits are described as aligned in value with the taxes they pay. When presented with various hypothetical candidates promising different ratios of government costs and benefits, a startlingly large percentage of Americans support the candidate who promises a roughly aligned combination of costs and benefits. Some even evaluate this candidate more favorably than a candidate who promises more benefits than costs.

Political knowledge, or the lack thereof, plays a considerable role in structuring the extent to which one prefers candidates who promise alignability. In two experiments, I've found a strong negative relationship between political knowledge and support for the candidate who promises alignable costs and benefits.

Those with less political knowledge are especially supportive of the alignability candidate—more so than they are supportive of a candidate who promises to provide greater costs than benefits. This suggests that, when evaluating political candidates' policy platforms, an "alignability heuristic" can affect choices about politics and policy, with less knowledgeable and less engaged voters particularly influenced by it.

If voters sometimes want their candidates to present government costs and benefits as aligned, might they also want the same from social programs? The two questions are related, particularly when the social programs in question are designed in detail by the politicians. If voters want programs to shower benefits on them without regard for cost, then politicians will have a reason to design programs in exactly this manner. Governments will routinely spend more resources than they have, as the voters demand an increasingly large share of their own benefits. Politicians will do what they can to downplay the costs of a program, if not hide them altogether. The result is the "fiscal illusion" that public choice scholars have long warned of, which could, theoretically, endanger economic health, and perhaps even democracy too (Buchanan and Wagner 1977).[3] On the other hand, one implication of my results thus far is that voters do not mind being reminded of the costs of government. Some voters even prefer it. By this standard, a politician who de-emphasizes a program's costs would be foolhardy.

In an experiment conducted in partnership with a health insurance program funded under the Affordable Care Act (or "Obamacare," as it is known colloquially), I show that framing the costs of a program as roughly alignable with the program's benefits can actually increase uptake in the program. In this experiment, I mailed residents of the large midwestern state in which the cooperative was based two promotional messages advertising the cooperative's health insurance. Some residents randomly saw a message merely promoting enrollment in the program; others randomly saw a message making clear that the insurance's benefits were aligned with its costs. The alignability message succeeded, causing people to enroll in the health insurance program being promoted. Participants who signed up for the advertised health insurance were committing hundreds of dollars a month to make the purchase, with all the obvious implications for their personal health and well-being. Alignability can have power not only over how people choose candidates, but how they make decisions about large policy programs that impact the most intimate aspects of their lives.

Vote Choice: Do Voters Go Shopping?

As a first attempt to find out if voters would ever choose candidates who promise cost-benefit alignability, in 2015 I conducted a study of U.S.-based respondents over Mechanical Turk in which participants were asked to choose between two candidates in a nonpartisan mayoral election. The survey explained that the mayor of the town in question had control over the town's taxes and the services that town government provided. Two candidates were then described as follows:

- "*Candidate A* wants to make the value of government services provided to each town resident roughly equal to the value of the taxes they pay. Under his plan, the average town resident would pay about $2,500 in taxes each year, and would receive about $2,500 worth of government services each year."
- "*Candidate B* wants to make the value of government services provided to each town resident be much greater in value than the taxes they pay. Under his plan, the average town resident would pay about $2,500 in taxes each year, and would receive about $5,000 worth of government services each year."

Candidate A was the candidate of cost-benefit alignability. Candidate B was the free-lunch candidate. Quite plainly, if you voted for the latter, you'd do better than if you voted for the former. This constituted an aggressive test of cost-benefit alignability's strength in the electoral arena. To choose Candidate A means that one would be willing to forgo government benefits worth twice as much as the taxes one had paid. After the candidates were described, participants were asked whom they would be more likely to vote for, and they were given a text box to share any thoughts they might have about the candidates.

Of the 169 study participants, 41% chose Candidate A, and the rest chose Candidate B. That is, 41% of subjects surveyed stated that they would prefer to forgo $2,500 worth of government services *beyond the taxes they paid*. To put this result in context, consider results from the dictator games in economics. In such games, a subject is provided with a sum of money, and this subject has sole, "dictatorial" discretion over how to split this money with another subject, if at all. Versions of this game have observed that about two-thirds of dictator subjects are willing to forgo individual benefits to themselves in the name of "fairness." The completely self-interested choice, wherein a subject would keep all the money, is almost never observed, regardless of how the rules of the game are set. (For an overview of the literature and a discussion of results under different rules, consult List [2007].)

Usually, however, the amount of money forgone in dictator games is trivial relative to the size of the total value of the pie that the dictator is allowed to divide. This is not the case here. Choosing the cost-benefit alignability candidate

amounts to eschewing a doubling of the money one has paid in taxes. To choose
Candidate A means to reject a very expensive free lunch.

Political Leaders and the Consumer Citizen

Where do consumer citizens come from? In previous chapters, I supposed that,
in part, they emerge because of the ubiquity of consumer decisions they face.
Here, I want to investigate another possibility: that consumer citizens can also be
forged by politicians. Politicians from both parties have trafficked in consumer
rhetoric. The Clinton administration pursued efforts to "put customers first";
President George W. Bush described his tax cut in consumer terms; President
Obama's signature achievement was the creation of a health insurance marketplace meant to achieve a semblance of consumer fairness (more on this below);
and President Trump's purported business acumen has been inseparable from
his rise to power. It stands to reason that consumer rhetoric is, at least in part, responsible for cultivating consumer citizens. When it comes to politics, everyday
people turn to their politicians for guidance. When they do so, they are especially responsive to politicians from their own party (Lenz 2012).

An experiment I fielded in 2020 measured whether, and to what extent, leading
politicians' rhetoric can lead people to strengthen their attachment to consumer
citizenship. The experiment depended on exposing, at random, some participants
to consumer rhetoric attributed to political leaders of their own party. This, in
turn, allowed me to study whether such rhetoric uttered by people's preferred
leaders can strengthen consumer citizenship, even when accounting for partisanship. If, say, I had only randomly assigned participants to be exposed to consumer
rhetoric from Donald Trump, any effects on consumer citizenship would be difficult to disentangle from their views on Trump. Republicans might respond positively, while Democrats would respond negatively, thereby giving the impression
that only Republicans were consumer citizens—and precluding inferences about
the effects of consumer rhetoric, measured apart from partisanship.

Both Democrats and Republicans respond to consumer rhetoric from their
own party by deepening their sense of consumer citizenship. This experiment,
conducted over Mechanical Turk, proceeded as follows. After identifying as
either Republicans or Democrats, participants read a brief news article.[4] At
random, the news article either featured a co-partisan leader speaking in consumer terms or, for a placebo, discussed a recent beauty pageant. Democrats
assigned to see a co-partisan leader read an article in which President Obama
was speaking in consumer terms, while Republicans read an article in which
President Trump was speaking in such terms.

The only differences between the articles was the identity of the president to which the consumer words were attributed, as well as his party. The article appeared as follows:

[Obama/Trump] Makes Case for [Democratic/Republican] Policies
MINNEAPOLIS, MINNESOTA
At a large political rally, [Barack Obama / Donald Trump] made his case for the Democratic Party / Republican Party]'s policies. He argued that only the [Democrats / Republicans] try to make sure that Americans get as much out of government as they put in.

"You're not getting enough for your tax money," declared [Obama/ Trump] at the rally. "It's important that we make sure all Americans get out of government what they put in. That's what [Democrats/ Republicans]' policies are based on—making sure the relationship between taxing and government spending is fair."

"We should think of government like a business," said [Obama/Trump]. "Like any business, its customers should get what they pay for."

[Obama/Trump] continues his tour of the state later this week.

The rhetoric supposedly uttered by either Trump or Obama hit several key consumer notes. People should get out of government what they put in. The amount people spend on taxes should be matched with government services of equivalent value—anything else would be unfair. Last but not least, government should be understood as a business, and government's "customers" should get what they pay for. Have Trump or Obama spoken in *exactly* those terms? No. But both of their parties have delivered similar messages over the years.

Such messages matter. To measure effects, I relied on a three-part Consumer Scale. On a 5-point scale, respondents were asked to agree or disagree with the following three statements:

1. "Government should be run like a business."
2. "Services provided per person should be equal to taxes paid."
3. "Americans who pay more taxes should get more services."

These questions were designed to capture some of the precepts of consumer fairness. Questions two and three in particular essentially asked respondents if they believed in the premise of alignability: that costs and benefits provided by government should roughly be equal. The first question, meanwhile, was meant to capture a general belief that government should be judged by the standards of the private sector. Participants' responses appeared to be tapping into a distinct underlying dimension, which we might think of as the overall strength of their consumer citizenship.[5]

Along the 1–5 index, the effect of being exposed to co-partisan consumer rhetoric was .31, in the direction of greater agreement with the consumer citizen position. On separate 1–5 scales, subjects exposed to consumer rhetoric were substantially more likely to agree with the propositions that government should be run like a business, services provided per person should be equal to taxes paid, and Americans who pay more taxes should get more services. All effects were significant at conventional levels. Complete results can be found in Table 3.1. Appendix Table A.16 provides descriptive statistics.

The effects were not concentrated among Republicans alone. To be sure, Republicans who had only read the placebo news article were more in agreement with consumer citizenship positions than their Democratic counterparts. On the index, the average Republican placebo response was about 31% greater than the average Democratic response in placebo. But compared to Democrats who hadn't seen the consumer rhetoric, Democrats who had seen the consumer rhetoric were about 13% in greater agreement with the items on the Consumer Scale. Interestingly, interaction models between partisanship and treatment suggest that the largest effects may have been observed among weak Democrats. Ultimately, however, the evidence from this experiment is clear: When uttered

Table 3.1 **Elite Rhetoric and the Consumer Scale**

	Dependent Variable	
	Consumer Scale	
	(1)	(2)
Treatment	0.310***	0.271***
	(0.081)	(0.071)
Constant	2.808***	2.882***
	(0.057)	(0.423)
Observations	838	838
Covariates?	No	Yes
R^2	0.017	0.343
Adjusted R^2	0.016	0.291
Residual Std. Error	1.167 (df = 836)	0.991 (df = 776)
F Statistic	14.799*** (df = 1; 836)	6.633*** (df = 61; 776)

Note: *p < 0.1; **p < 0.05; ***p < 0.01

by co-partisans, consumer rhetoric can compel members of both parties to more strongly identify as consumer citizens.

Trump Voters and Consumer Attitudes

But is consumer citizenship more strongly associated with members of one party more than another? Intuitively, we might suspect the answer to be yes: After all, if we're interested in politicians who embody values that might be appealing to consumer citizens, we can look at Donald Trump. Prior to running for president, President Trump was a salesman par excellence, standing atop an empire of name brands. He sold real estate, he sold steak, and he sold ties at Macy's. While his campaign kick-off speech is often remembered for its vituperative attacks on immigrants, it also managed to weave in numerous references to Trump's business experience, such as it was. "I am not a politician," he explained. "I have worked in business, creating jobs and rebuilding neighborhoods my entire adult life" (Trump 2015). He has repeated claims like this ever since.

A nationally representative survey conducted in the summer of 2018 indicated that about 38% of Americans believe that government should be run like a business. That question appeared on a longer omnibus survey, which included the other two items on the Consumer Scale. Respondents were also asked for their 2016 vote, as well as their then-current level of approval of President Trump.

The relationship between agreeing with the propositions of the Consumer Scale and attitudes toward Trump was quite strong.[6] In fact, the size of the relationship between responses to those statements and attitudes toward Trump was stronger than the relationship between various key demographic variables and attitudes toward Trump.

In Figures 3.1 and 3.2, I've presented results from two models that show relationships between predictors of attitudes toward Trump and support for him. On the left-hand side are the estimated coefficients of a model of the determinants of voting for Trump, while the right-hand side are the estimated coefficients of a model of the determinants of Trump approval. The accompanying models are estimated in Appendix Table A.15.

As the reader may recall, in the first chapter I discussed Sides, Tesler, and Vavreck's (2018) contention that "racialized economics" helps explain Trump support. Racialized economics relates to beliefs about whether nonwhite and/ or immigrant groups receive more than they deserve. One question in the current survey taps similar attitudes. This question reads, "Blacks have gotten less than deserved," with subjects agreeing or disagreeing on a 1–5 scale, with higher numbers indicating greater disagreement (and therefore a more racially conservative response). While the question is not a perfect proxy for racialized

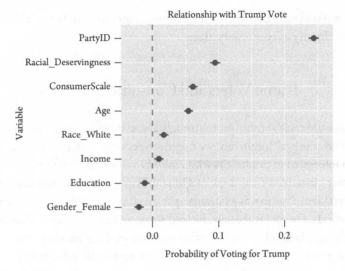

Figure 3.1 Models of self-reported Trump vote, as of July 2018. Variables standardized for comparison. Corresponding models, and details on variable construction, can be found in the Appendix.

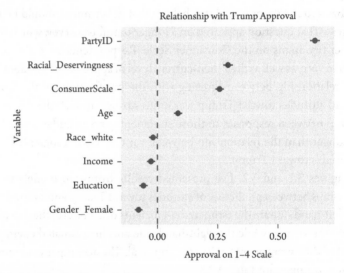

Figure 3.2 Models of self-reported Trump approval, as of July 2018. Variables standardized for comparison. Corresponding models, and details on variable construction, can be found in the Appendix.

economics, it does refer to both race and deservingness at the same time, and will thus suffice for our purposes.

Self-reported voting histories are notoriously inaccurate, and presidential approval is a slippery thing. Moreover, this was not a survey experiment, preventing the kind of causal analysis I offer elsewhere in the book. Despite these limitations, the results are illuminating. In both figures, I've standardized the variables, which allows us to compare the magnitude of the relationship between each independent variable and the dependent variable. As one might expect, the standard 7-point party identification scale blows everything else out of the water. And yet the Consumer Scale outpaces—that is, the magnitude of its relationship is greater—than household income, race, education, gender, and age. As both figures show, the relationship between the Consumer Scale and the outcomes is about as large as the relationship between the outcomes and feelings related to race and deservingness.

On average, self-reported Trump voters scored about 27% higher on the Consumer Scale than those who did not vote for him. This, in turn, was part of a broader pattern related to partisanship and the Consumer Scale, whereby stronger levels of agreement with the scale were somewhat positively associated with identification with the Republican Party.[7] This correlation is not surprising. Yet the fact that it is not especially strong underscores the point that reliance on consumer concepts is related to, but substantively distinct from, partisanship.

To further understand the extent to which responses to the Consumer Scale are distinct from partisanship, consider how evaluations of Trump differ among Democrats based on their placement on the Consumer Scale. Democrats whose position on the Consumer Scale lay above the median were 28% more approving of Trump than Democrats whose position on the scale was below the median. Similarly, Democrats who scored below the median on the Consumer Scale only had a 2% probability of voting for Trump; for Democrats above the median, the probability jumps to 10.1%.

On their own, analyses like these hardly end debate. The challenges of observational survey data are well known. Without rehashing the entirety of the debate, suffice it to say that survey data alone cannot identify causes. We certainly can't say that people's responses to the Consumer Scale questions are *causing* them to support Trump. It may be the other way around: people like Trump, the businessman-turned-politician, and as a result come to change their views about the relationship between government and business. As the prior study in this chapter showed, people respond to political leaders' use of consumer rhetoric by becoming more attached to tenets of consumer citizenship. Either way, in this case, the evidence indicates that supporting Trump, almost halfway into his presidency and on election day, is related to the conflation of government and private firms, as well as supporting a version of alignability.

Who is the consumer citizen? To a large extent, the consumer citizen is likely a Trump supporter or a Democrat who is surprisingly sympathetic toward

Trump. This is in no way guaranteed to last, however: if Democratic leaders were to offer more consumer rhetoric, Democrats would probably strengthen their attachment to consumer citizenship.

The Alignability Candidate Experiment

The second and third questions on the Consumer Scale ask respondents about alignability. Based on the earlier results, it would seem that a large share of people are willing to say they like alignability. But in a survey setting, expressing a preference for alignability may be little more than cheap talk. To meaningfully *prefer* alignability is a taller order. To show meaningful affinity for it, a person must prefer that their government costs and benefits roughly match. In a survey, agreeing with it may only have been a way for Trump supporters to signal their support for the president. And in the experiment with both Obama and Trump, co-partisans may have voiced stronger attachment to consumer rhetoric after treatment not because they actually desired alignability, but because they were eager to follow any signals offered by their political leaders. The substance of alignability, then, may have played a very small role.

An experiment I conducted, however, offers evidence that some people do indeed prefer their political candidates to espouse alignability, holding everything else constant. Some people—specifically, people with less political knowledge than others—seem sincerely enamored with the idea of alignability when it is voiced by political candidates. In fact, these people prefer alignability—even when such support means they would receive fewer government benefits than they would otherwise.

For this experiment, participants were randomly assigned to one of three conditions. Unlike the previous experiment, in which I relied on actual politicians, here I told subjects in each condition about a hypothetical candidate named Sean Woods, running for mayor in a nonpartisan race.[8] The race was described as nonpartisan out of a fear that invoking partisanship would preclude understanding of a preference for alignability. In a controlled experiment in which little information is shared about the candidate, it seems likely that respondents would have reached for the familiar partisan brand and evaluated the candidates largely on that basis.

Participants were randomly presented with one of three versions of Woods to evaluate. In the *Alignability* condition, they were told that Woods wanted to make the cost of the average tax burden and the value of government services roughly alignable in value, with each worth about $2,500. In the *2xBenefits* condition, they were told that Woods wanted to make taxes about $2,500 a person, but provide each town resident about $5,000 worth of benefits. And in the 3xBenefits condition, they were told that Woods wanted to make services worth about $7,500 per person, and taxes about $2,500.

The treatment slide looked like this:

> Sean Woods wants to make the value of government services provided to each town resident be [roughly equal in value to / greater in value than / much greater in value than] the taxes they pay.
>
> Under his plan, the average town resident would pay about $2,500 in taxes each year, and would receive about [$2,500 / $5,000 / $7,500] worth of government services each year.

After being exposed to their treatment assigned, participants were asked to use a 0–100 slider to rate how likely they would be to vote for Woods. They were then asked to evaluate Woods along four affective dimensions. They were asked to agree with statements that Woods "cares about people like me," "is qualified for public office," "shares my values," and "is someone I can trust." To minimize idiosyncratic interpretations of these questions, I then averaged responses, creating what I call an *Affect Average*. In addition, prior to treatment, I also asked all participants to complete the ANES Political Knowledge Battery. The Political Knowledge Battery asks respondents five questions about the organization of American government, such as the length of Senate terms, and asks them to identify four prominent political office holders.[9]

Conducted in February 2016 over Mechanical Turk, 239 U.S.-based respondents completed the experiment. Participants in the *Alignability* condition reported a 49.9% likelihood of voting for Woods, and gave him a mean *Affect Average* score of 60.4. Those in the *2xBenefits* condition reported a 55% likelihood of voting for him, and gave him a mean *Affect Average* score of 67.4. And those in the *3xBenefits* condition reported being 58.4% likely to vote for him, and gave him an *Affect Average* score of 72.9. The 12.5-point difference in *Affect Average* scores between the *Alignability* candidate and the *3xBenefits* candidate is statistically significant, as is the 8.4% difference in the likelihood that participants would vote for such a candidate. The differences between the *Alignability* candidate and the *2xBenefits* candidate are not significant on these questions. (Descriptive statistics appear in Appendix Table A.18.)

Many people, it seems, *do* like the candidate who promises them more benefits than costs. That is all well and good; it would be truly stunning, and frankly implausible, if majorities of people preferred candidates to give them fewer benefits. Yet a large number of participants were, on average, content with a candidate who promised them the same amount of government benefits as costs. The picture becomes even more complicated when we begin to incorporate participants' political knowledge responses. Levels of political knowledge govern people's attitudes toward the Alignability candidate, with less knowledgeable people much more in favor of this candidate than more knowledgeable people.

To arrive at this conclusion, I scrutinized responses to the political knowledge questions in two ways. First, responses were judged correct if any obvious permutation of the correct answer was included in their response. For example, the person who answered "Chief Justice SCOTUS" was judged as providing the right identity of John Roberts. Then, to avoid the mistakes of earlier evaluations of political knowledge that applied unreasonably ungenerous standards of accuracy (Gibson and Caldeira 2009), all responses were read individually. For the most part, this resulted in subjects who misspelled "chief" or "justice"— sometimes with quite creative alternatives—as being counted as having provided correct answers. (My generosity has its limits, however; contra one person, John Roberts is not a "poolboy.")

On the resulting 9-point knowledge scale, the mean knowledge score was 5.9, with a median of 6. With that in mind, I consider participants who scored below a 6 as "low knowledge" and those who scored above a 6 as "high knowledge." High-knowledge participants gave the Alignability candidate an Affect Average score of 44.15. However, low-knowledge participants gave the same candidate a score of 58.3. This 14-point difference is statistically significant at conventional levels. No other candidates yielded such stark differences between high- and low-knowledge participants. In fact, low-knowledge participants preferred the Alignability version of Sean Woods most of all.

To better understand the role that the interaction between political knowledge and treatment condition is playing in the results, I estimated a model with interactions between treatment assignment and political knowledge. Full results appear in Appendix Table A.17. The effects of the interaction between knowledge and assignment to alignability is large, -4.90, and significant (with a p-value below .05). In context, this means that, for those randomly assigned to the Alignability condition, a 1-point increase in their knowledge score reduces their affinity for Woods by about 5%. In Figure 3.3, I present interaction plots of political knowledge and Affect Average for each candidate. As political knowledge increases, so does opposition to the Alignability candidate—and vice versa.[10]

By decomposing the Affect Average measure into its constituent parts, we can better understand precisely how participants' differential levels of knowledge explained their feelings toward the Alignability versions of Woods. When re-running the model that interacts all available demographic information with political knowledge, but making the aligned version of Woods's perceived

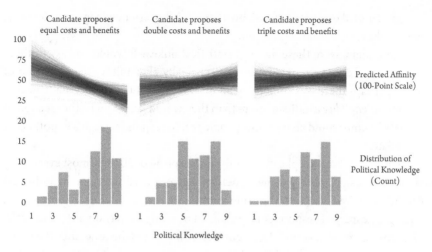

Figure 3.3 Predicted affinity for each candidate (bootstrapped).

trustworthiness the dependent variable, we find that, conditional upon being assigned to that condition, a 1-point increase on the knowledge index degrades subjects' trust level by 5.34 on this 0–100 scale. Similarly, a 1-point increase in the knowledge index reduces their belief that the aligned version of Woods cares about voters like them by 6.0 on that 0–100 scale. A 1-point increase in knowledge among subjects in the *Alignability* condition reduces their belief that Woods shares their values, too.[11]

The relationship between political knowledge and the preference for cost-benefit alignability is further underscored by looking at the results for the version of Woods who promised to double the average value of government services relative to the average tax burden. While affinity for the *Alignability* version of Woods decreased with an increasing knowledge score, the pattern here is reversed, with more knowledgeable participants viewing the *2x* version of Woods more favorably. For every 1-point increase in political knowledge, participants' affinity for this version of Woods increased by 3.38 percentage points.

The direction of the relationship between knowledge and voting is the same as it was for the *Affect Averages*, with less knowledgeable people saying they would be more likely to vote for the *Alignability* version of Woods than the Woods who promised to double or triple benefits relative to taxes. Conversely, higher-inclined people become more inclined to vote for Woods if the ratio of benefits to costs he promises grows. The failure of participants to respond systematically to the Woods who promised to triple the value of benefits relative to taxes may have been a product of sample size. Alternatively, it may be attributable to respondents viewing this candidate as especially unrealistic. On this matter, I can only speculate. All I know is that higher-knowledge participants regard the

$3x$ version of Woods more favorably than their lower-knowledge counterparts, but the difference is not significant.

In the main, were these findings statistical flukes? It would be easy to think so. Perhaps I'd just stumbled upon an especially alignability-friendly group of folks; perhaps there was something about the spring of 2016 that made people like the *Alignability* candidate more than they would later. Maybe the election of Donald Trump would change how people would respond to such a hypothetical candidate.

To find out, I ran a replication study in the spring of 2018. Almost everything about the design was the same as before. Again, I used the same hypothetical candidate, paired him with the same treatments, measured the same outcomes, and again captured respondents' political knowledge levels on a 9-point scale. I had to change what counted as a "correct" response; in the time since the initial study, Theresa May replaced David Cameron as U.K. prime minister, and no less importantly, Donald Trump had been elected president.

But the basic story remained the same. While people still liked best the candidate who promised three times more benefits than costs, indicating they wished to vote for him and generally had a more positive affinity for him, those who had less political knowledge did not feel this way. Indeed, people who had less political knowledge viewed the candidate who promised town residents *less*— the *Alignability* candidate—more favorably than the candidate who promised residents *more* benefits. On the knowledge scale, the median score was again a 6. People below this median said, on average, that there was a .55 probability that they would vote for the *Alignability* candidate. People above the median said there was only a .4 probability they would do the same. Unsurprisingly, people below the median also liked the *Alignability* candidate, as reflected by the various measures that make up the Affect Average measure described above, more than the other candidates—and more than people above the median. On the whole, as political knowledge increases, attitudes toward the *Alignability* candidate become colder, and so do attitudes toward the candidate who promises to double the amount of benefits relative to costs.[12]

Crucially, these results hold when I include study participants who could not, at the end of the study, recall the precise combination of costs and benefits that the hypothetical candidate they had seen described, and when I exclude such participants. This isn't just a question of low-knowledge survey respondents paying less attention to the study and answering randomly. It's tapping into a dividing line in how people evaluate candidates' promises regarding government costs and benefits.

Table 3.2 summarizes participants' feelings toward the *Alignability* candidate in both the original 2016 experiment and the 2018 replication. For both studies, the median level of political knowledge was 6, measured on a 9-point scale, and

Table 3.2 **Feelings about Alignability Candidate, by Knowledge, in 2016 and 2018 Studies**

	Alignability Candidate Affect (High Knowledge)	Alignability Candidate Affect (Low Knowledge)	Difference
2016 Study	44.1	58.3	14.19**
2018 Replication	39.3	53.4	14.14***

Note: *p < 0.1; **p < 0.05; ***p < 0.01

so I've separated individuals into high- and low-knowledge groups, with the median serving as the dividing line. The difference between how high-knowledge and low-knowledge respondents evaluated the alignability candidate was strikingly similar across both studies: those with lower levels of political knowledge felt much more fondly about the *Alignability* candidate than did their high-political-knowledge counterparts.

Different people—less politically knowledgeable people—are comparatively more susceptible to the allure of alignability in their political candidates. From the consumer realm, they probably have heard something like, "If something is too good to be true, it probably is," or "There is no such thing as a free lunch." Such rules, however vague they may be, inform the consumer decisions they make far more frequently, and their evaluation of political candidates. Conversely, more politically knowledgeable people seem to evaluate political candidates qua political candidates, and are quite content to support the candidate who promises to give them more than what they paid.

Why Are Low-Knowledge Voters Especially Susceptible to Alignability?

In the candidate experiments described above, participants who lacked political awareness, as evinced by their relatively poor performance on a political knowledge battery, proved most susceptible to the candidate whose policy platform promised alignability. Two possible, interrelated explanations beckon. The first focuses on the lack of familiarity that low-awareness participants have with political decisions. They are not used to evaluating objects in political environments or contexts, and thus bring to bear the evaluative strategies they employ when evaluating objects in other, more familiar environments. This reading extends the logic of John Zaller and Philip Converse. Converse (and Zaller) find that "awareness of contextual information is likely to depend on general levels of political awareness" (Zaller 1992, p. 45). Here, it seems as if those who lacked political awareness were more likely to import techniques from an environment with which they were more familiar. Facing a deficit of contextual information, low-awareness people applied contexts from a different environment. Chaiken (1980, p. 753) wrote, "Heuristic information processing may involve the use of relatively general rules (scripts, schemata) developed by individuals through their past experiences and observations." In this case, low-information participants took a general rule from one environment, one they'd used before, and brought it into another environment.

The second, related explanation depends on my decision to deprive participants of partisan cues. A copious body of research tell us that, when evaluating candidates, Americans are overwhelmingly likely to rely on their partisan affiliation. Party identification is often formed early in life, and endures for a long time, and certainly from election to election (Campbell et al 1960; Norpoth 2008). By one account, partisan attachments are analogous to ethnic or religious attachments, insofar as they persist for decades and usually remain invulnerable to contrary empirical evidence (Green, Palmer, and Schickler 2002). Partisanship's role in structuring vote choice may only have grown over time (Bartels 2000; Abramowitz 2010). Researchers frequently invoke the language of "brands" to describe ordinary people's relationship with the parties (e.g., Lavine, Johnston, and Steenbergen 2012; Lupu 2013), although this language is kept at the level of metaphor. People identify with those brands that they believe most closely match their own self-image (Green, Palmer, and Schickler 2002). While there is reason to think that the effect of partisanship on vote choice has occasionally been overstated when compared to the effect of policy voting (Fowler 2017), even this skeptical take on partisanship paints it only as *an equal* to policy.

Without partisanship, voters lose a factor that would otherwise be essential in their decision-making process. In their look at ANES panel data from six presidential elections, including 2012, Don Kinder and Nathan Kalmoe find that party affiliation helps shape voting *regardless of the amount of political information at subjects' disposal*—"for the poorly informed, for the well informed, and everyone in between," partisanship matters a great deal (Kinder and Kalmoe 2016, pp. 99–100). Without partisanship, low-information voters have little to fall back on. In Zaller's canonical model (1992), people with fewer predispositions about politics are easier to persuade. In presidential elections and otherwise high-salience partisan elections (Rahn 1993), the party itself can provide the kind of cue to which low-information voters respond. In general, low-information voters seek out heuristics to minimize the cognitive costs of candidate selection. By virtue of having weak partisan attachments, such voters are more interested in seeking out heuristics to reduce their decision-making under their comparatively greater uncertainty (Mondak 1993).

Forced to make use of other signs, low-information voters turn to alignability to help them make their decision. After all, they are already familiar with alignability from their time as consumers. Low-knowledge voters regard the *Alignability* candidate most favorably, including over other candidates who promise to heighten the value of government benefits well beyond the cost. But as knowledge increases, support for the *Alignability* candidate wanes. Without the crutch of partisanship, voters who have fewer predispositions will be more likely to rely on what they know from their time as consumers. An "alignability heuristic," informed by their consumer experiences, evidently has pull over their electoral choices, particularly in nonpartisan settings. Those under its spell will support candidates whose policies promise them *fewer* government benefits, compared to candidates who promise them more.

The Obamacare Experiment

In and of itself, this result is surprising. I've shown that, conditional upon possessing low levels of political knowledge, voters respond positively to electoral candidates whose platforms promise cost-benefit alignability. But in the real world, with real stakes, it is surely possible that voters behave differently. And while it *seems* like President Trump was able to capture a large number of people who might be described as consumer citizens, he did not campaign on alignability explicitly. In fact, for a Republican candidate, his willingness to defend government programs was unusual. If government programs that involve money and consequences are involved, do voters still respond positively to alignability? In other words, does *Homo Emptor* go shopping for social programs, just as she might go shopping for goods at Walmart or on Amazon? If so, will appealing to the norms of consumer fairness make *Homo Emptor* more likely to enroll in such programs?

The policy architects of the Patient Protection and Affordable Care Act (Affordable Care Act, ACA, Obamacare) certainly seemed to think so. The Affordable Care Act is built around certain periods of open enrollment, during which government-subsidized health insurance is available for purchase. In the first open enrollment period in 2014, an aggressive advertising campaign was deployed to try and convince Americans to sign up for health insurance as the law mandated. Professional sports stars, including Lebron James, participated in the commercial; the president recorded a promotional video skit with actor and comedian Zach Galifanikas. In the first period of open enrollment, the federal government spent more than $50 million to persuade Americans to sign up for

health insurance (Shear and Vega 2014). Yet the ACA's creators trusted advertising only so much, as they paired the advertising campaign with a mandate to
purchase health insurance. Under this mandate, Americans who did not have
health insurance would have to pay a penalty.

The ACA advertising campaign largely focused on affordability. "Affordability
is a big issue in terms of how people make decisions," explained U.S. Health
and Human Services administrator Sylvia Mathews Burwell as the ad campaign debuted nationwide (Pear 2015). She was right—to a point. Affordability
matters, but it's not the only thing that matters. Presumably unbeknownst to
her, Burwell was echoing those who view citizens as clamoring for the largest
possible benefits at the smallest possible cost. Insofar as people like to pay as
little as possible, Burwell was right. But as we've already seen, that's not *all* they
like. Sometimes bringing the cost to the surface—and communicating the
alignability of the cost to the value of what one gets in return—also leads to satisfied customers.

It might stand to reason that if government programs could be described in
this way, people would view them more positively. Yet the U.S. government seems
inept on this front, failing to communicate successfully the benefits it provides
(Howard 1997; Mettler 2011). The consequences for government program use
are significant, if unsurprising: Large swaths of people fail to take advantage of
programs for which they qualify (Soss 1999). And even when they do, they often
leave before their eligibility has expired (Blank and Ruggles 1993). One explanation holds that the "stigma" of government programs depresses enrollment in
them (Moffitt 1983). Under this theory, people would rather refrain from using
government programs than risk the embarrassment associated with them.

The failure of government to advertise its wares effectively only mirrors the
failures of private-sector companies to do the same. The academic literature has
ranged from skepticism to outright pessimism about the possibility of advertising affecting purchasing behavior. This is likely true when the content of the
advertising is political (Ashworth and Clinton 2007; Krasno and Green 2008;
but see Spenkuch and Toniatti 2016), but it has also been the case when the content is commercial. Reviews of the advertising literature have noted that most
of the studies claiming statistically significant effects are lab-based and thus
lack much external validity (Chandy et al. 2001). As Gentzkow and DellaVigna
(2009) summarize the literature, "The results of these marketing studies provide
little support for the view that there is a consistent effect of advertising spending
on sales." If, say, Coca-Cola has trouble converting advertising into revenue,
there would seem to be little hope for government. Coca-Cola's products are
much easier to understand than government's. They're tastier, too.

What compelling evidence there is on behalf of advertising's effectiveness has
come from field experiments. Bertrand et al. (2010) worked in partnership with

a South African consumer lender to test the effects of advertising by mail. The researchers found that mailing postcards increased loan uptake, that customers preferred less expensive loans, and that those recipients whose postcards featured photos of attractive women were more likely to purchase loans. Others have used Internet-based experiments to show advertising's effectiveness (Lewis and Reiley 2011). Perhaps there is hope for advertising yet.

More recently, scholars have observed some positive effects from advertising campaigns about public services. An environmentally friendly energy firm, Opower, randomized message distribution to customers, with some randomly assigned messages containing information about the energy use of their neighbors. One author found that such messages reduced overall energy consumption by 2 percentage points (Allcott 2011). Relatedly, Bolsen et al. (2014) distributed "pro-social" messages to a random swath of citizens in the United States during a drought, emphasizing the need to conserve water. The messages had a positive effect on conservation.

When it comes to private goods such as consumer loans, or utilities married to prosocial messages, the Don Drapers of the world can breathe sighs of relief. Advertising works, or at least it can. Yet whether appealing to citizens with advertising can also affect uptake of public programs remains an open question.

To help investigate this question, in January 2015 I ran a study in partnership with a midwestern cooperative funded by the ACA. The aim was to conduct a field experiment, modeled on Bertrand et al. (2010), to see if cost-benefit alignability could be wielded to increase uptake of an expensive social program. The cooperative I worked with was one of twenty-three health insurances cooperatives founded nationwide by the ACA. The ACA used federal funding to jump-start statewide cooperatives in order to increase insurance rates in notoriously limited markets. Such co-ops received $2.3 billion in federal funds, of which our partner organization received about 5%.

Those who purchased insurance from our partner bought plans that followed the ACA's metallic scheme. There were four tiers of metals. Plans in the highest tier, platinum, offered a combination of high premiums and low deductibles, while plans in the lowest tier, bronze, offered the opposite.[13] Membership growth in our partner organization's insurance was slow at first—there were only 4,000 customers in 2014, the year before this study was conducted—but quickly swelled to more than 55,000 by the time we fielded our study.

The study was premised on the idea that citizens would respond positively, and indeed sign up for the health insurance being sold, if it were described as offering a level of benefits aligned with its level of costs.[14] To translate this admittedly abstract expectation into concrete language, before putting any messages in the field, I curated a tournament of messages online, in order to statistically determine which messages were most persuasive.[15]

To Whom It May Concern:

We are writing to tell you about our company,
     We're a nonprofit. Our plans are priced to reflect
their costs. We aim to provide fair coverage for you and your
family.

We believe that everyone in   deserves access to affordable,
high-quality health care. Our plans offer generous benefits and
high-quality coverage.

Enrollment in   for this year will close on
February 15th. If you sign up by then, you will have coverage
starting on March 1st.

To sign up for one of our plans, call us at
You can also visit our website, at

-Your Friends at

Figure 3.4 Obamacare treatment postcard.

I then took the winning messages to the partner cooperative's legal counsel. (Lawyers are even more powerful than political scientists.) We settled on the messages portrayed in the postcards displayed in Figures 3.4 and 3.5. The treatment postcard makes clear that the cooperative's prices are reflective of costs— thereby meeting a key tenet of consumer fairness, as noted by some of the earliest work on the subject (Kahneman, Knetsch, and Thaler 1986a; 1986b). This postcard also uses the word "fair," highlighting the concept that I expected to motivate people to actually purchase health insurance. Figure 3.5, meanwhile, is a placebo message, designed to convey the basic message used by our partner cooperative in other promotional efforts but without making reference to anything like alignability. Without such a placebo, any possible increases in enrollment observed among those who received the fairness message might be attributable to the fact that those who received the message simply had more information about the cooperative. A placebo ensures that both treatment and nontreatment subjects have information about the cooperative, allowing us to better distinguish the effects of consumer fairness in particular.

Note that neither message made mention of the ACA or Obamacare. This was for three reasons. First, the preliminary data indicated that mentioning either Obama or the ACA had no effect on attitudes about enrollment. Second,

---

Dear Neighbor:

We are writing to tell you about our company,
:   '. **We were founded in 2012. We service all residents
in the state of**   .

We believe that everyone in   deserves access to affordable,
high-quality health care. Our plans offer generous benefits and
high-quality coverage.

Open enrollment in   for this year will
close on February 15th. If you sign up by then, you will have
coverage starting on March 1st.

**To sign up for one of our health plans, please visit our website
at** :   .

-Your Friends at

Figure 3.5   Obamacare placebo postcard.

the partner organization made no mention of either in their standard promotional material. On the whole, the leeway that ACA-funded health insurance organizations had to distance themselves from the ACA remains one of the better accomplishments of the law. If use of social programs does indeed decline because users feel a stigma associated with it, as Moffitt (1983) argued, then it was to the program's advantage to minimize individual users' connections to the program.

After settling on the messages, the cooperative and I hired a mailing company to distribute and send the postcards to 10,000 randomized residents of the state in which the partner cooperative operated. Five thousand residents received the treatment postcard; 5,000 received the placebo. To be clear, I had no idea if the 10,000 people we selected already owned health insurance. Privacy regulations on health insurance are justifiably onerous. This meant, however, that any effect I did find was likely to be on the conservative side. In all likelihood, I mailed postcards to many people who were somewhat satisfied with their health insurance and would have been resistant to any message I sent them.

The experiment ran during the open enrollment period that lasted from November 15, 2014, to February 15, 2015. The postcards were mailed on January 8, 2015. I removed some addresses that could not be verified. To verify distribution I added my own address to both the treatment and placebo lists. I received both postcards on January 10. After open enrollment ended, and after removing myself from the results file, I analyzed what I'd found.

Before turning to those results, however, it's worth dwelling on the subtlety of the intervention. Perhaps the most controversial aspect of ACA was its mandate and the attendant penalty for noncompliance. This penalty is a blunt object, essentially designed to coerce people into buying health insurance. In contrast, the alignability message we sent relied only on altering a few sentences on a postcard. To be clear, at the time of the experiment, recipients of both postcards were obligated to buy health insurance under the law. But the alignability postcard connected the implicit coercion of the law to a consumer fairness message.

While the postcard is a familiar tool of the experimental literature, the outcome variable in this study was unusually costly. Rather than looking at voter turnout, as previous canonical experiments involving postcards as treatments have done (e.g., Gerber, Green, and Larimer 2008), this study looked at whether individuals respond to treatment by purchasing a monthly health insurance plan. Many plans purchased in our experiment carried monthly premiums of between $400 and $500. Moreover, the study did not revolve around which candidate or party would best advance one's interests, but how to best preserve or advance one's own life. This experiment, in other words, repurposed a treatment often used in get-out-the-vote experiments and applied it to a much more expensive and consequential outcome.

In total, thirty-one state residents who were sent a postcard signed up for health insurance with our partner cooperative, implying an overall enrollment rate of .31%. Of the thirty-one subjects who enrolled posttreatment, twenty had been sent the treatment postcard, with the remaining eleven coming from the placebo group. This difference, however small it may appear, offers strong evidence that being sent a fairness message can, on its own, increase enrollment in the ACA. Compared to those who received a message containing just information about the health insurance cooperative—information similar to that which they would have encountered elsewhere through the cooperative's marketing efforts—the people who received the consumer fairness message were almost twice as likely to sign up.[16]

The detailed results appear in Table 3.3. I estimate four models. In column 1 of Table 1 I present the results of a simple linear probability model. In column 2 I rely on one of the few pretreatment variables at our disposal: recipients' zip codes. Collection of pretreatment covariates was limited by Health Insurance Portability and Accountability Act (HIPAA) and Institutional Review Board (IRB) requirements. Given these limitations, zip codes are the best available proxy for important geographic and socioeconomic heterogeneity in the results. As such, I estimate the same ordinary least squares (OLS) model in column 2,

Table 3.3 **Alignability Message and ACA Enrollment**

	Dependent Variable Enrollment in ACA			
	(OLS)	(OLS)	(Logit)	(Logit)
Alignability Message	0.002*	0.002**	0.58*	0.74**
	(0.001)	(0.001)	(0.38)	(0.425)
Constant	0.002***	0.001	−6.1***	−2.54***
	(0.001)	(0.06)	(0.30)	(1.1)
Observations	9,926	9,926	9,926	767
Zip-Code Fixed Effects?	No	Yes	No	Yes

Note: *p < 0.1; **p < 0.05; ***p < 0.01

but add in zip code–fixed effects. In column 3 I estimate the model from column 1 but with logistic regression, and in Column 4 I provide logistic regression estimates with zip code–fixed effects. Across models I find the same thing: the alignability message had a detectable, positive effect on whether people actually signed up for health insurance or not. To visualize the effect I present Figure 3.6, which overlays the obtained effect estimates for both conditions on top of 1,000 bootstraps of the linear model (without covariates) in Table 3.3.

The reported estimates are all made in what is known as an Intent-to-Treat (ITT) framework. I cannot say for sure whether recipients received or read their messages, although I have reason to be confident that the mail vendor did distribute them. All I can say is that we *intended* to send a randomly assigned group of state residents the treatment postcard, while an equally sized group of state residents were assigned the placebo postcard. The estimates, therefore, only account for the effects of being randomly assigned to be sent an alignability message. In addition, I only had access to the partner's posttreatment membership records; it is possible that the message spurred people to purchase health insurance from other vendors whose data I could not access. In sum, the estimated effect is likely quite conservative.

To put the cost and benefits to the provider in perspective, the partner organization spent $2,000 distributing the fairness postcards, implying an advertising-cost-per-enrollee of $100. Given the average monthly premiums, the fairness messages more than paid for themselves. The same is true of those who received placebo messages. Sending 5,000 placebo postcards also cost $2,000, implying an advertising-cost-per-enrollee of $181.82. Overall, to net thirty-one new enrollees, the partner organization spent $129.03 on advertising per new enrollee. To be sure, the enrollment rate among treatment subjects was quite

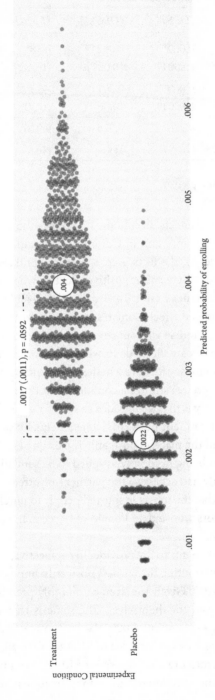

Figure 3.6 Consumer fairness messages and ACA enrollment (bootstrapped).

small. But the difference between treatment and control in advertising-cost-per-enrollee, $81.82, is substantial. In addition, our research partner also provided us with details about the cost of the coverage that our subjects had purchased. Subjects who were sent the placebo postcard purchased health insurance with, on average, $471.23 monthly premiums; those who purchased insurance after being sent treatment postcards purchased insurance with less expensive premiums ($420.94). However, this difference is not statistically significant when reestimating the models described above.

The burden for this test was steep. It is not likely that many people could ever be persuaded to sign up for health insurance on the basis of a postcard alone, regardless of the vendor in question or the message conveyed. But as we found, some people can be persuaded on just that basis. Alignability is powerful enough to persuade people to take expensive actions that have long-term implications for their health and well-being.

Though it has received immense criticism since its inception, perhaps the ACA deserved more credit for its design than not only its critics but also its supporters gave it. Politicians from both parties have long been attuned to the demands of the consumer citizen. The ACA was specifically designed to treat citizens as customers free to choose their own health insurance. In describing the ACA to Congress, President Obama asserted that his "guiding principle" held that "consumers do better when there is choice and competition" (Obama 2009). There was, to be clear, no mention of anything like alignability in the initial marketing of the policy. But the president's impulse was largely correct.

Whether they are shopping for, say, snow shovels (Kahneman, Thaler, and Knetsch 1986a) or health insurance, consumer fairness can influence outcomes. The findings presented here echo previous work on advertising's ability to affect behavior related to public services, such as energy consumption (Allcott 2011) and water consumption (Bolsen, Ferraro, and Miranda 2014). But as far as I know, this is the first study to show that consumer fairness criteria can influence purchasing decisions in the policy domain, just as it does in the consumer domain. If the promoters of the ACA had viewed the consumer as a consumer citizen, in the same way the law's creators seemed to intuit, perhaps the program would have been more successful.

This experiment, after all, was conducted while the ACA still required all Americans to buy health insurance or face a small financial penalty, a provision that would be repealed at the end of 2017. In designing this aspect of the law, the ACA's architects relied on coercion, among the bluntest tools at government's disposal: either follow the law and purchase health insurance—or face the consequences. The evidence here suggests that coercion coupled with references to consumer fairness could have increased ACA enrollment more than coercion alone.

Drilling Down into the Health Insurance Results

What, specifically, made the treatment postcard comparatively appealing to the residents who received it? The treatment postcard featured three sentences at the top, and in bold, that the placebo postcards did not. While the placebo postcards told recipients that the company had been founded in 2012, the treatment postcards described the company as "a non-profit." Also, the placebo postcards noted that the company served all residents in the recipient's home state, while the treatment postcards declared that the company's plans were "priced to reflect their costs." Finally, the treatment postcards promised that the company would "aim to provide fair coverage for you and your family."

In a perfect world, we would be able to go back in time, win the cooperation of the company's legal counsel, and send out a different treatment postcard for each sentence that distinguished the treatment postcards from the placebo ones. Unfortunately, we do not live in that world. As a next-best exercise, I fielded an online survey experiment in which people were asked about a hypothetical health insurance company. At random, the company was described with only one of the distinctive descriptions used in the field experiment, including a placebo sentence. Specifically, people were told, "We're interested in your views on a health insurance company. This company says [it is a non-profit / its plans are priced to reflect their costs / its aim is to provide fair coverage for you and your family / it was founded in 2015]."[17]

I then asked all participants to evaluate the hypothetical health insurance company with a feeling thermometer, and I inquired how likely they would be to buy insurance from the hypothetical company. Compared to the placebo sentence, each sentence culled from the treatment postcard worked like a charm. People not only viewed more favorably the companies described with sentences from the treatment postcards, they were also far more likely to indicate a willingness to buy insurance from the company. For example, compared to the placebo, being told that the hypothetical health insurance company was a nonprofit increased by 31% participants' willingness to say they would buy the insurance. Being told the company's plans were "priced to reflect their costs" increased by 21% their willingness to buy. And the pledge of fair coverage increased such willingness by 39%. Similarly large positive effects were observed on people's general feelings toward the company that had been described. Complete regression results appear in the Appendix at Table A.19.

In sum, *all* elements of the postcards seemingly helped convince people to buy the health insurance they were being sold. When it comes to policy, people respond not only to idiosyncratic, divisible reminders of consumer fairness and alignability; they are responsive to lots of them.

Conclusion

When it comes to politics and policy, how far does consumer fairness go, and do different people respond to it differently? In the Obamacare study, effects were observed on average, across all study participants. The effects as they relate to electoral candidates were more heterogeneous. As we saw with the experimental data about candidates, on two occasions, less-knowledgeable voters were most moved by the candidate who pledged alignability. In fact, in those experiments, low-knowledge voters preferred the *Alignability* candidate most of all. People who know less about politics have good reason to rely on heuristics to aid their decision-making (Mondak 1993; Lupia 1994). Here, low-knowledge voters' electoral preferences reflected consumer fairness norms. In doing so, these voters came to support, most of all, the candidate who plainly promised to give them the least. While there is a voluminous debate about whether heuristics lead to positive social outcomes or incomes in an individual's self-interest (e.g., Gigerenzer and Todd 2000; Kuklinski and Quirk 2000), it would seemingly be hard to argue that low-information voters are personally well served by relying on an alignability heuristic when they select a candidate to support. After all, the candidate supported proposed policies that were plainly contrary to their self-interest.

When voters take positions against their self-interest, they are often described as lacking in requisite information. Larry Bartels, for example, claimed that support for the Bush tax cut of 2001 "derived in considerable part from unenlightened considerations of self-interest among people who did not recognize the implications of President Bush's policies for their own economic well-being" (Bartels 2008, p. 181). That is, people who would not benefit from the tax cut believed they would, and this basic error led them astray. There is surely something to this explanation. As Bartels points out, among Democrats, more-informed voters were much less supportive of the tax cuts than less-informed voters—with the implication being that, had they been informed, their preferences might have been different.

Among Republicans, however, no such pattern was evident. Support for Bush's tax cuts was largely stable across information levels. Doubtlessly much of that can be explained by the effects of partisanship. President Bush was a Republican, and his fellow Republicans wanted to support their man. Yet some Republicans may have been motivated by a sincere preference for having a sense that government was giving them fewer benefits, or benefits aligned with the taxes they paid. Of course, they may have inflated or misperceived the taxes they actually paid. But so too they might have neglected the full benefits that government gave them. This would have been, as Bartels put it, a sort of "unenlightened consideration of self-interest."

But as my evidence regarding Trump voters suggests, their attitudes toward Bush's tax cuts might also have been part and parcel of their broader belief that government should be run like a business—that government should match costs to benefits, even if that means they themselves would get less than otherwise. As of this writing, such a belief matters in predicting support for President Trump. Some of that support may be misinformed, but some may come from a belief in something like alignability—even when alignability cuts against ostensible self-interest.

In addition, as this chapter shows, political leaders from both parties can help cultivate consumer citizenship. Political scientists often speak of the allure that partisan leaders have on everyday Americans, and at times, leaders from both parties have spoken in consumer terms. Here, I've shown that when partisan leaders—the current Republican president, the most recent Democratic president—speak in such terms, their co-partisans listen. Indeed, when articulated by political leaders, consumer rhetoric can cause Americans from both parties to more stridently believe that government should be run like a business, that people who pay more taxes should get more government services, and that, in general, the value of government services should be equivalent to the amount of taxes paid. In other words, although less knowledgeable, more Republican voters may be more likely to be consumer citizens, but we should not view Democrats as immune to the power of such rhetoric.

Nor should we regard consumer citizens as always working against their interests. Alignability may be an unusual idea, but it does not necessarily lead people astray from politics and policies that would serve them. The health-care experiment is a case in point. In that study, alignability prompted people to sign up for government-provided health insurance. I observed those effects across an entire random sample, not just among the less well-informed.

In political campaigns, low-information voters may be more under the sway of an alignability heuristic than their better-informed counterparts, even if the heuristic cuts against their interests. But all individuals, regardless of their level of political knowledge, can be affected by consumer fairness norms when they are asked to enroll in complex social programs. Consumer fairness rhetoric can cause members of both parties to more strongly identify as consumer citizens. Consumer fairness can change how people view government spending, how much they're willing to pay in earmarked taxes, and even the candidates they support. Consumer fairness can go far indeed.

4

The Consumer Citizen, Political Knowledge, and Political Attitudes

While less-knowledgeable voters appear to be the most affected by consumer thinking, it is not as if most voters are particularly well informed. For decades, scholars have observed stunningly low levels of political knowledge—levels not accordant with common expectations of prosperous, educated democracies. In this chapter I investigate whether or not political knowledge can be increased by appealing to people as consumers. To do so, I rely on the taxpayer receipt discussed in the Chapter 2. In two new experiments, administered in the United States and abroad, participants were provided with itemized, per-capita estimates of the uses of their tax money. In both cases, the receipts made recipients more knowledgeable about how government spent their tax dollars. Specifically, the receipts made people's perceptions more accurate about how much their government spends on items such as education, foreign aid, and welfare.

This result, in and of itself, is no small thing. Having an informed citizenry is often described as a prerequisite for democracy (e.g., Hochschild and Einstein 2015). Political knowledge is not just a good on its own, but is vital for the attitudes and behaviors that follow. As Michael Delli Carpini and Scott Keeter (1997) explain, without a modicum of knowledge about the world around them, citizens will have trouble identifying their interests, distinguishing those parties and policies that serve to advance those interests, and connecting the two. A citizen lacking political knowledge will not know what he wants politically—and even if he figures that out, he will not know what to support, and what to oppose, in the name of achieving the desired outcome.

Yet in the same experiments in which I find that taxpayer receipts can increase political knowledge about government spending, I also find that such approaches do not change political attitudes about redistribution. In a sense, this echoes my previous forays into studying the taxpayer receipt. The receipts can improve knowledge, but they can't change redistributive preferences.

The Consumer Citizen. Ethan Porter, Oxford University Press (2021). © Oxford University Press.
DOI: 10.1093/oso/9780197526781.003.0004.

What, if anything, can? As we know from previous chapters, alignability can do the trick. In this chapter I introduce a new possibility: that the everyday pressure that people experience in consumer life can change how they feel about redistribution. In a study outlined in this chapter, I found that priming people to think about overdue bills and underfunded bank accounts can prod them to become more supportive of redistribution. Attitude changes, it turns out, do not have to be preceded by changes in political knowledge. They can come from everyday consumer life.

The Taxpayer Receipt and Political Knowledge

Much of the evidence gathered in social science indicates that the quantity of political knowledge that the public possesses is perilously small. In perhaps the most influential study of mass political ignorance, Philip Converse reports that people have trouble understanding how and why the parties can be described as "liberal" or "conservative." In Converse's study, one respondent thought Republicans "liberal" because of "the money they have spent in this last [Eisenhower] administration." Another respondent declared Republicans conservative because they "try to hold down the spending of government money," which prompted the person performing the survey to ask how they held spending down. "By having no wars," the respondent replied, casually consigning the Korean War to the fiction section (Converse 1964, p. 24).

Many observers have echoed Converse's conclusion: the public knows "astonishingly little" about politics (e.g., Delli Carpini and Keeter 1997). This is true about matters of ideology and policy (Kinder and Kalmoe 2016), but also matters that should be more straightforward. They have trouble correctly identifying passages from the U.S. Constitution and naming the members of the Supreme Court. A 2016 survey by the American Council of Trustees and Alumni found that, among other examples of ignorance, 10% of U.S. college graduates believe that Judge Judy, of the eponymous syndicated television show, is actually a member of the Supreme Court (American Council of Trustees and Alumni 2016). A 2002 Columbia Law School survey reported that about two-thirds of Americans think the Marxist dictum "From each according to his ability, to each according to his needs" appears in the U.S. Constitution (Cole 2002).

To be sure, pessimism about political knowledge has at times been exaggerated. On several occasions, measurement error has led to excessively large estimates of ignorance (Achen 1975; Gibson and Caldeira 2009). (The possibility for similar measurement is why I was exceptionally careful in coding responses as accurate or not in the studies described in the previous chapter.) Yet this revisionist take has hardly challenged the general point: even in an advanced democracy like the

United States, ordinary people don't know much about politics. Perhaps more alarmingly, some citizens are not only ignorant but have great difficulty learning new facts about politics. In lab studies, only the most aggressive techniques—described as "hitting subject between the eyes"—have occasioned increases in knowledge (Kuklinski et al. 2000).

People seem to know comparatively more about picayune matters than they do politics. In the early 1990s, for example, while 86% of voters knew the name of George H. W. Bush's family dog, and 89% knew the television character whom Vice President Dan Quayle had attacked, only 5% knew that both Quayle and Bush supported repealing the capital gains tax (Delli Carpini and Keeter 1997, p. 63). Yet this should not be nearly as stunning, or even as sad, as it might first sound. People like dogs and television far more than policy. More precisely, they seem to enjoy thinking about dogs and television more than policy. (Some days, it is hard to blame them.) *Homo Emptor*, as we understand him, spends far more time thinking about consumer decisions than political ones. What if this could be leveraged to increase *Homo Emptor's* supply of political knowledge? Rather than merely ruing the political ignorance of everyday people, we might be able to mitigate their ignorance—by appealing to them as consumer citizens.

As the reader may recall from the discussion of the taxpayer receipt in Chapter 2, taxpayer receipts are designed to parsimoniously represent the uses of government spending by mimicking the properties of a consumer receipt. If the receipt could not produce the large gains in trust I expected it to, perhaps it could still make people aware of the facts it conveys. None of these facts are, in the language of Carmines and Stimson (1989), "easy"; rather, taxpayer receipts present per-capita estimates of individuals' contributions to individual spending categories. Survey data show that voters are often bewildered by questions about government spending. The amounts that government spends dwarf those that consumers are likely to encounter in everyday life. As of 2016, for example, only 3% of Americans knew that "foreign aid" constitutes less than 1% of total federal spending. The average guess was 31% (DiJulio et al. 2016). As journalist Ezra Klein once put it, misconceptions about the size of foreign aid have morphed into "the budget myth that just won't die" (Klein 2013).

In the fall of 2016 I tried to see if the taxpayer receipt could be used on U.S. subjects to increase their political knowledge. To do so, I asked U.S.-based Mechanical Turk respondents to select their household income from eight possible options, and then presented the respondents with a taxpayer receipt based on their selection. To present the per-capita data, I relied on the last available version of the White House taxpayer receipt (thanks to 2011 spending caps, spending had not changed all that much in the intervening years).

I randomly varied the kinds of taxpayer receipts that people would see. Members of the Standard Receipt treatment group saw a version of the receipt with categories broken down to their (estimated) overall tax contribution. For example, for the health-care category, those assigned to this condition who made less than \$37,000 were told that \$636.05, or 27.49% of their tax bill, went to health care. Meanwhile, people randomly assigned to the Percentage-Only Receipt were shown only the percentage of their tax money that had gone to each item. Naturally, those in this condition did not see any personalized information, as the percentages were universal. Still others were shown *only* their per-capita contribution to environmental matters, expressed as both a percentage of the total and the dollar figure. This Environment-Only Receipt was created on the supposition that, upon seeing a receipt about one item, people would be spurred to think more critically about the other items. Finally, participants in the control group saw no information about spending. (Images of examples of the different receipts appear in Appendix subsection "Examples of U.S. Receipts in 2016 Study," as Figures A.6, A.7 and A.8.)

Afterward, I then asked all participants, "What percentage of your tax money does the U.S. government spend on the categories below? For each category, drag the slider to the value you believe best represents what percentage of your tax money the U.S. government spends on each category." Each spending category had a separate slider that respondents could adjust from 0 to 100.

I'd anticipated that people who saw the Environment-Only Receipt would at least remember the information conveyed to them about the environment. That seemed like a safe assumption: people's attention spans are limited, and asking them to remember lots of information seemed like a more demanding ask than asking them only to remember one specific thing. Similarly, I expected people who saw the percentage version to do somewhat better than the people who saw the Standard Receipt. Percentages are not easy, but converting numbers to percentages is even harder.

Since there is no reason to expect or desire citizens to know *exactly* how much of their taxes go to each spending item, as a first cut at measuring effects I consider answers within 10 percentage points of the correct answer to be correct. In turn, I build a 15-point scale for overall political knowledge, with each point consisting of a binary measure for whether subjects correctly estimated the percentage amount of their tax money that goes to the point in question.

Results appear in Table 4.1. Descriptive statistics are in Appendix Table A.21. The Standard Receipt—that is, with subjects' personalized information presented alongside percentages—caused a significant increase in people's political knowledge. On a 15-point scale, the Standard Receipt caused a 1.74-point increase, in a model without covariates, and a 1.88-point increase in a model with covariates. Participants who saw the percentages only receipt did markedly better, improving their score by 2.62 points in a no-covariates model and 2.69 points in a regression-adjusted model. On perhaps the most infamous example

Table 4.1 **2016 U.S. Taxpayer Receipt Results**

	Dependent Variable	
	Correct Overall Total	
	(1)	*(2)*
Standard Receipt	1.740***	1.882***
	(0.331)	(0.316)
Percentages Receipt	2.605***	2.693***
	(0.328)	(0.313)
Environment-Only Receipt	−0.320	−0.047
	(0.330)	(0.317)
Constant	5.644***	0.555
	(0.237)	(1.372)
Observations	1,224	1,224
Covariates?	No	Yes
R^2	0.083	0.242
Adjusted R^2	0.081	0.200
Residual Std. Error	4.048 (df = 1220)	3.776 (df = 1160)
F Statistic	36.916*** (df = 3; 1220)	5.864*** (df = 63; 1160)

Note: $^*p < 0.1$; $^{**}p < 0.05$; $^{***}p < 0.01$

Covariate details: The model with covariates includes age, education, race, household income, sex, education, employment status, U.S. state, party ID, and ideology.

Covariate details: Further variable details can be found in appendix subsection "Mechanical Turk Demographic Questions."

of citizen ignorance about public budgeting—the extent to which they overestimate the amount spent on foreign aid—similar results were observed. Exposure to the Standard Receipt increased the likelihood that subjects would correctly estimate the foreign aid budget by 8.5% while those who saw the Percentage-Only Receipt were 15% more likely to do so.[1] (All reported effects are significant by conventional levels.)

The Environment-Only Receipt had no impact whatsoever on the overall battery. Most interestingly, nor did it affect accurate knowledge of environmental spending specifically. The Standard Receipt and the Percentage-Only Receipt did just that. Participants who saw the Standard Receipt were 8.7% more likely than the control to estimate the size of environmental spending accurately, while those who saw the Percentage-Only Receipt were 13.7% more likely to be accurate. In contrast, those who saw just the Environment-Only Receipt were only 0.5% more likely to estimate the amount of environmental spending accurately, an estimate that falls short of any reasonable standard of significance. In other words, people who *just* saw how much of their tax money had gone to environmental spending were hardly better at knowing that amount than people who had not seen any such information. And they were far worse at knowing than people who had seen that information *and* lots of other information.[2]

Figure 4.1 displays effects, by condition, on accurate knowledge about environmental spending only. (The accompanying model can be found in the first column of Appendix Table A.20.) The Taxpayer Receipt, whether displayed with personalized information or with general percentages, is unusual in its ability to increase political knowledge. Information conveyed via a Taxpayer Receipt is sticky in a way that receiving more category-specific information is not. The figure further suggests that people enrolled in this study were not merely engaging in a recall exercise. If they were, surely those in the Environment-Only condition would have done better on the question about environmental spending. Rather than causing people to think more critically about the entire exercise, people in the Environment-Only condition effectively tuned out all the subsequent questions, *including the one pertaining to the information they had just seen.*

In addition, I found no evidence that people were especially affected by the personalized numerical details. Just communicating the information as a percentage was slightly more powerful than communicating personalized information. People's political knowledge increased as a result of the receipt—but it didn't seem to matter if the receipt was personalized to them. What mattered was that the receipt displayed information about multiple government programs at

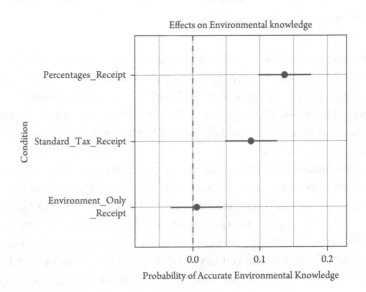

Figure 4.1 Effects on environmental knowledge only.

once. The effective versions of the Taxpayer Receipt try to capture the entirety of the costs that people put into government, and the value of that which they get back.

When administered over the Internet as part of a randomized experiment, Taxpayer Receipts can have large effects on political knowledge. But can they do the same outside of a lablike environment? And can the effects endure beyond the artificial environment of the survey experiment? Quite unexpectedly, the British government allowed me to find out.

The Taxpayer Receipt across the Pond

When President Obama announced that the U.S. government would produce for its citizens a version of the Taxpayer Receipt, I was thrilled. As you'll recall, however, the receipt that the White House produced was only visible on the White House website. On their own accord, people interested in learning about the uses of their tax money could log on, enter information about their income, and then see a personalized receipt. The problem, of course, is that the kind of people who are most driven to do that sort of thing are already likely tremendously politically engaged. They probably already know a lot about politics. In short, they are the opposite of the sort of people who are most prone to bring their consumer experiences into politics.

The British government took the concept of the receipt and did the American government one better. Rather than rely on people to seek out their receipts, in 2014 the British taxing authorities used snail mail to send personalized taxpayer receipts to all taxpayers. This effort was, at least theoretically, capable of affecting the views of all kinds of people, including those with less political knowledge. What would the effects of a receipt be, if any, when sent by the government? Would we witness gains in political knowledge? And if so, might we also witness changes in attitudes—precisely the kind I had not witnessed in the United States?

Prior to this study, I had not investigated the consumer citizen outside of the United States. Perhaps the consumer citizen speaks only with an American accent. The consumer has played a pivotal role in American politics since the nation's founding. While other nations can rely on ethnic and religious bonds to tie them together, the United States cannot. Commercial practices may be all that we share (Glickman 2009), yet the influence of the consumer has loomed large elsewhere too. In *Empire of Things* (2016), historian Frank Trentman argues that desires for ordinary consumer objects have long been the engine of global capital, tying together disparate continents and people. According to Trentman, the history of consumption is often reduced to a history of postwar consumption in America, when in fact that history should encompass not just the United States but also "African kingdoms . . . Japan and West Germany," all of which displayed differing dispositions to the interdependent consumer world (Trentman 2016, p. 11).

The United Kingdom has been at the forefront of turning its subjects into consumers. Broadly, the modern American approach to consumption is indebted to the earlier British model (Trentman 2016). In the 1990s, as part of his reform efforts, Prime Minister Tony Blair pursued the "consumerization" of government services. By improving the quality of government services—by enhancing the customer experience—electoral benefits redounded to Blair and his pro-government Labour Party (Trentman 2016, p. 549). During his 2001 reelection campaign, Blair (2001) described "build[ing] public services around the consumer" as one of his party's paramount goals. The taxpayer receipt does not in and of itself improve government services, but it communicates information about them in terms familiar to consumers worldwide.

While Blair had championed the effort to "consumerize" government for the Labour Party, the taxpayer receipt was introduced by the competing Tories. In 2012 Ben Gummer, a Conservative Member of Parliament (MP), became the first to propose taxpayer receipts as a universal, by-mail policy in the United Kingdom. Gummer argued that the receipt would aid in the functioning of democracy. "We would not for a moment think of paying a bill in a supermarket or of setting up a mobile phone direct debit if we did not receive an itemized receipt in exchange," he argued. "Yet for tax, the largest outgoing for most people, we get nothing—no total account of how much we have paid and no detail of where it has gone" (House of Commons 2012).

The argument sounded familiar. Yet unlike me, Gunner believed that the receipt would not communicate to people all the services that government provides, but instead mostly remind them of the costs that government extracts. The conservative chancellor George Osborne also framed the receipts in this way when introducing them. The receipts, he said, would "show how hardworking taxpayers have to pay for what governments spend" (Mason 2014).

In the fall of 2014, the British version of the IRS, Her Majesty's Revenue and Customs (HMRC), mailed twenty-four million taxpayers individualized receipts. Figure 4.2 displays an example of what was sent out. The receipts detailed how income tax and National Insurance payments were calculated, and then showed a breakdown of the spending categories supported by that revenue. (National Insurance payments are akin to Social Security contributions, collected via payroll tax.) The spending categories included defense, overseas aid, and welfare and health care. The spending-side items were personalized, based on actual government data housed by HMRC or by self-reports from self-assessed returns.[3]

HM Revenue & Customs

Your Annual Tax Summary 2013-14

Mrs A N Smith
1 Anystreet
Anytown
WX1 2YZ

Dear Mrs Smith
For the first time we are sending you an Annual Tax Summary. This is to show you how your Income Tax and National Insurance contributions (NICs) are calculated and how your money is spent by the government.

This is for your information. You do not need to contact us as this is not a demand for payment.

This is how we worked out your tax for 2013-14

Your taxable income		
Total income from employment		£60000.00
Your income before tax		**£60000.00**
Less your 2013-14 tax free amount		£9440.00
You pay tax on		**£50560.00**

Your tax was calculated as

Income Tax		
Basic rate Income Tax	£32010.00 at 20%	£6402.00
Higher rate Income Tax	£18550.00 at 40%	£7420.00
Total Income Tax		**£13822.00**
National Insurance contributions (NICs)		**£4414.40**
Total Income Tax and NICs		**£18236.40**
Your income after tax and NICs		**£41763.60**

Your employer pays

National Insurance contributions (NICs)		**£7217.95**

For more information
go to www.gov.uk/ annual-tax-summary
Go to our website to find out more about your Tax Summary, and for a list of indirect taxes such as VAT.

Your taxable income
£60000.00
We know this from information supplied to us by you, your employer(s) or your pension provider(s).

Tax free amount
£9440.00
After your allowances, deductions and expenses your total tax free amount for 2013-14 is £9440.00. This is the amount you received in the 2013-14 tax year without paying tax.

Your tax and NICs
£18236.40
This is 30% of your taxable income. For every £1 of income, you paid 30p in Income Tax and NICs.

Your income after tax and NICs
£41763.60
This is your income after Income Tax and NICs.

The table on the other side of this page shows how the government has spent your taxes.

Tax Summary for **Mrs A N Smith** for the tax year **2013-14**

HMRC 08/14

Figure 4.2 The U.K. Taxpayer Receipt.

As with the U.S. version, the British version is essentially a clever fiction. When collected, tax revenue is not actually divided by "spending category" and distributed accordingly. The receipt presents estimates that divide the total amount of tax money paid by an individual by the same overall shares of spending across categories. To the consumer citizen, however, the artificiality of the exercise should matter little; what matters is the familiarity of the manner in which the information is communicated.

Along with my colleagues Lucy Barnes, Avi Feller, and Jake Haselswerdt, we devised a plan to study the effects of the receipts that were distributed.[4] The receipts were sent by mail between November 21 and mid-December 2014. The long time frame for delivery of the receipts was attributable to the enormous scale of the operation; the government printers were not capable of operating any faster. All taxpayers who pay taxes through PAYE, the tax payment system that private employers use, received a receipt in the mail. People who file their own taxes in the United Kingdom do so through the Internet; they received an online statement.

Assessing the causal impact of nationwide policy interventions is difficult. The difficulty is only compounded in this case because the intervention consists of political information. Outside the lab, there are systematic differences in the observable characteristics of highly informed individuals. Many policies designed to further transparency depend on citizens' willingness to seek out disclosed information. The taxpayer receipt in the United States certainly depended on this willingness. Yet individuals who know about such policies, let alone those who are willing to act on them, are likely systematically different from those who are not aware of such polices and those who choose to seek out the disclosed information.

No one was permitted to opt out from receiving the receipts in advance, thereby obviating the kind of selection issues endemic to transparency-on-demand policies such as the U.S. version of the receipt. This was also a time-limited opportunity; in 2015 HMRC distributed receipts again, but permitted individuals to opt out. Furthermore, unlike many similar studies, the taxpayer receipt was a real-world policy initiative. In lab and survey experiments, participants face fewer competing demands for their attention, and greater incentives to pay attention to any information provided. Moreover, they often do so in a compressed time frame, with dependent variable data collected shortly after treatment. The distribution of receipts in the United Kingdom in 2014 represented a golden but limited opportunity to draw inferences about the possibility of increasing political knowledge and changing attitudes, with far greater external validity than similar studies, including those I've conducted in the United States.

In addition, because the receipt was distributed by the government, we'd get to learn if effects differed depending on the sender. Much has been written about the power of source effects. More credible message-senders are capable of generating larger effects than less credible ones (Druckman 2001). This could operate in either direction: the arrival of the information on the doormat with the official HMRC imprimatur may make recipients more attentive to it and thus give the information it contains more credibility. On the other hand, a skeptic of government might disbelieve any official information precisely because they do not trust the government to be honest. Either way, this kind of dynamic is a particular limitation of lab-based approaches to the study of political knowledge. In this study, we were able to directly assess the impact of an information provision that actually occurred.

Our study consisted of two survey waves, as well as a message delivered to panelists between the waves. During this time, we stayed in regular contact with the HMRC officials responsible for distribution, to ensure that we would collect pretreatment data before treatment and posttreatment data after treatment. The first survey wave was administered from November 12, 2014, to November 18, 2014, just as the first batch of statements was being distributed. The interstitial messages were disseminated in the first week of December. The second survey wave was administered from December 17, 2014, to January 5, 2015, after all receipts had been distributed.

We embedded a randomized experiment into the survey. After completing Wave 1, individuals were randomly assigned to receive or not receive an encouragement to read the taxpayer receipts that they would soon be receiving in the mail. We compare outcomes of interest in Wave 2 for individuals in each condition, yielding an Intent-to-Treat (ITT) estimate, similar to what I relied upon for the ACA study discussed in Chapter 3.[5]

All participants in Wave 1 saw one of two messages. Individuals randomly as-signed to the control group were exposed to a placebo message telling them they had been selected to be in a study and urging them to take the study seriously, with no mention of the study's substantive focus. For completing the study, they would be entered in a raffle to win an iPad. Meanwhile, individuals in the encouragement group received a message that told them about the receipts they were soon due to receive, and urged them to read the receipts upon their arrival. Those in the treatment group were further told that, at the end of the receipts' distribution, they would be asked about the amount the government had spent on budgetary categories detailed in the receipt, and that those who answered correctly would be entered in a raffle to win an iPad. (Complete text of all encouragement and placebo messages are included in the Appendix subsection "U.K. Taxpayer Receipt Experiment Messages to Subjects.")

As we were staying in touch with HMRC officials throughout this process, midway through the distribution of the receipts we sent new messages to all participants. Those in the encouragement group were reminded that they were part of a study about the receipts; those in the control group received a message reminding them that they were enrolled in a study. Finally, as part of the solicitation process for Wave 2, people in the encouragement group were told that the survey they would take was part of the study on tax receipts in which they were enrolled, while people in the control group were told they would answer questions about "important social and political matters." Both encouragement and control subjects were reminded about the iPad raffle. They were then directed to take the same survey they had completed in Wave 1, with one crucial difference: At the end of Wave 2, all participants were asked if they recalled receiving a taxpayer receipt over the previous six weeks.

The survey contained questions meant to measure respondents' political knowledge, their attitudes toward government and taxes, and their willingness to participate in politics. To measure political attitudes, we asked questions familiar from previous chapters. Among others, we asked the trust-in-government-spending question from the American National Election Study (ANES), and more general questions about trust in taxes and government overall. To measure willingness to participate in politics, we asked about respondents' voting plans in the upcoming election, and we asked if they wished to send a message to their elected officials.

To measure political knowledge, we used a battery of three questions, all with the same structure, asking respondents to estimate the share of government spending allocated to the budget categories we had specified in our preregistered hypotheses. We asked,

> Over the past twelve months, what percentage of the tax money that you paid would you say the government actually spent on [overseas aid] [national defence] [health]?

Participants were directed to a box in which they could provide numerical estimates. Given that many individuals evince low levels of numeracy (Citrin and Sides 2008; Ansolabehere, Meredith, and Snowberg 2013; Lawrence and Sides 2014), this was an aggressive test of the idea that receipts could actually cause knowledge gains.

Indeed, public knowledge of government budgets has proven no less woeful in the United Kingdom than in the United States. A 2013 survey in the United Kingdom revealed that roughly one-quarter of subjects believed overseas aid constituted one of the top three budget items. In that same study, most respondents thought the government spent more on overseas aid than education and pensions. Respondents also drastically underestimated the costs of social services (Ipsos Mori 2013). People don't know much about numbers in general, and they really don't know much about numbers relating to government budgets—whether in the United States or the United Kingdom.

YouGov UK, the preeminent survey firm, was responsible for implementing the survey and collecting responses. Via an online, nationally representative panel, 2,529 people completed the survey in Wave 1. A total of 2,072 people completed the survey in Wave 2. Between Waves 1 and 2 we maintained 82% of the panel, with some evidence of differential attrition (more on this point appears shortly).[6] A wealth of self-reported demographic information was made available to us about all participants. In particular, we received details about participants' household income, present employment status, gender, age, education level, ethnicity, geographic region, household size, and political party affiliation. Descriptive statistics, available in Appendix Table A.23, make clear we were well balanced across treatment and control.

Our randomized encouragement indeed changed behavior, successfully incentivizing treatment participants to read their receipts. Twenty-nine percent of the encouraged group recalled receiving the taxpayer receipt, compared to 24% of the control group.[7] Because we wanted to determine the impact of the statements on "correct" budget knowledge, we needed to differentiate correct from incorrect answers. As specified in our preregistration plan, we scored responses as correct if they came within 10 percentage points of the true value, with nonresponses graded as incorrect. This was the same approach I used in the study previously described in this chapter. Once again, the results remained robust across more and less generous approaches to scoring responses as correct.

Under this approach, we found that the randomized encouragement to read the receipt had significant positive effects on political knowledge. This result remained robust to the inclusion of numerous covariates, and when we accounted for participants who left the study between Waves 1 and 2 (what is known as "differential attrition"). When estimates were judged correct if they fell within 10 percentage points of the true value, we found that respondents in the encouragement group offered 1.01 correct estimates on average out of 3, compared to .903 correct estimates provided by those in the treatment group. In other words, being randomly exposed to an encouragement to read the receipt increased participants' political knowledge by 12.2%. Upticks in correct estimates were observed across all three budget categories. Furthermore, as we discussed at length in the resulting paper, the knowledge gains were not sensitive to how strict we were with what counted as correct. Under both more and less generous approaches, we still observed significant gains (Barnes et al. 2018).

To better account for demographic characteristics, we estimated linear models that incorporated the demographic data available to us. This data included not only demographic data such as gender and region but, importantly for this study, education. We also account for participants' political knowledge, as measured by the same battery, at Wave 1, before treatment.

As the first column in Table 4.2 shows, the regression-adjusted estimate of being randomly exposed to the encouragement is .097. In the second column, although the aforementioned model accounts for subjects' education levels, we incorporate political knowledge levels as observed at Wave 1. When we do so, we estimate the effect of being randomly exposed to the encouragement as 0.074. (For ease of interpretation I have omitted the covariate coefficients from this table. For the same models with covariates displayed, see Appendix Table A.22.)

While this effect may appear small, the demographic data indicate otherwise. The encouragement increased a respondent's expected number of correct answers by an amount similar to the increase that would be observed with a one-level increase in education. In other words, the knowledge increase caused by the receipt is similar in size to the knowledge difference between completing some college courses and obtaining a university degree. "Don't graduate college—get a taxpayer receipt!" is probably not ideal advice, however, unless one's goal in life is to know how much the government spends on certain items.

Given our two-wave design, differential attrition was a concern. In other words, we were worried that people leaving the study before it was over would affect our conclusions. We observed slightly higher levels of attrition in the treatment group, 22.5%, than in the control group, 14%. To address this, we followed a strategy recommended by Gerber and Green (2012) and weighed respondents by the inverse probability of missing an outcome.[8] When accounting for differential attrition, and when taking into account all plausible covariates, the effect of being exposed to treatment is .08. This result appears in column 3 of Table 4.2.

Table 4.2 **U.K. Taxpayer Receipt Knowledge Results**

	Wave 2 Knowledge Index		
	Model 1	Model 2	Model 3
Treatment	0.097**	0.074**	0.080**
	(0.042)	(0.035)	(0.037)
Constant	0.168	0.091	0.067
	(0.137)	(0.116)	(0.118)
N	2072	2072	2072
R^2	0.120	0.367	0.372
Adjusted R^2	0.108	0.358	0.362
Residual Std. Error	0.941 (df = 2042)	0.798 (df = 2041)	2.050 (df = 2041)
F Statistic	9.618***	39.447***	40.239***
	(df = 29; 2042)	(df = 30; 2041)	(df = 30; 2041)

Note: *p < .1; **p < .05; ***p < .01

To what extent, if any, do knowledge gains depend on whether participants recalled actually receiving the receipt or not? As described, Wave 2 was administered six week after the distribution of the receipts began. Inevitably, some in our sample received their receipts much earlier than others, likely diminishing if not altogether eliminating any positive effects on knowledge. Indeed, less than 5% of participants reported receiving their statements in the week prior to completing the Wave 2 survey. Those in treatment who heeded our directive to read their receipt scored a 1.24 on the knowledge index. This represents a 28% increase over subjects in treatment who did not recall receiving their receipt. The 35% difference between those in control who do not remember receiving their receipt and those in treatment who do is even larger. The differences were significant at conventional levels.[9]

What about their political behaviors? To determine if the distribution of the U.K. taxpayer receipts had an effect on political participation, we asked respondents if they planned to vote in the then-upcoming elections, and if they would be interested in writing a message to their political leaders. We asked the question about participation in both waves; we asked subjects if they wished to write their representatives only at the end of Wave 2. Asking participants to write two separate messages to officials, even six weeks apart, would have, in our minds, overstepped the boundaries of plausibility.[10] Our evidence on this was inconclusive.[11]

An encouragement to read the taxpayer receipt, sent by U.K. snail mail, increased people's political knowledge—but here was the rub. When we asked people for their views on redistribution, we did not observe any effects. We attempted to measure changes in redistributive preferences in a variety of different ways. We asked subjects if the government was providing a fair value for their tax money, the extent to which they trusted how government was using their tax money (a question imported from the ANES), how they felt about their overall tax burden, and their feelings about tax progressivity. On all of these questions, we failed to find the taxpayer receipt making a dent.[12]

Participants, we can say confidently, learned from their receipts—or at least from the encouragement to read theirs. But their attitudes about redistribution did not change. How, then, can the consumer citizens' attitudes toward redistribution change?

Redistributive Preferences and the Consumer Citizen

We already know part of the answer to the question just posed. Based on experiments described in Chapter 2, framing government costs and benefits as achieving alignability caused participants to become more supportive of higher levels of taxation and feel warmer about taxes in general. That finding offers both a narrow lesson about the power of alignability and a broader lesson about the limits of Americans' supposed opposition to redistribution.

This opposition—or supposed opposition, depending on your point of view—has a long and distinguished pedigree. In *The Federalist Papers*, Alexander Hamilton wrote that it would be "impracticable to raise any very considerable sums by direct taxation" (Hamilton, Jay, and Madison 1788 [2011]). He was voicing what would become a defining feature of politics in the United States: the mass public's opposition to government spending and taxing—or, taken together, their opposition to redistribution. In Hamilton's lifetime, this opposition would manifest itself in the form of the Whiskey Rebellion. In ours, it comes in the forms of the Reagan Revolution (Sears and Citrin 1986) and the Tea Party (Skocpol and Williamson 2012). While Americans have not been in "perpetual tax revolt," a fact noted by Ellis and Stimson (2012, p. 29), U.S. history has been punctuated by groundswells of opposition to redistribution. A general aversion to redistribution on a mass scale is, by one understanding, what makes America exceptional in the international system (Foner 1984; Lipset 1996). Unlike our European cousins, we do not have a popular socialist party, nor has there been long-standing support for policies that would approximate socialism. As a share of gross domestic product (GDP), the tax money collected by the U.S. government lags well behind most countries in the Organisation for Economic Co-operation and Development (Organisation for Economic Co-operation and Development 2020). Growth in inequality (Piketty and Saez 2003, 2007) has not measurably increased support for redistribution, despite theoreticians' predictions (Meltzer and Richard 1981; Bonica et al. 2013).

But as my findings about alignability suggest, American opposition to redistribution is not fixed. Many have sympathetic views of the poor (Piston 2018); a surprising number may even view paying taxes as a civic responsibility that they are proud to undertake (Williamson 2017). For the consumer citizen, much depends on the precise mixture between the perceptions of government costs and government benefits. When government's costs are said to exceed government's benefits, citizens will, unsurprisingly, become less trusting of government taxing and spending. But citizens' support for taxes can increase when benefits and costs are said to roughly align with one another. In the case of earmarked taxes, citizens may even countenance higher tax rates. In this book, we've seen that occur on Internet surveys, when costs and benefits are artificially manipulated, as well as at city of Chicago bus stops, where the costs and benefits referred to map onto actually existing government services.

The existing literature offers several powerful explanations for Americans' attitudes toward redistribution. One explanation focuses on the deep roots of political culture. Louis Hartz (1955) argued that Americans are naturally anti-government because of their liberal, nonfeudal origins. À la Alexis de Tocqueville, Americans view themselves as "born equal" (Tocqueville 2001, p. xxx) and therefore do not require government to step in and level the playing field. Empirical evidence for the "Lockean liberal" view has been offered by, among others, Feldman (1988) and Lipset (1996). The latter uses public opinion data to claim that a normative commitment to liberal individualism precludes Americans from supporting taxes at rates observed in other industrialized nations.

Another perspective focuses on the connection between attitudes toward government spending and racial attitudes. Here, the view is that antitax and antigovernment spending perspectives are really proxies for racial hostility. By opposing taxes and government spending, white Americans get to oppose the interests of those who are not white (see, e.g., Gilens 2000; Alesina, Glaeser, and Sacerdote 2001; Piston 2018). Generally, more ethnically diverse societies offer less generous social welfare programs (Luttmer 2001). Immigration rates also seem to drive down the amount of redistribution (Eger 2010), which seems to hammer home this point: support for redistribution appears contingent on people believing their resources are being redistributed to people like them. Still another camp argues that large-scale political and demographic trends—the kind that take place over the course of generations—account for people's views of redistribution. Business interests that disfavor redistribution have become much more adept at the use of procedural tools to advance their interests (Hacker and Pierson 2010).

All of these explanations have much to offer. But if we wish to understand Americans' attitudes about redistribution, thinking of them as consumer citizens also helps. Doing so makes clear that *Homo Emptor*'s redistributive preferences are susceptible to short-term changes in the information presented to them. As we know from prior chapters, when that information describes government costs and benefits as meeting alignability, people become more supportive of redistribution. Here I introduce a new finding: people can become more supportive of redistribution when everyday consumer pressures—in the form of information about bills they cannot afford and payments they cannot make—intrude into their lives.

Everyday Consumer Stresses and Redistributive Preferences

Consumer life can be a source of considerable stress. Managing a budget, deciding what we can afford and what we cannot afford—not to mention simply deciding what we want—are activities that demand a fair amount of cognitive effort. Such activities, for example, require us to do a good bit of math in our heads. Although people are surprisingly capable of maintaining calculators for government taxing and spending, few people actually enjoy it. In general, many people are innumerate. For this reason, it is no wonder that, when they go shopping, people tend to make use of heuristics, even if those heuristics lead to perhaps-less-than-optimal outcomes. Car buyers, for example, are more likely to buy convertibles on sunny days (Busse et al. 2015).

In their work on scarcity, Mullanaithan and Shafir argue that having scarce material resources depletes cognitive resources (2013). After less-well-off study participants were presented with "tough" consumer choices that reminded them of their limited material resources, they displayed less cognitive capacity when compared to better-off study participants (Mani et al. 2013). This finding corroborates earlier work of Mullanaithan and Shafir, in which they find that poor people's attention levels are shaped by their poverty, leading to overborrowing and other suboptimal behaviors (Shah, Mullanaithan, and Shafir 2012).

Yet consumer choices are not uniquely cognitively demanding on those with fewer resources. Even those with more resources have to utilize considerable cognitive bandwidth when making consumer choices, particularly when those choices are difficult. For both the poor and nonpoor alike, consumer decisions, especially when they impose a burden on the decision-maker, make a demand on cognitive load—that is, they consume people's limited mental energies.[13]

Moreover, even though we often treat it as such, income is hardly static. Over the last thirty years, the number of Americans experiencing sharp year-to-year fluctuations in household resources has increased significantly (Hacker, Rahm, and Schlesinger 2013). Economic security, or the lack thereof, has a broad impact on attitudes toward the welfare state in the United States and abroad (Rehm et al. 2012). Income volatility likely increases support for regressive taxation (Hosek 2015). Having sufficient resources at one time is no guarantee that one will in the future. Particularly in an age of sharp income volatility, it may be the case that, when forced to make a hard consumer choice—a choice that would require using a large amount of money—people of all income ranges change their political attitudes. Even if people are well-off now and can afford to expend large amounts of material resources, they may not be able to do so tomorrow.

To understand how the everyday stresses of consumer life might affect redistributive preferences, I conducted a study in which participants were encouraged to think about hypothetical bills they could not afford and hypothetical unexpected costs they could not bear. These questions were not about the goods that consumers desire, but about situations in which the pressures of everyday consumer life come crashing down. It turns out that being reminded about the bills one has to pay, when those bills are particularly onerous, can lead one to support increasing taxes on the rich.

For this experiment I used the same primes as in Anandi Mani, Sendhil Mullainathan, Eldar Shafir, and Jiaying Zhao's work on scarcity (2013), applying them to questions related to progressive taxation and policy preferences. I found that exposure to "hard" consumer decision-making primes—primes that ask people to make choices involving comparatively larger amounts of money— makes them significantly more likely to support higher taxes on the rich. Unlike Mullanaithan and Shafir, this finding does not depend on dividing the sample into high- and low-income individuals, nor does it come from a convenience sample. Rather, it obtains across a nationally representative sample and remains robust across household income levels. Hard consumer choices, in other words, affect not only the cognitive capacity of the impoverished. They also shape the redistributive preferences of those with more money.

My study was designed to mimic the Mani et al. (2013) research, with different primes and outcome variables. Participants were randomly assigned to read one of two sets of primes. In the easy primes, people were presented with a series of dilemmas related to consumer life—what would you do, for example, if your car needed a $150 repair—and asked to explain how they would respond. The hard primes presented subjects with the exact same set of dilemmas, but the amount at stake was far greater. The $150 repair, for example, became a $1,500 repair.

The full text of the primes appears in the Appendix subsection "Scarcity Study Primes." To summarize, the first prime asks participants to think about a hypothetical cut in their salary; the second asks them to consider an unforeseen expense; the third tells them to imagine they need to pay for a car repair; and the fourth asks them about urgently needing to replace a refrigerator. After each prime, participants were provided with a text box in which they could explain how they would respond to the consumer dilemma described. Critically, at no point did the treatments make explicit or implicit reference to redistribution, taxation, or government spending.

Just reading the responses provided in the text boxes is instructive. Those who responded to the easy primes mostly reported that, in such hypothetical scenarios, they might have to cut back on unnecessary expenses—eating out, taking long vacations—but otherwise would be unaffected. Indeed, some came out and said outright that they would not be troubled much at all. Those who read the hard primes, on the other hand, told a different story. They'd have to go in debt, they'd have to exhaust their savings, or they'd have to count on family, friends, or their church for help. In many cases, they detailed rather elaborate plans about how they'd cope. Some were just bleak: "No I would not be able to maintain at all," wrote one subject. "My husband makes decent money now and we still live paycheck to paycheck."[14]

After responding to their primes, participants answered a variety of questions about their attitudes toward progressive taxation. They were asked if they supported increasing taxes on the rich, with answers ranging from "definitely not" to "definitely yes," along a 5-point scale. In February 2016 the survey firm Survey Sampling International (SSI) administered this experiment on a nationally representative online sample. (SSI maintains detailed demographic records on its panelists; they were appended to the resultant data set and used in the analysis that follows. Appendix Table A.24 displays descriptive statistics.)

Results appear in Table 4.3. The first column displays effects without covariates; the second displays them with covariates. Across both models, those exposed to the hard primes were significantly more willing to tax the rich than those exposed to the easy primes. On our 5-point scale, the model without covariates estimates that the effect is about .17; in the model with covariates, the estimate rises to .22. It is not "scarcity" as experienced by the impoverished alone that is driving these results (a point underlined in the Appendix, by Figure A.9). In general, people become more supportive of taxing the rich when they're compelled to make difficult consumer choices.

If people are made to feel economically trapped, they wish to punish those who have more money. The less well-off wish to punish the better-off—an age-old story, with tax rates standing in for pitchforks. What is interesting is that this evidence shows just how sharply preferences can fluctuate based on life's

Table 4.3 **Consumer Decisions and Taxing the Rich**

| | Dependent Variable | |
| | Tax the Rich | |
	(1)	(2)
Hard Choices	0.172**	0.220**
	(0.087)	(0.100)
Constant	3.725***	4.176***
	(0.061)	(0.466)
Observations	808	644
Covariates?	No	Yes
R^2	0.005	0.102
Adjusted R^2	0.004	0.018
Residual Std. Error	1.233 (df = 806)	1.217 (df = 588)
F Statistic	3.916** (df = 1; 806)	1.209 (df = 55; 588)

Note: *$p < 0.1$; **$p < 0.05$; ***$p < 0.01$

Covariate details: Covariates included are employment status, age, sex, race, education, income, and U.S. state.

Covariate details: A table of descriptive statistics can be found in Appendix table??.

everyday consumer inconveniences. Trouble with your car? Need a new refrigerator? Such frustrations may be all that is required to propel people to want to confiscate the income of the most affluent.

Everyday consumer experiences, even when they lack any political content, can shape redistributive preferences. Redistributive preferences are not nearly as static as Louis Hartz would have us believe. They are malleable, and consumer experiences can play a large role in shaping them. In one well-worn description, Americans are "operationally liberal" but "philosophically conservative" (Ellis and Stimson 2012). The evidence presented here indicates that Americans may be better thought of—philosophically and practically—as *consumers*.

Conclusion

Increases in political knowledge alone do not necessarily prompt changes in political attitudes. The taxpayer receipt pushes people to know more about how government spends their tax money, but it does nothing to alter the attitudes that people have about redistribution, as broadly understood. In past chapters, we've seen that subtle consumer-inspired changes to descriptions of government costs and benefits can shape such attitudes. And the last study of this chapter shows that similar attitudes can be changed because of everyday consumer pressure.

Canonical accounts of Americans' redistributive preferences tend to point to timeless factors, such as the influence of racism and the endurance of Lockean liberalism. The evidence gathered suggests that daily consumer experiences also matter. Why do Americans not yearn for the confiscatory tax rates of Europeans, or at least tax rates closer to the average of OECD nations? They might, actually— when they're reminded of the pressures of consumer life, or when they're told that costs and benefits are aligned.

Scholars have also argued that Americans would have different views toward redistribution if they were better informed (e.g., Gilens 2001). As the previous chapter explained, Larry Bartels argued that some Americans supported the Bush tax cuts because they lacked adequate information. "Had the public as a whole been better informed, public support for the [Bush 2003] tax cut would have been significantly lower than it actually was," he wrote (Bartels 2008). In the taxpayer receipt studies, however, informing people had no effects on their proximate political attitudes. In the U.K. study, even as people had more accurate knowledge about the amount that government spends on foreign aid—thereby correcting an overestimation of significant magnitude—they did not become supportive of more foreign aid spending.

But while the taxpayer receipts that provided ample information about taxes and government spending did not move attitudes about such items, the treatments in the scarcity study did—even though the treatments made no mention of such items at all. All the latter did was bring to mind the ordinary consumer pressures that people might face when going about their everyday lives. *Homo Emptor's* redistributive preferences can fluctuate with only a small consumer prompt, encountered when far away from politics, as he is going about his everyday life as a consumer. This can be true even when consumer prompts have no distinctly political content. Some scholars assume that political attitudes must be the byproduct of evaluations of overtly political objects, such as policies, candidates, or parties. A substantive link, it is thought, must exist between an object of evaluation and the result of that evaluation. But in the scarcity study, such a link is not readily apparent.

The success of the taxpayer receipt at increasing political knowledge should not be minimized. Political knowledge matters, even if it doesn't necessarily translate to attitude shifts. Mimicking the format of a receipt appears to be crucial for the taxpayer receipt's success at increasing knowledge. Simply telling people about government spending in one category and then asking them to estimate the spending just on that category does not work. Rather, people are superior at retaining information, including about that one category, when it is presented alongside all the other information that government spends.

Why does the receipt work better than an approach that, on its face, seems less cognitively demanding? The evidence is consistent with my theory: because the taxpayer receipt is similar to the receipts that people encounter constantly, it requires less cognitive effort than one might assume. Whereas asking people to remember specific information about a particular category might resemble a school test, asking people to retain information from a receipt is asking them to use a modified version of a format they use all the time. One of the reasons that people may conflate consumer and political decisions is the superficial similarities between the two. By presenting people with a receipt, I leveraged those similarities—and the public responded by learning more about politics than they would otherwise.

The failure of knowledge to change attitudes corroborates seminal work on the effects of military propaganda on soldiers (Stouffer et al. 1949) and more recent research into corrections of factual misinformation. Providing people facts, even when people accept those facts and even when those facts undercut the assertions of their preferred politicians, can have no downstream effects on their political attitudes (Porter and Wood 2019). Treating consumer citizens as they are, and trying to improve the political knowledge they retain, does not mean necessarily changing their views on redistribution. Such views can change, however, when the burdens of the consumer world intrude—but those changes are not dependent on increases in political knowledge.

5

The Consumer Citizen, Trust, and Operational Transparency

So far, we've learned that appealing to citizens as consumer citizens can make them more supportive of taxes and government spending, as well as increase their amount of political knowledge. It can even cause them to sign up for government-funded health insurance. We've also learned that less politically knowledgeable citizens might be especially reliant on an alignability heuristic familiar to them from their consumer experiences, at the expense of the amount they benefit from government. We've appealed to what they've learned as *private* consumers—and, in doing so, shaped their public preferences. However, we still don't know if appealing to people as consumer citizens can change their underlying attitudes toward government. We also don't know if such appeals can make them more trusting of political processes, government bureaucrats, and the entirety of government itself.

Trust in government has been in steady decline for decades. There have been predictable partisan differences, with Democrats generally trusting government more than Republicans. Figure 5.1 illustrates this pattern over time. (This is the companion figure to Figure 1.3, which shows these trends without conditioning on party.) Members of both parties, as well as self-identified independents, have grown distrustful of government in general and skeptical about the uses of government. As the reader will see, there plainly seems to be something to the notion that trust fluctuates with partisan control (e.g., Keele 2005), with partisans becoming more trusting when their party is in power. For example, as the bottom panel of Figure 5.1 shows, during the George W. Bush administration, Republicans were actually more trusting of government than Democrats. An increase in trust was also observed among all groups in the immediate aftermath of the attacks of September 11, 2001.[1] By the end of the Obama administration, however, the predictable partisan divide was apparent once again, with Democrats trusting government far more than their Republican counterparts.

The Consumer Citizen. Ethan Porter, Oxford University Press (2021). © Oxford University Press.
DOI: 10.1093/oso/9780197526781.003.0005.

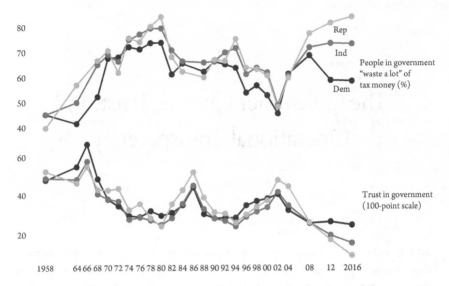

Figure 5.1 ANES Trust in Government Measures, by party. The top panel shows attitudes toward government's use of tax money, while the bottom displays an aggregate measure of trust in government.

Partisan differences relating to government spending have followed a similar pattern; they became especially stark during the Obama years, as the number of Republicans who believed that government was wasting "a lot" of their tax money exploded, reaching nearly 80% by the end of Obama's term.

Perhaps trust in government and confidence in government spending would prove resistant to any intervention. Short of a national tragedy, it is possible that nothing—and certainly nothing in the social scientist's toolbox—can reverse a decades-long trend. The same might also be true of the partisan divide on such measures. I'd begun this project, however, motivated by the idea that appealing to citizens as consumer citizens could change their attitudes toward government. Perhaps I needed to test something even more consumer-friendly than a receipt.

To do so, I worked alongside Michael Norton and Ryan Buell, professors at Harvard Business School and experts in consumer psychology, and an advertising firm called Chi Donahoe. Together we designed a sort of advertisement for government itself. Our advertisement was inspired by a concept called "operational transparency" that Buell and Norton had pioneered in the study of private enterprises. We took the concept and applied it to government services, to see if using operational transparency could improve trust in government.

Many governments today do engage in transparency efforts, broadly defined. When doing so, they often give lip service to the notion that their efforts will improve trust. Yet many of these efforts are just large data dumps that make little effort to cater to the needs, abilities, and limitations of potential users. The

Chicago Data Portal, for example, offers users a wide array of information about what the city spends. This information, however, is contained in download-able spreadsheets—195, to be exact, as of this writing—on questions related to finance and administration that require a not-insubstantial level of technical acumen, not to mention free time, to unpack.

Operational transparency requires a more refined approach. If you're not fa-miliar with the term, however, you might have observed it anyway, in recent ad-vertising campaigns in which companies underscore the efforts that have gone into making their products. Walmart, for example, has routinely highlighted its employees in its advertisements. Other companies have followed suit. More subtly, many Internet companies have websites that are meant to tell users about all the work—the sweat equity—that the company is putting into delivering your product. When you search prices on any number of price-comparison websites, for example, the sites are happy to tell you about all the possibilities they are looking into on your behalf.

This trend in advertising is no accident. Scholars of consumer psychology have observed that people are more likely to view a company favorably, and per-haps become even more likely to buy its products, if the company engages in operational transparency (e.g., Buell and Norton 2011). The premise of opera-tional transparency is straightforward. To engage in it, all a company needs to do is illuminate the efforts that have gone into making a product. In other words, the company needs to visually shed light on its internal operations. Only when operations are made transparent can consumers appreciate the effort that goes into them—and by extension into the company's products and services.

This basic premise builds on copious research. By making clear the effort they are putting in on your behalf, companies hope to win your patronage and loyalty. "We have worked for you; now we hope you will like us more, or even buy our products more frequently." That, essentially, is the claim. When consumers are given a more transparent look at the details of a firm's operations, they are more likely to think higher of the firm (Kruger et al. 2004). Just observing the amount of time that has been devoted to the delivery of a service can increase ratings of outcome quality (Kruger et al. 2004; Chinander and Schweitzer 2003).[2] All of this research is indebted to a set of earlier experiments, in which Kahneman, Knetsch, and Thaler (1986a; 1986b) showed that consumers presented with more details of a firm's costs are more likely to forgive higher prices.

Enter Ryan Buell and Mike Norton. They've found that operational trans-parency can have significant positive effects on consumer attitudes and beha-vior. What consumers respond to, the researchers found, was the *appearance* of effort. People want to see the labor that has gone into producing what they are about to purchase. In one study, Buell and Norton recruited participants to test a modified version of a travel website, modeled on Kayak.com. All participants searched for the same travel itinerary, but those participants assigned to experience a version of the site that clearly communicated all the searching that the site was doing—the version that made clear the site was performing extensive price comparisons for the user—regarded the site as offering the most value. In another study, participants were asked to choose between an operationally transparent travel website and a standard travel site. Most chose the former—and the effect is not limited to travel websites. Buell, Kim, and Tsay (2017) found consumers also seeming to prefer operational transparency when buying food in a cafeteria.

If applied to government, what might operational transparency's effects be? In the corporate world, advertising campaigns that have used operational transparency-like messages have aimed to bolster consumers' trust. When Walmart introduced an advertising campaign predicated on making transparent the efforts that its employees undertake to serve customers, its CEO said that trust in the company would increase as a result. "We have wanted to do this for a long time because we know that people trust Walmart even more when they understand the opportunities we provide our associates, who the customers are that shop with us, and how we deliver low prices," explained Bill Simon, the company's CEO, when announcing the campaign (Walmart 2013). Yes, the campaign probably helped stave off complaints about Walmart's treatment of its employees—but as Simon said, communicating the work that Walmart workers do for customers might make people *trust* the company more.

The nature of government services would seem to make them a ripe target for operational transparency. People know very little about such services, even when they benefit from them directly (see, e.g., Mettler 2011). Moreover, even if citizens are aware that government is engaged in service delivery, there are limited opportunities to observe such delivery in action. Residential mail delivery and trash collection often occur during working hours when homeowners may be away. Traffic is typically rerouted around major construction projects, and work zones are generally cordoned off from pedestrians. And a bevy of governmental services, from cleaning the air to certifying the health of restaurant foods, are by design meant to be as unobtrusive as possible. In all those cases, governance requires *minimizing* operational transparency. The state, in the colorful language of Richard Titmuss (1958), is "submerged," akin to an iceberg that has most of its mass underwater, outside the view of observers.

In this chapter I report on two efforts to bring operational transparency to government. First, I teamed up with Ryan Buell and Mike Norton, the psychologists behind the leading papers on operational transparency, to see what would happen when we applied operational transparency to government services. We created a video simulation of a generic American town, which we called "Anytown," that amounted to an advertisement for government.[3] In the simulation, we illuminated all the government services that are typically obscured. For example, viewers of the simulation were told about the road and the university systems, but they were also informed about environmental and restaurant regulations. Viewers were even told about the home mortgage interest deduction—the government benefit that, according to Mettler (2011), beneficiaries were least likely to identify as coming from government.

What we found affirmed the impulse behind the study. Applying operational transparency to government services—that is, shedding light on the services that people either forget about or never knew about in the first place—has large, positive effects on people's levels of trust in government. People who saw our video simulation also became more supportive of taxes and government spending. The effects were not only positive and statistically significant, but were also large in size.

But there are limits to operational transparency. As John Hibbing and Elizabeth Theiss-Morse argued in their groundbreaking *Stealth Democracy* (2002), Americans have strong feelings about government processes. They don't just care about "outputs"—the services we made operationally transparent in the Anytown study—but they also care about the process by which the inputs are made. As Hibbing and Theiss-Morse describe, citizens' attitudes toward government can be understood as a function of their location in "process space," as distinct from the "policy space" that political scientists usually use to understand political attitudes. In their recent research into consumer preferences, Buell, Kim, and Tsay (2017) have found that applying operational transparency to processes—in their case, the processes that go into making food in a cafeteria—can enhance perceptions of the value of the resulting food. It was not clear whether the same would be true for government.

In this light, for a second study I applied operational transparency to the U.S. Congress. I took advantage of a recent news leak that detailed how incoming Congress members are expected to spend their days. As the original news article detailed, first-year Congress members are expected to spend a large amount of time fundraising. I showed study participants either the original article, which illustrated how often members fundraise, or a slightly modified version that made clear how much time, in total, Congress members work. The results were clear: when operational transparency is applied to the political process, and when the process portrays politicians as mostly engaging in fundraising for their own self-interest, people become less trusting of government. Visually emphasizing all the work that Congress members do as Congress members—and they do quite a lot—had no discernible effects, either positive or negative, on any quantity of interest. Operational transparency can be a powerful tool when applied to government services that can make people trust government, yet when applied to political processes, the effects run in the opposite direction.

Operational Transparency
and Government Services

In a sense, the Anytown study was a study of an advertisement that government could run for its own services. In the United States, governments rarely self-promote the services they provide. Compared to the nation's largest companies—like, say, Apple or Amazon, both of which take in far fewer annual revenues than the sum of all federal receipts—government is a miserly self-promoter. Outside of military recruitment spending, federal procurement of advertising services totaled $892.5 million in 2013, the last year for which comprehensive figures are available (Kosar 2014). That same year, the military reported spending $556.3 million on advertising for recruitment purposes (Office of the Under Secretary of Defense 2012). These are not entirely insignificant amounts. Indeed, the combined total would place them just outside the top twelve of all advertising spenders that year.[4] On the other hand, compared to overall federal spending, it is a small drop in a very large bucket.

Local and state governments sometimes get in on the act. States and cities spend to promote themselves as active tourist destinations, and all levels of government spend to promote specific policies. Again, the amounts spent are not microscopic. New York State, for example, recently spent about $50 million annually on messages designed to attract visitors (Spector 2016). Many government advertising messages, however, are clumsy or poorly considered. In 2003, for example, Medicare was ridiculed for spending $600,000 on a blimp to promote its services (Pesca 2003). (Look up! It's a bird.... It's a plane.... It's a blimp promoting government benefits?)

Sporadically, governments do try and make us appreciate that certain benefits originate with them. After President Obama signed the American Recovery and Reinvestment Act into law—known popularly as "the stimulus" of 2009—notices appeared adjacent to highway construction sites that the work was funded through the law, notifying passersby that the stimulus was responsible (Karl and Simmons 2010). Yet even the wisest government advertising attempts do not try and sell Americans on government in general. Government ads might try and convince us to sign up for Medicare, they might ask us to adopt one of their cities as our next vacation destination, or they might make us appreciate that our tax dollars are funding a highway renovation. Yet, as far as I can tell, at least in the United States, such ads never make clear to us the diverse range of services that government is performing on our behalf at any one time.

Anytown was designed to rectify that. Anytown is a computer simulation that depicts the construction of a generic American town (hence the name). With visuals modeled on the popular computer game *SimCity* from the 1990s, Anytown tells a five-minute story focused on the services that government provides. Anytown presents an "operationally transparent" government, one that discloses the services it provides. As is clear in the full video (with the complete script in Appendix subsection "Anytown Script"), we intended to "hit subjects between the eyes" (Kuklinski et al. 2000) and give them little doubt about government's role in performing various services for them.[5]

Across six scenes, the viewer watches an allegorical town evolve from a blank landscape into a flourishing metropolis, while a voice-over describes the otherwise hidden work that government is doing to support the needs of the town's citizens.

The Anytown video emphasizes certain kinds of governmental services and benefits, such as the home mortgage interest deduction, that are viewed as classically submerged, while also portraying government as the provider of more traditional transfer benefits. In addition, the video shows government's role in providing the public goods of a clean environment and food safety that, by definition, benefit everyone. Most importantly, the video frames the government as being responsible for shepherding Anytown from a small splotch of land to a fully functioning, desirable place to live.

In the first scene, the viewer finds a green space waiting to be filled. In the second scene, the camera scrolls back, and shows the construction of basic infrastructure: pipes, roads, bridges, schools, a town hall, and a fire station. The voice-over attributes these developments to the role played by the government. Figures 5.2 and 5.3 display how the town develops throughout the Anytown video.

Figure 5.2 A screenshot from the beginning of the Anytown video.

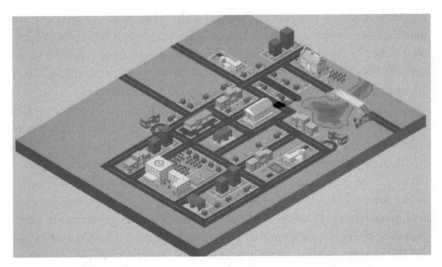

Figure 5.3 A screenshot from about halfway through the Anytown video, after the town has developed more.

The narrator explains that the government accommodates Anytown's growing population with more roads and more plumbing, by organizing an electrical grid, and building parks and a hospital. For the plumbing and electrical items, a close-up shot is offered to make these items more tangible to viewers. A similar close-up shot is presented to show the fire department extinguishing a fire.

In a subsequent scene, the government is shown confronting the problem of pollution with a regulatory solution. The narrator explains that when the air and water become polluted, Anytown's government works to make businesses adopt practices that are more friendly to the environment. Recycling becomes the rule, and businesses and individuals both abide by it. As the recycling symbol proliferates throughout the city, the town becomes noticeably less polluted.

Later in the video, Anytown's government is shown to be providing the home mortgage interest deduction—which, judging by survey evidence, can be described as the most submerged government service (Mettler 2011). The Anytown narrator explains that, as more residents want to buy homes, the town government reduces the taxes of new homeowners. More residents move into Anytown, and the government increases local offerings in postsecondary education. In the next scene, in addition to expanding the town's transit infrastructure, the government tackles the problem of food safety by mandating restaurant inspections. The government is also said to be providing aid to the homeless and impoverished. According to Mettler (2011), surprisingly large numbers of people have trouble crediting government for offering such benefits. The video concludes with the narrator reminding viewers of how Anytown has grown and the role that government has played in its growth, including the provision of infrastructure, a clean environment, and basic municipal services.

Meanwhile, participants not assigned to view the Anytown video viewed a placebo video meant to imitate the look and feel of Anytown without sharing any of its content. In this case, because the look of the Anytown video was inspired by the *SimCity* computer games of the 1990s, the placebo video was an narrated video of equal length of another popular computer game from that period, *Myst*.

We recruited for the study over Mechanical Turk 554 U.S.-based participants. Descriptive statistics can be found in Appendix Table A.29. After they watched their randomly assigned video, all participants responded to the trust in government battery from the Pew Center for the People and the Press Trust in Government Survey. This fourteen-question battery, the full text of which appears in the Appendix subsection "Pew Trust in Government Questions," measures participants' attitudes about government's role in their everyday lives, government's role as being positive or negative, the quality of civil service, and whether they trust government to do what is right, among similar items.

We also tried to measure whether the ad could change their views about taxing and spending. Once again, participants were asked a question from Hansen (1998): "Do you favor increases in the taxes paid by ordinary Americans in order to increase spending on domestic programs like Medicare, education, and highways?" And of course, they were asked our old friend from the American National Election Study: "Do you think that people in the government waste a lot of money we pay in taxes, waste some of it, or don't waste very much of it?"

The Anytown video had strong positive effects on multiple measures of trust in government. Participants who saw the video also came to have more positive views on government taxing and spending and were more likely to favor tax increases to support greater domestic spending. I've broken the results into two tables and a figure. Table 5.1 shows the effects across Pew trust items. All items have been rescaled so that positive responses are pro-trust and standardized to allow for comparability. Anytown had large, positive effects on people's perceptions of government performance, belief that government programs should be increased, view that government has a positive effect in their daily lives, and whether government generally plays a positive role. The final column of Table 5.1 reports effects on a composite trust measure, consisting of all Pew items averaged. On this well-known battery, the Anytown video was capable of generating large and significant effects, all in the same, more trusting direction. The table presents results with our standard set of covariates (with coefficients omitted for ease of display); readers interested in results without covariates can consult Table A.25 in the Appendix. The results remain substantively

Table 5.1 **Anytown Pew Trust in Government Results**

	Dependent variable:				
	Performance	Increase Programs	Daily Life	Positive Role	Comp. Trust
	(1)	(2)	(3)	(4)	(5)
Anytown	0.262***	0.275***	0.214**	0.220**	0.238***
	(0.086)	(0.077)	(0.088)	(0.085)	(0.083)
Constant	−0.533	0.236	0.604	−0.900*	−0.094
	(0.526)	(0.477)	(0.545)	(0.525)	(0.509)
Observations	549	551	551	550	544
R^2	0.194	0.338	0.137	0.196	0.253
Adjusted R^2	0.089	0.253	0.025	0.092	0.155
Residual Std. Error	0.954 (df = 485)	0.866 (df = 487)	0.989 (df = 487)	0.953 (df = 486)	0.920 (df = 480)
F Statistic	1.847*** (df = 63; 485)	3.953*** (df = 63; 487)	1.224 (df = 63; 487)	1.882*** (df = 63; 486)	2.575*** (df = 63; 480)

Note: *p<0.1; **p<0.05; ***p<0.01

Covariate details: All models include covariates for age, income, sex, race (white), education, ideology, party ID and U.S. state.

Covariate details: Further variable details can be found in appendix subsection "Mechanical Turk Demographic Questions."

unchanged. Figure 5.4 showcases that the Anytown video had on specific Pew trust measures.[6]

In Table 5.2, I present the effects of Anytown on participants' trust in government spending and their support for tax increases. Again, the video has pronounced positive effects. The taxpayer receipt repeatedly proved unable to generate effects on these exact same outcomes, which is not the case here. When applied to government services, operational transparency can not only increase trust in government, but can also increase support for government taxing and spending, even if the survey question makes clear that the respondent may have to bear increased costs.

It's worth emphasizing how this result departs markedly from what a free-lunch perspective might have anticipated. From that viewpoint, Anytown might have been able to please people in its description of benefits, but there would be no expectation of Anytown increasing support for tax increases. The opposite might even have been expected, with the video depressing support for

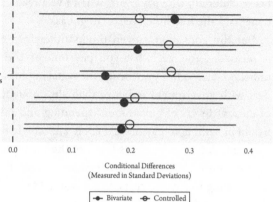

Overall, would you say the agencies and departments of the government are doing an excellent, only fair or a poor job?

Where on the following scale of 1 to 6 would you place yourself? Government programs should be cut back / Government programs should be maintained

Which would you rather have? Bigger government, more services / Smaller government, fewer services

In general, is the government's effect on your life positive or negative?

How much effect do you think the government's activities—the laws passed and so on—have on your day-to-day life?

0.0   0.1   0.2   0.3   0.4

Conditional Differences
(Measured in Standard Deviations)

–●– Bivariate   –⊖– Controlled

Figure 5.4 Effects of Anytown on questions from Pew's trust in government battery, measured both with and without available covariates.

Table 5.2 **Anytown Government Spending Results**

	Dependent Variable			
	Trust in Government Spending		Support for Tax Increases	
	(1)	*(2)*	*(3)*	*(4)*
Anytown	0.674***	0.665***	0.203**	0.277***
	(0.080)	(0.083)	(0.085)	(0.081)
Constant	−0.343***	−1.564***	−0.103*	0.405
	(0.057)	(0.498)	(0.060)	(0.496)
Covariates?	No	Yes	No	Yes
Observations	554	551	554	551
R^2	0.114	0.229	0.010	0.282
Adjusted R^2	0.112	0.138	0.009	0.190
Residual Std. Error	0.942	0.928	0.996	0.901
	(df = 552)	(df = 492)	(df = 552)	(df = 487)
F Statistic	70.796***	2.517***	5.767**	3.042***
	(df = 1; 552)	(df = 58; 492)	(df = 1; 552)	(df = 63; 487)

Note: $^*p < 0.1$; $^{**}p < 0.05$; $^{***}p < 0.01$

Covariate details: Models with covariates include age, income, sex, race (white), education, ideology, party ID, and U.S. state.

Covariate details: Further variable details can be found in the Appendix subsection "Mechanical Turk Demographic Questions."

taxes. "After all, why pay more, when I've already received all of these splendid benefits?," the free-lunch seeker might ask.

But the consumer citizen thinks differently. She sees these benefits and is pleased. "You get what you pay for," as the saying goes—and, perhaps unbeknownst to her previously, she is paying for a good product. In short, her deal with government is better than she thought. She is both more trusting of current levels of government spending and taxes as a result, *and* she now would be willing to pay more. People are acutely familiar with the costs of government; Anytown reminds them of the quality of what they get back. *Homo Emptor* doesn't just want more services at no costs. He wants *good* services, and he is willing to pay the costs. What worked for Walmart works for government services—and then some.

To understand just how powerful the Anytown treatment was, recall the partisan differences highlighted in Figure 5.1. Democrats and Republicans generally have very different levels of confidence in government spending. In this study, among those who *did not* see Anytown, we observed similar differences. Among Republicans in the placebo group, 70.4% believed that government was wasting "all" of their tax money. Only 45.5% of Democrats in the placebo answered similarly. In contrast, among Republicans who'd seen the Anytown video, 42.6% believed that government was wasting all of their tax money. In 2015, at the height of Republican hostility toward government's use of their tax money, Republicans randomly assigned to see Anytown became essentially as confident in government spending as Democrats who were in the placebo condition. Similar results were observed on the composite trust in government measure. Based on that, Democrats assigned to the placebo condition trusted government 13% more than Republicans in the placebo measure. Yet when we compare Republicans who saw Anytown to Democrats in the placebo, the difference in trust levels shrank to 6.5%—cutting the partisan distance in half.[7]

Operational Transparency and Government Processes

There is more to government than the services it provides, however. There's also the processes that produces the services—the "slow and difficult drilling of holes into hard boards" (Weber 2020, pp. 115): that makes such services possible, even if the process itself is messy. There's reason to think that Americans have strong attitudes about these processes. In *Stealth Democracy* (2002), John Hibbing and Elizabeth Theiss-Morse argue that scholars of American politics have focused too much on government outputs, or services of the sort studied above, at the expense of political processes. According to Hibbing and Theiss-Morse, Americans' views toward such political processes are quite cogent. By and large, people want government processes to be fair and neutral, and they loath policymakers who prioritize their own narrow interests. "People would most prefer decisions to be made by what we call empathetic, non-self-interested decision makers," they write (2002, p. 83).

This suggests that applying operational transparency to government processes may yield two different results. If such transparency portrays the people who make policy—the legislators—as hard-working public servants, it stands to reason that trust in government could be improved, and perhaps attitudes toward government taxing and spending could be affected as well. What works for Walmart might work for Congress members too. On the other hand, if operational transparency reveals public servants to be engaging in self-dealing, the effect might be deleterious for attitudes toward government.

Fortunately, the real world allowed for a test of these competing hypotheses. In 2013, the Huffington Post published an article about a leaked presentation given by congressional leaders to new Congress members. According to the presentation, in their ten-hour days, new representatives could expect to spend four hours each day on "call time," making calls to potential donors. New members would spend more time raising money each day than they would on any other activity, including engaging with their congressional duties and meeting constituents. As the Huffington Post article explained, call time isn't restricted to new members; higher-ranking members also get in on the act. They don't like it—one high-ranking congressperson compared it to "putting bamboo shoots" under his fingernails—but they do it nonetheless (Grim and Siddiqui 2013). The Huffington Post article about the demands of call time featured a screen shot from the actual PowerPoint presentation given to new Congress members.

The leaked schedule afforded me a perfect opportunity to test whether operational transparency, when targeted at processes rather than outputs, can affect trust in government. Hibbing and Theiss-Morse's work suggests that such transparency would have an effect on trust—and, if the operational transparency revealed the kind of behavior described in the Huffington Post article, that effect might very well be negative. Americans do not like their political process to feature much in the way of self-dealing, and Congress members devoting their days to enriching their campaign coffers would be doing just that. According to Hibbing and Theiss-Morse, some Americans mistakenly believe that politicians who raise money are raising money for themselves, not their campaign accounts. More broadly, "In the public's eye, [after being elected] politicians become

enmeshed in a Washington system in which they spend time with special interest leaders, they solicit money from them, and they pander to their whim"
(Hibbing and Theiss-Morse 2002, p. 123).

But Congress members don't *only* fundraise. Whether their constituents
know it or not, Congress members often work long hours, splitting time between Washington, DC, and their home districts. Many members are known
to actually sleep in their offices. As recently as 2018, newspapers reported
on the "increasing" number of Congress members who were sleeping in their
Capitol Hill offices, "on everything from cots in closets to futons stashed
behind constituent couches" (Schultz 2018). As the original Huffington
Post article noted, members have a "bleak work life" that allows them little
time off.

Recall that one of the central tenets of operational transparency relates
to the way it communicates effort performed on a recipient's behalf: When
people see the work that goes into providing a product, and that work is
visualized by pointing to the employees who produced the product, people
view the product more favorably. In this case, Congress members are the
workers, and legislation is the product. Making people aware of the work that
Congress members do—the hours they put in—might affect how people view
government broadly.

In a July 2018 study I presented U.S.-based Mechanical Turk participants
with one of three potential news articles. Two articles were modeled on the
original Huffington Post article. In one version, which I think of as "negative
procedural transparency," the essential details of the story were unchanged.
A presentation to new Congress members had leaked; in this presentation,
new members were told to expect to spend about one-third of each day di-
aling for dollars. The article concluded with a tally of all the money incumbent Congress members had raised since the beginning of the current
congressional term.

I created two treatment articles. The "positive procedural transparency"
treatment article took the liberty of removing any mention of fundraising from
the article and instead dwelled on the laborious model schedule the presentation revealed. "Congress Members Spend Hours Every Day Raising Money,
Documents Show," read the headline of the negative treatment article; "Congress
Members Abide Grueling Schedule, Documents Show," read the headline of
the positive version. And where the former had concluded by tallying up the
money incumbent Congress members had raised—$831 million—the latter
ended by noting that the current Congress had passed 219 bills into law, and also
passed 609 resolutions. (The complete text of all articles is in Appendix subsection "Procedural Operational Transparency Newspaper Articles.") In addition
to the positive and negative procedural operational transparency conditions,

I assigned some study participants to a placebo condition, which consisted of reading an article about a local beauty pageant. (I always feel bad for the people assigned to the placebo condition.) As the original article featured a screen shot of new members' actual likely schedules, I created congressional schedules of my own, one for the positive and one for the negative conditions. In the positive condition, I replaced the hours meant to be spent on fundraising with more hours on outreach to constituents, and I added "floor time" as another way for Congress members to pass their days. Figures 5.5 and 5.6 display the schedules that treatment participants saw. After viewing their assigned article, participants answered the same Pew battery I'd used in the Anytown study. They also replied to the same questions meant to tease out their redistributive preferences.

What works for government services, I found, does not work for governmental processes. Or, if it works, it does so in reverse: only the negative kind of operational transparency was able to affect attitudes, and it did so by diminishing trust. The positive kind of operational transparency, which communicated to participants just how hard their representatives worked for them—at least as

Model Weekday Schedule—D.C.

✓ 4 Hours—Constituent Visits

✓ 3 Hours—Committee Time

✓ 2 Hours—Floor Time

✓ 2 Hours—Strategic Outreach

✓ 1 Hour—Lunch/snacks/recharge

Figure 5.5 The positive daily congressional schedules shown to participants in the procedural operational transparency study.

Model Weekday Schedule—D.C.

✓ 4 Hours—Fundraising/Call Time

✓ 3 Hours—Constituent Visits

✓ 2 Hours—Committee Time

✓ 2 Hours—Strategic Outreach

✓ 1 Hour—Lunch/snacks/recharge

Figure 5.6 The negative daily congressional schedules shown to participants in the procedural operational transparency study.

Table 5.3 **Procedural Operational Transparency**

	Dependent Variable	
	Composite Trust	
	(1)	(2)
Positive Treatment	−0.013	−0.013
	(0.036)	(0.034)
Negative Treatment	−0.074**	−0.095***
	(0.037)	(0.034)
Constant	0.028	0.267*
	(0.025)	(0.146)
Observations	952	952
Covariates?	No	Yes
R^2	0.005	0.263
Adjusted R^2	0.003	0.207
Residual Std. Error	0.463 (df = 949)	0.413 (df = 884)
F Statistic	2.293 (df = 2; 949)	4.698*** (df = 67; 884)

Note: *p < 0.1; **p < 0.05; ***p < 0.01

Covariate details: Covariates included are age, sex, race (white), Party ID, ideology, household income, education, and U.S. state.

Covariate details: Further variable details can be found in appendix subsection "Mechanical Turk Demographic Questions."

hard as Walmart tells us its employees work for us—had almost no discernible effect. Table 5.3 displays models, with and without our standard covariates, for the effect that each condition had on the composite trust scale. Whereas Anytown moved people sharply in the positive direction, the negative procedural transparency condition pushed them to trust government less. Yet the effect was substantially smaller (we can compare coefficients because they are standardized and refer to the same outcome variable). The negative effect of negative procedural operational transparency was about one-third the size of the positive effect of the Anytown video.[8] Descriptive statistics can be found in Appendix Table A.30.

What items on the Pew battery were specifically affected by the treatment? Table 5.4 has the answers. The negative treatment made people more likely to say they would want "smaller government, fewer services"; that they could "trust the government to do what is right" less of the time; and that they viewed government as playing a more negative role in their life. Again, the coefficients are

Table 5.4 Congressional Operational Transparency (Specific Items)

	Dependent variable:					
	Small/Large Gov		Gov to Do Right		Gov Pos. Role	
	(1)	(2)	(3)	(4)	(5)	(6)
Positive Procedural Operational Transparency	-0.125	-0.163**	-0.049	-0.043	-0.010	-0.021
	(0.078)	(0.071)	(0.078)	(0.074)	(0.078)	(0.076)
Negative Procedural Operational Transparency	-0.151*	-0.216***	-0.154*	-0.156**	-0.183**	-0.236***
	(0.079)	(0.072)	(0.079)	(0.075)	(0.079)	(0.077)
Constant	0.090	0.021	0.065	0.844***	0.062	0.187
	(0.055)	(0.298)	(0.055)	(0.309)	(0.055)	(0.319)
Covariates?	No	Yes	No	Yes	No	Yes
Observations	954	954	954	954	954	954
R^2	0.004	0.280	0.004	0.223	0.007	0.172
Adjusted R^2	0.002	0.228	0.002	0.167	0.005	0.112
Residual Std. Error	0.999	0.879	0.999	0.912	0.998	0.942
	(df = 951)	(df = 889)	(df = 951)	(df = 889)	(df = 951)	(df = 889)
F Statistic	2.125	5.396***	1.957	3.994***	3.310**	2.886***
	(df = 2; 951)	(df = 64; 889)	(df = 2; 951)	(df = 64; 889)	(df = 2; 951)	(df = 64; 889)

Note: *p < 0.1; **p < 0.05; ***p < 0.01

standardized, and again, the effects are small. But they all point in the same direction. Interestingly, as columns 3 and 4 of Table 5.4 show, the *positive* procedural operational transparency condition also made people more likely to say they wanted a "smaller government" with "fewer services."

Before running the experiment, I expected the treatments to, at minimum, have effects on attitudes toward Congress itself. To measure these possible effects, I included feeling thermometers for the three branches of government.[9] But on no branch, including Congress, did either of the treatments have any effects. The treatments did not merely prime people to think negatively (or positively) about Congress; they changed people's underlying trust in government instead.

One way to understand these results is to view them as owed, at least in part, to the low levels of trust in Congress exhibited by subjects across conditions. It is possible, if not likely, that shortly before the experiment, many participants were exposed to some outside information that may have cast Congress in a bad light. Perhaps Congress had passed a bill that respondents disliked; perhaps Congress had not passed enough bills. Whatever the precise cause or causes, animosity toward Congress runs deep and may have effectively precluded any positive effects from emerging. Such potential "pretreatment effects" (Druckman and Leeper 2012), though not directly observed, may nonetheless be shaping the outcome here—putting a ceiling on the potential of operational transparency to shape attitudes. Under this explanation, operational transparency may be strong, but distrust in Congress is stronger. The implication of this study remains the same, however: when applied to political procedures, operational transparency decreases trust.

Conclusion

What works for Walmart *can* work for government. Across a broad range of measures, operational transparency can increase people's trust in government. The effect is sizable enough to lessen, though not always entirely eliminate, the divide that often separates partisans on these questions. Yet the effect is limited to *government services*. When people are hit over the head with information testifying to all the work that their legislators do on their behalf—all the labor they put in—they hardly bat an eye. As Hibbing and Theiss-Morse (2002) knew, people's views on governmental processes are more coherent than many researchers give them credit for. As those scholars make clear, people care about outputs *and* inputs. But they have little appetite for or interest in the details of the decision-making process. Operational transparency only makes a positive difference when it is trained on services.

Why? Two possible explanations are available. The first is simply that people know less about government services. It's not the government *in general* that is submerged; it's the specific benefits that the government provides. This distinction is easy to gloss over, but it matters. There are always news stories about self-dealing Congress members furiously trying to raise money; there are almost never stories about the home mortgage interest deduction. The Americans whom Hibbing and Theiss-Morse (2002) interviewed described politicians—even new politicians, elected with the best of intentions—as participating in a "corrupt system." Yet the same interview subjects had little grasp of policy outcomes. The increase in trust that we witnessed with Anytown may be related to the sheer amount of learning that people are doing when they watch the video. There just isn't that much more they can learn about political processes.

Yet this explanation is not entirely satisfying. People who saw their taxpayer receipt were also learning new information. As we've seen in both the United States and the United Kingdom, people managed to learn and remember what's on their receipt. Yet in those cases, no changes in attitudes, including on trust, were observed. A second explanation therefore presents itself. Government *services* are especially alluring to the consumer citizen. A government that is offering such services is engaging in precisely the kind of transactional behavior that appeals to consumers. Such a government is giving consumers something for their hard-earned dollars—something that they might not previously have realized they were getting. The receipt, while transactional, is also vague and ambiguous. What is "defense" (or "defence," as the British put it)? What is "foreign aid?"[10] What can one take away from these small phrases, beyond the numbers placed next to them?

There is nothing vague or ambiguous about Anytown. It details exactly how government services affect, and intervene in the lives, of everyday Americans. A viewer of Anytown might think of government as giving them a surprisingly fair deal—*all this, just for my tax money?* Having judged the deal to be fair, those who watched were then much more eager to willingly part with their tax money for government programs. Those exposed to the newspaper article conveying negative procedural operational transparency, however, likely concluded the opposite: the government comprises corrupt self-dealers. Even those who saw the positive operational transparency article saw government reduced to a set of hardworking legislators who, no matter how well-intentioned they may be, are not providing *Homo Emptor* much in the way of a deal. Walmart employees don't just work hard for the sake of hard work; they do so while providing you with goods that you want to buy. Without the latter, operational transparency runs aground. The consumer citizen wants government services, not political processes.

Years before conducting these studies, I had expected taxpayer receipts to improve trust in government. While that expectation was proven incorrect, the assumption underlying it was not. People's trust in government can be changed when they are approached as they are: as consumer citizens.

6

Consumers and Citizens

Some of our classical forebears, those who first articulated notions of citizenship, would likely be disappointed in all that I've described to this point. They did not envision citizenship as being enmeshed with consumer life. Quite the opposite, actually. In his *Politics*, Aristotle takes pains to emphasize that citizens are meant to be more than mere residents of a geographic territory, more than mere repositories of legal rights. Properly understood, citizens are actively committed to the community they share. "What effectively distinguishes the citizen proper from all others," he wrote, "is his participation in giving judgment and holding office" (Aristotle 1962, p. 169). For Aristotle, citizens are those who, by dint of their political engagement and participation, uphold the state itself.

Almost by definition, consumers qua consumers do not uphold the state. And only inadvertently might they be said to be committed to their community, as their individual purchasing decisions create the macroeconomy. Individual consumer decisions are, by and large, private, personal experiences. Of course, we often buy goods for other people. And of course, we sometimes go shopping in public places—in malls and on Main Street. Yet the number of malls has rapidly declined in recent decades (Cohen 2003). More than ever, we are shopping by ourselves on the Internet. The informal and spontaneous social world of the shopping center has given way to the small, isolating screen of the smartphone app.

Consumer decisions are made in private, with intended effects only on the consumer making the decision, while political decisions are made in public, with effects, potentially, on all of one's fellow citizens. In distinguishing between the public and the private, John Dewey argued that when an action is believed to have *indirect* consequences, regulations usually follow, and "something having the traits of a state come into existence. [But] when the consequences of an action are confined, or are thought to be confined, mainly to the persons engaged in it, the transaction is a private one" (Dewey 1927, pp. 12–13). This distinction has been made widely, across time and place. The ancient Greeks drew a sharp

The Consumer Citizen. Ethan Porter, Oxford University Press (2021). © Oxford University Press.
DOI: 10.1093/oso/9780197526781.003.0006.

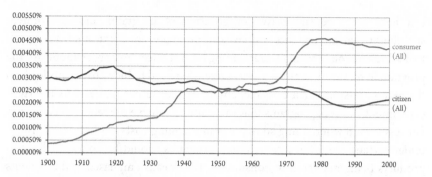

Figure 6.1 A Google "n-gram" of the words "consumer" and "citizen" that shows their usage in the English language corpus over time. The figure is not sensitive to case. Source: Michel et al. 2010.

line between the *polis*, or the public sphere, and the *oikos*, the private domain of the hearth and home; in the sixteenth century, the Germans borrowed from the Romans to carve out *privat*, which they viewed as separate from the authority of the state (Habermas 1989). The evidence presented in this book suggests that the boundaries between these two concepts appear to have eroded.

Indeed, by one metric, consumerism has come not to complement citizenship so much as displace it altogether. Figure 6.1 displays how often the terms "consumer" and "citizen" have appeared in the English language corpus since 1800. The pattern is unmistakable: as the term "citizen" declines in usage, "consumer" rises.

Insofar as his approach to citizenship is based on lessons from his time as a private consumer, *Homo Emptor* would thus seem wildly ill-equipped for the duties and obligations of citizenship. Citizens make decisions that affect others. Consumers, by and large, do not. They make decisions about themselves as individuals, not as citizens.

This dynamic would seem to pose tremendous dangers to political and civic life, and to public life in general. How can consumers form a common world? As the consumer triumphs, can citizenship survive?

The Only Way out Is In

If we wish to aid *Homo Emptor*, then we must treat him as we find him. Rather than merely decrying the encroachment of market life into the public sphere, we can use aspects of the consumer experience to improve the quality of democracy and public life. For policymakers, this would mean crafting policy with several lessons of this book in mind. First, remember the lesson of alignability: people can become more supportive of government programs and government spending when the benefits *and* costs of programs are mentioned. When the two values are roughly equal, mentioning both at once can boost support for the program in question. In those cases, there is no need to hide costs. This leads to the second lesson: when possible, emphasize consumer fairness. As the ACA experiment showed, programs that can claim to achieve the tenets of consumer fairness—even when doing so requires mentioning costs—will do well. Third, under certain conditions, government programs should be conceptualized as products being marketed to consumers. This means emphasizing the benefits that programs provide and clarifying the effort that goes into those programs, while ensuring that programs can be used efficiently and effectively (as Herd and Moynihan 2018 emphasized).

This proposal—to recast government programs as products—is likely to strike some as not befitting the spirit of democratic governance, an example of a solution that would only exacerbate the underlying problem. Such a criticism, however, would neglect the full history of the relationship between the consumer and the citizen. In the first chapter, I described *Homo Emptor* as akin to an uninvited dinner guest who nonetheless affects the evening conversation. Uninvited though he may be, if the conversation involves politics, he has not always been a stranger. The public sphere, as we understand it, would not exist for the consumer and the market world in which he lives. In proposing to use the consumer world to uphold and restore the public world, I am returning to the origins of the latter.

As Jurgen Habermas described, following the Renaissance, the need for commercial merchants to exchange information laid the groundwork for the emergence of "the news," or media that exist to convey information about current events between people. Printed communications concerning, say, the price and supply of a particular good gave way to political periodicals. As he explained it, it was no coincidence that "the great trade cities became at the same time centers for the traffic in news" (Habermas 1989, p. 16). And the economy too, which previously had been thought of as only a private matter—a task "proper to the *oikodespotes, the paterfamilias,* the head of the household"—became not only a ward of the state but its chief area of oversight (Habermas 1989, p. 20). The consumer who had once acted in private, or in exchange only with his neighbors, fell under the authority of the state that he had helped create. Quite simply, the private consumer helped birth the public sphere.

In the early days of the modern public sphere, governments explicitly corralled media to serve their interests. In some cases they took over existing newspapers; in other cases they produced their own. Their aim was to use the press to make announcements about rules and regulations, and to provide important economic updates, such as those relating to stocks, the price of goods, and even excise taxes. In short, government aimed to inform readers about the political and economic developments of the public sphere (Habermas 1989). The Viennese government, for example, issued this decree to a journal editor in 1769: "In order that the writer of the journal might know what sort of domestic decrees, arrangements, and other matters are suitable for the public, such are to be compiled weekly by the authorities and are to be forwarded to the editor of the journal" (as quoted in Habermas 1989, p. 22). Other European governments behaved similarly. They were not revealing the submerged state, emphasizing services provided or benefits unappreciated; they were constituting the public's relationship to the state.

The early public sphere, however, would give way to the welfare state, and with it the state's submersion (Titmuss 1958). And "in a social-welfare state that above all administers, distributes, and provides, the 'political' interests of citizens constantly subsumed under administrative acts are reduced primarily to claims specific" only to those aspects of the government that pertain specifically to the person making the claim (Habermas 1989, p. 211). The result, ultimately, is the phenomenon measured by Mettler (2011): people receive individual government benefits but never connect those benefits to the state from which they originate.

If we wish to transform *Homo Emptor*'s relationship to the entirety of government, *beyond* specific claims he may have on specific government benefits, we would be well advised to return to governmental strategies of the early, pre–welfare state public sphere. Governments should be encouraged to advertise themselves and their services, making clear what they do and, in turn, providing the groundwork for a public. Government, in short, should promote itself and its wares no differently than a private firm; if anything, government should be leaps and bounds more aggressive about such self-promotion. If spoken to about government in this manner, *Homo Emptor* might betray a smile of recognition that, in an irony of history, he created the political world from which he now seems so distant. Underneath *Homo Emptor* remains *Homo Politicus*, and the only way to get to the latter is through the former.

This would amount to a massive new approach to civic education—and not just for high school students. Concerns about the quality and quantity of civic education are perennial—and often wrapped up in concerns about the poor state of political knowledge (e.g., Galston 2001). As we've seen, appealing to the citizen as *consumer* citizen may be able to help. Such appeals can boost political knowledge about otherwise frustratingly complex topics. Efforts like the distribution of taxpayer receipts, if rolled out nationwide as a part of a broader civic education campaign, could lead to upsurges in political knowledge among Americans.

A government campaign to promote its own virtues and enhance political knowledge should not consign itself to television. The relationship between television and diminished civic engagement has long been noted (Putnam 1995; Velez and Newman 2019). One does not have to view the Internet as a panacea to speculate that, relative to television, its impact on political engagement can be positive (as Karpf [2012] suggested). This government effort to promote itself could attempt to implement the programs described by Michael Neblo, Kevin Esterling, and David Lazer in their book, *Politics with the People* (2018)—but with a consumer spin. Neblo and his coauthors use online town halls to directly connect citizens with their representatives. In these town halls, constituents exercise their deliberative capacities while engaging in substantive exchanges with their elected officials about policy matters. Scaling up such efforts would not only dramatically increase the share of young people who report participating in democratic processes or simulations thereof—a number that, as of late, has been woefully low (Hansen et al. 2018, p. 24)—but could very well enrich civic life for the broader population.

Neblo and his coauthors conceive of citizenship as being opposed to consumer life, arguing that their online town halls offer participants a way to act "as *citizens*, rather than just as consumers. Contemporary democracy asks little more of citizens than their votes and money, and so it is no wonder that many citizens share a sense of dissatisfaction and disconnection from public life," they wrote (Neblo, Esterling, and Lazer 2018, p. 3). This is a common complaint. But from the perspective of the consumer citizen, it is a false choice. Deliberation is indeed a virtue of democracy. But meeting people where they are, as consumers, requires that political virtues such as deliberation be marketed alongside other goods. Some may find that this degrades deliberation, but what good is deliberation, or any particular political virtue for that matter, if few people are making use of it?

A consumer citizen approach could be profitability applied to virtual town halls. Think of how markets, despite the countless differences between individuals, draw people into a common space. The campaign I am outlining should take advantage of this feature. Most civic education efforts focus on public schools. On one hand, this make sense. Public schools are government-funded public spaces. On the other hand, by focusing on schools, civic education efforts lose out on most of the population before they begin.

A civic education campaign modeled on consumer citizenship could meet citizens in the markets where they congregate. Imagine short, complimentary civic education classes offered to the large, diverse shoppers at Costco (adjacent to the complimentary snacks). Or think of the government mandating that large online retailers periodically offer users the ability to directly engage with their elected representatives, via online town halls.

We use Amazon.com for nearly everything already. We should use it—and its successors and competitors—for democracy too.

Implication for Models of Attitude Formation

My approach has several implications for more general ways of understanding political attitude formation. First, it's worth considering the way in which my argument intersects with the standard model of attitude formation. Formally, this model can be presented as $\Sigma \; v_i * w_j$, with v standing for the value of an individual attribute, and w standing for the weight the respondent attaches to that attribute (see, e.g., Chong and Druckman 2007). I suggest here an addition to the model. Not only do people form attitudes based on attributes and attribute-specific weights; they also base their attitudes on the extent to which they are familiar with, or have had recent or repeated exposure to, both the object and attributes under evaluation. One supposition of mine is that, when a respondent's level of familiarity with the object she is evaluating is low, she is more likely to turn to evaluative techniques developed elsewhere with which she is more familiar.

If she is familiar with the attributes but unfamiliar with the object, then it stands to reason she is more likely to make biased or otherwise "incorrect" evaluations. Think here of how, in Chapter 3, the people with low political knowledge seemed to like the *Alignability* candidate most of all, even though this meant they would receive few benefits personally. "Incorrect" is deployed here in the spirit of Anthony Downs's (1960) article, aptly titled "Why the Government Budget Is Too Small in a Democracy," in which he argued,

> It is good for the citizens in a democracy to get what they want, and to base their wants on as much knowledge as possible. It is not good for them to get something they would not want if they knew more about it. That is the extent of my ethical foundation, and I think it is compatible with almost every normative theory of democracy. (Downs 1960, p. 545)

It is hard to believe that many people actually want fewer benefits rather than more. We also know that, in this case, knowing more about politics would be associated with wanting more government benefits. But here we have not just an information deficit, of the kind that initially concerned Downs, but an inappropriate reliance on consumer lessons when evaluating a political object. With this in mind, at minimum, we could add an f term to the standard model, as specified by Chong and Druckman, to account for the general role that familiarity plays—or we could model expected "incorrect" responses, as understood by Downs, by weighting attributes and values by respondents' familiarity with the object under evaluation.

My approach also has ramifications for John Zaller's *RAS* (Receive-Access-Sample) model. Zaller's model is built on four axioms, each one concerning, respectively, reception, resistance, accessibility, and response (Zaller 1992, p. 58). Regarding accessibility, Zaller writes that people will be able to call a consideration to mind more quickly when it has been thought about more recently. For Zaller, considerations consist of "*any* reason that might induce an individual to decide a political issue one way or the other" (Zaller 1992, p. 40, emphasis added). The evidence presented in this book emphasizes that a consideration can indeed consist of *any* reason that might propel a subject to take a particular position on an issue.

Even if a consideration has no obvious political content, it still seems capable of affecting political choices. For example, the consideration of whether an earmarked tax meets the criterion of source-use alignability has no obvious political content. Yet this consideration can affect attitudes toward earmarked taxes nonetheless. The same is true for whether a candidate pledges to achieve cost-benefit alignability, or if a health insurance cooperative promises benefits approximate to costs. And the consumer pressures tested in Chapter 4 never mention politics. But as we've seen, the considerations they tap into can affect political outcomes nonetheless.

Even people who cannot access political considerations easily may be able to access other considerations with ease. For those people, such nonpolitical considerations are more likely to bubble to the surface and make an impact on their choices when they are asked to respond to a political query. Zaller seems to assume that political responses are mostly, if not always, products of political considerations. I do not think this is necessarily the case. Indeed, those who may lack awareness of politics may have high awareness of the consumer world—say, what products are on sale, what they want to buy, what brand they like best— and vice versa. When prompted to respond to a political choice, those with high awareness of nonpolitical matters, such as those that relate to their lives as consumers, will probably rely on considerations from the domain with which they are more familiar.

In Summation

In seeking to unpack political attitudes and behaviors, political scientists should not restrict their focus to the same old places. Given our reasonable confidence in the idea that few people think about politics in sophisticated ways (or in ways similar to political scientists), we should turn our attention to the sources of the ways that most people think about politics, even if those sources have no obvious political significance. As of this writing, it was only about fifteen years ago that a reality television show, *The Apprentice*, catapulted an already-famous businessman into upward of twenty million households a week. At that time, imagining Donald Trump as president would have been a laughable exercise. The show contained no overt political messages. No one then would have regarded the show or its popularity as auguring anything about American politics. Yet as of this writing, its star sits in the Oval Office.

Political scientists have begun to grasp this point: political attitudes and behaviors can come from very strange places. Reality television, of the sort typified by *The Apprentice*, has begun to receive scholarly attention (Kim n.d.). More broadly, Eric Oliver and Thomas J. Wood (2018) show that many political beliefs are correlated with "magical thinking," or the extent to which one's beliefs deviate from reason. In other words, we can better understand how Americans think about politics if we recall that many of them believe in angels. Magical thinking, consumer thinking: these are but two kinds of thinking that might affect politics, even if we do not expect them to, let alone want them to. Politics does not only occur when and where we believe it should. There is a deservingly rich literature on the effects of "politically irrelevant events," such as shark attacks and college football games, on vote choice (e.g., Busby, Druckman, and Fredenall 2017; Achen and Bartels 2016; Healy, Malhotra, and Mo 2010).

This literature has provoked a spirited debate (Fowler and Montages 2015; Fowler and Hall 2018). Yet lacking in this debate has been a systemic theory about the nature of the "irrelevant" events, or stimuli, more likely to have political effects. Is it just the case that citizens make meaningful political decisions based on *anything* that comes in front of them? Or are there meaningful patterns to discern? This book has argued that citizens' political preferences are related to their consumer experiences, because of the much greater time and cognitive resources people devote to the latter than the former, the superficial similarities between the two, and the consumer-tinged rhetoric of political elites. This premise could serve as the basis for a broader theory, directing us how to sift through all the possible, seemingly irrelevant events that could affect politics. Eventually, we could precisely identify what distinguishes sources of political influence, and the extent to which *seemingly* irrelevant forces are indeed irrelevant.

The debate about irrelevant events has mostly side-stepped the question of what should follow a verdict. If indeed irrelevant events can affect politics, then what should the response be? No matter what, the response does need to be one of resignation. In the previous chapters, I outlined how the consumer world, a world apart from politics, can be leveraged to affect, and indeed sometimes improve, meaningful political outcomes. Trust in government can be increased by appealing to citizens qua consumer citizens. So too can people's feelings about taxes and government spending be made more positive. They can become more willing to sign up for social programs, and they can increase what they know about politics. These findings are offered in the spirit of a search for a more solutions-focused social science (Watts 2017; Lenz 2018)—one that does not merely identify and measure political phenomena, but attempts to change them.

Appendix

THE STRUCTURES OF CONSUMER AND POLITICAL DECISIONS

For the citizen who considers politics only peripherally, political and consumer decisions are easy to conflate in part because of their surface-level structural similarities. Both present individuals with a limited set of choices and ask them to identify which one they prefer. There are, of course, other possible choices outside what is presented. The consumer could, if he wished, leave the store, just as a citizen could write in her own candidate on the ballot, or offer the pollster a policy preference not on offer. But what of those citizens whose interest in politics is limited to begin with? They are not likely to propose alternative policies or to offer serious write-in candidates. They are likely to choose from what is available—that is, what is on the menu. In both cases, people spend most of their time evaluating a finite set of choices.

Similarly, the *objects* of political decisions are often framed in terms familiar to consumers. When they speak about policy in particular, politicians refer to some set of benefits and some corresponding set of costs. The same is true when they are discussing partisan affiliation: the opposition party costs you money and gives you little in return. While not all policies are discussed in this manner, many are. The framing of policies as related to costs and benefits may have cumulative effects. We can think of costs and benefits as being *transaction considerations* of both consumer and political decisions. There are additional normative considerations in both contexts.

Table A.1 summarizes both the superficial similarities and differences between consumer and political decisions. To understand how consumer and political decisions might appear similar to people who do not engage in politics frequently, consider the following. When a private firm asks you, as a consumer, to make a purchase, it is effectively asking if you will part with some of your money for one of their goods. Of the choices before you, will you pay a cost, in the form of the price, to receive a benefit, in the form of a good? Likewise, a politician who asks you if you would be willing to part with your money in the form of a tax is asking you if you want to receive a good in return. The good being offered by the politician is, of course, different from that being offered by the private firm. A furniture company might be selling a sofa; a politician might be selling a road. But the considerations—especially for those who think about politics less frequently—are similar.

Yet, fundamentally, government is *not* a provider of goods akin to companies. And here is where the trouble starts. Albert Hirschman (1970) laid the groundwork for this perspective, describing three possible actions that allow individuals to express themselves in sociopolitical or economic settings: exit, voice, and loyalty. To *exit* means to leave, to take one's marbles and go home. *Voice* refers to our capacity to give our opinion, and *loyalty* refers to our capacity to remain true. Sometimes, these mix together.

In our private-sector example, a furniture company has promised to deliver a good in exchange for the voluntary receipt of your money. Rarely, though, does the government make a similar promise—and when it does, you have little choice but to accept it or leave at significant cost. Exit in response to one particular policy would be extraordinarily costly. A new highway would, on its own, hardly prompt someone to leave town. I can blow off the furniture salesman much more easily; on the whole, I can exit from private-sector decisions at little cost. Exiting to express my political opinion, however, is cost-prohibitive—literally so, with moving costs; and less literally but no less consequential, with the costs associated with leaving behind friends, family members, and all that is familiar.

There are also differences in assigning credit, or "tracing" benefits to their origins (Arnold 1990). For example, financing of road construction is a byzantine process, involving multiple levels of government. A politician from one level of government who promised to build a road would likely have to rely upon the cooperation of others, at other levels, to see her promise through. Many government services, including tax expenditures designed to achieve some policy end, are likely to have such "traceability" problems, with ordinary people unable to trace or attribute the services to their proper political origins (Arnold 1990; Mettler 2011). The reverse is also true, as politicians are blamed for problems that they had no role in creating (Sances 2017). The high costs of acquiring correct political information are well known, and only exacerbated by federalism (Popkin 1991).

If Americans are inclined to view politics through the consumer lens, then it stands to reason that they may well underestimate the value of what government provides them. They will be little different from a customer who has paid for a sofa but not received one in return—a customer who has *not* paid willingly. And if Americans are inclined to view politics through the consumer lens, it stands to reason that they will be generally displeased with government. Exit is costly in a way that voice is not, and so they will express their displeasure by speaking out against taxes and government spending, decreasing their trust in government, or preferring candidates who would, if elected, redistribute less. As discussed in Chapter 2, Anthony Downs recognized this dynamic some sixty years ago (Downs 1960, p. 546).

The objects under evaluation in consumer and political decisions are quite different. When making a consumer decision, an individual is usually being asked to evaluate a discrete, tangible object. Questions about government policies, of the type familiar to surveys, usually ask about topics that are nondiscrete and nonunitary. Do you support a recently passed law? How do you feel about your local government? An individual asked to respond to such questions—or an individual who develops responses without provocation—is evaluating objects that are neither discrete nor tangible.

There are consequential differences between the perceptibility of government costs and benefits and those costs and benefits that come to us as consumers. By *perceptibility*, I mean the extent to which we can see or otherwise have explicit, immediately available evidence of a cost or benefit. When a consumer good is purchased, the benefits it affords are often, but not always, easily perceptible. As possible benefits, the cup of coffee offers the coffee itself, the caffeinated rush that soon follows, or—depending on quality—the flavor. Perceptibility also has a temporal aspect. In consumer environments, the benefits arrive rather quickly, or I have near-certainty of when they will arrive. If I purchase a cup of coffee, I have a good idea about when its benefits will come. Purchase and consumption happen close together, often simultaneously. This is only rarely true for government. More often than not, payments to government bear little relationship to consumption of government. Costs and benefits are perceptibly intertwined in consumer decisions, in a way that they are not when it comes to decisions involving government.

Government benefits—even its social programs that involve disbursing material benefits—are rarely easy to discern (e.g., Mettler 2011). Part of the reason that governmental benefits and costs are not easy to discern is that they are distributed and extracted, respectively, over a widely varying time horizon. Costs are extracted via taxes on biweekly payrolls; they are also extracted every mid-April, and they are extracted via various governmental fees. Meanwhile, even material cash benefits are not disbursed to correspond with the schedule in which costs are extracted; Medicare and Social Security payments are not disbursed at the time that the cost is extracted for them. This brings us to another reason that government costs and benefits are not easy to discern: their nontangible quality. This helps explain why, among those items not recognized by subjects as government benefits by Mettler (2011), the least recognized benefits are those, like the home mortgage interest deduction, that do not appear in any tangible form, but instead show up as a reduced tax burden to the individual.

Public goods pose special problems for the perception of government costs and benefits. Consumer goods are, by definition, excludable and rivalrous; public goods are neither. Imagining a coffee shop in which public goods are sold is thus an exercise in surrealism. The shop would have to give away coffee to all those who wanted it, and it would have to do so for everyone who wanted it. The coffee-shop-as-government only becomes slightly less surreal when something other than public goods are sold. As the link between government costs and benefits is very wide, the Government Coffee Shop would give customers coffee well before or long after they had paid for it (if they paid for it all). In the Government Coffee Shop, a customer would walk in, have to pay, and not necessarily receive—or not know they have received—coffee in return. And they might harbor the sneaking suspicion that everyone else was getting their coffee for free.

Policy has not been designed to reflect the perspective of the consumer citizen. Government taxes sporadically, and government disburses benefits sporadically, rarely making the latter as clear as the former. There are, of course, exceptions. After the stimulus bill passed in 2009, the federal government went out of its way to advertise which projects were being funded as a result. At the same time, however, the tax cuts included in the package were infamously tied to payroll taxes and *not* promoted as such, leading many people to disbelieve they had received a cut (Mettler 2011). By and large, though, while candidates for elected office may sometimes intuit the centrality of consumer life, policymakers do not. Citizens are rarely treated by their government as they would be were they customers of an ordinary firm.

When it comes to government benefits, there is no equivalent of April 15, a date devoted to the extraction of costs. As Kahneman and Tversky (1979) made clear, people are more sensitive to losses than gains. Analogously, *even if* government costs and benefits were equally salient, we might expect the former to matter more than the latter. But this is not the case. Once a year, or on a quarterly basis, most Americans feel the pain of writing the government a check. And for many, government takes a bite every other week, as one's take-home pay is reduced even further by the hand of Uncle Sam.

All this is not to say that *all* of government lacks any and all similarities to common consumer experiences. Everyday municipal services, such as public transit, offer citizens an opportunity to witness costs and benefits existing in close proximity. (And as is apparent in the bus-stop study described in Chapter 2, the role of consumer decision-making in structuring political attitudes is apparent at such locations.) Buying a bus ticket and then being transported to one's preferred destination is roughly equivalent to purchasing a good and immediately receiving the benefits of that purchase. But even in that case, a person would not be faulted for taking for granted the roads, the traffic lights, and the stop signs—all government-provided elements that made her trip possible. In summary, underlying structural similarities are only one of three forces contributing to the conflation of consumer and political decisions. The ubiquity of consumer decisions and the consumer rhetoric of political leaders play large roles, as this text attests. But as the above discussion indicates, the extent to which the *seeming* structural similarities mask deeper differences also may help explain some common American attitudes, primarily opposition to redistribution and distrust in government.

Table A.1 **Consumer vs. Political Decisions**

Features	*Consumer Decisions*	*Political Decisions*
Superficial Structural Similarities		
Number of Objects to Evaluate	Finite (e.g., items on a menu or goods in a store)	Finite (e.g., candidates on a ballot or policy choices in a survey)
Transaction Considerations	Costs, benefits, and norms	Costs, benefits, and norms
Underlying Structural Differences		
Extraction of Costs	Tied to provision of benefit	Divorced from provision of benefit
Provision of Benefit	Tied to extraction of cost	Divorced from extraction of cost
Exit Costs	Low	High
Punishment Options	Refusal to pay; negotiation	Support antigovernment policies or candidates
Traceability	Straightforward	Obscured
Kind of Objects to Evaluate	Most are discrete and tangible	Few are discrete and tangible

A Note on Methodology

On matters of methodology, I consider myself an experimentalist, whose work relies on the random assignment of a treatment to make causal discoveries. Generally speaking, *treatments* can be anything, from the distribution of money to the distribution of medicine to exposure to psychological primes, provided that their assignment is orthogonal to other characteristics of the subjects being experimented upon. To assess the causal effects of a treatment, we compare subjects who received or were otherwise assigned to receive the treatment to those who were not, on some measure collected after the treatment. The resulting quantity is called a "treatment effect."

But this book is not only about designing and testing experiments. It is also about articulating and describing the boundaries of a novel theory about political behavior and attitudes. For an experimentalist, such a task might pose a challenge. Experiments often go awry or produce results unexpected by theory. Sometimes, they produce no results at all. A book of failed experiments might be a humorous addition to social science libraries, yet perhaps not much of a contribution to the advancement of knowledge. Conversely, a book comprising only successful experiments might be initially greeted with applause yet ultimately prove to be less than meets the eye, when it turns out that the experimentalist had swept all the failed results under the rug.

I use experiments in this book to both argue that my theory has empirical validity—and, more specifically, that its implications *cause* changes in political attitudes and behavior. When resources permit, I've tried to replicate my findings; experiments described in Chapters 2 and 3 have been successfully replicated, while the taxpayer receipt's effects on knowledge have been observed in both U.S. and U.K. contexts. I also use experiments to map the limitations of my argument. For example, I find that taxpayer receipts can affect trust in government, as I believed they would. Enrico Fermi, the great physicist, is reported to have once said (perhaps apocryphally) that while "experimental confirmation of a prediction is merely a measurement, an experiment disproving a prediction is a discovery" (Fripp et al 2000). He probably overstated things, but I like the sentiment.

Experiments are not always possible, for reasons of ethics or practicality. In some cases I was fortunate enough to run experiments on large, nationally representative random samples. In several other experiments, I used Amazon's Mechanical Turk service to recruit participants. Mechanical Turk is a platform that offers people around the world the opportunity to complete small tasks for small amounts of money. It has been widely used across the social sciences for experimental work similar to the research that animates this book. Psychologists, political scientists, and economists have all made use of it (e.g., Kuziemko et al. 2015).

While there have been concerns about Mechanical Turk samples' external and internal validity, the available literature suggests that such concerns are unwarranted. Regarding external validity, Berinsky, Huber, and Lenz (2012) demonstrate that experiments conducted over Mechanical Turk produce results similar to those obtained on nationally representative samples. Several scholars have subsequently replicated this insight, including Coppock (2017) and Mullinix, Leeper, Druckman, and Freese (2015). Regarding internal validity, concerns have related to the Mechanical Turkers' attentiveness (Berinsky, Margolis, and Sances 2014) and even the possibility that some responses are provided by bots. All the Mechanical Turk models provided in this book are robust—that is, they remain statistically and substantively identical—to aggressive re-estimation strategies in which problematic responses, broadly defined, are removed.

Is Mechanical Turk a convenience sample? Yes. It is certainly convenient—and cheap. But its superiority to standard convenience samples, such as those consisting of undergraduate samples, is worth emphasizing. It recruits from a far broader population, with participants coming from all ages, races, geographic regions, and political ideologies. It does skew younger and liberal, but not disastrously so. For a study I conducted that has no relationship to this book, my research partners and I administered the same experiment simultaneously over Mechanical Turk and a nationally representative sample (Nyhan et al. 2017). What we found astounded us: without any manipulation of the data after collection, the results from Mechanical Turk were statistically indistinguishable from the results obtained from the nationally representative sample. If our interest is in *level differences* between treatment and control—which indeed it is for most of this book—Mechanical Turk is hard to beat as a convenience sample.

Mechanical Turk Demographic Questions

Please describe your level of education:

- No formal education (1)
- Attended pre–high school but not high school (2)
- Attended high school but did not graduate (3)
- High school graduate (hold diploma) (4)
- Some college, no degree (5)
- Associate degree (6)
- Bachelor's degree (7)
- Master's degree (8)
- Professional or doctorate degree (9)

Please describe your race or ethnicity:

- White, Non-Hispanic (1)
- Black, Non-Hispanic (2)
- Other, Non-Hispanic (3)
- Hispanic (4)
- 2+ races, Non-Hispanic (5)

Please describe your gender:

- Male (1)
- Female (2)

Please state the total number of people in your household:

- 1 (1)
- 2 (2)
- 3 (3)
- 4 (4)
- 5 or more (5)

Please indicate your household income from the ranges below:

- Less than $5,000
- $5,000 to $7,499
- $7,500 to $9,999
- $10,000 to $12,499
- $12,500 to $14,999
- $15,000 to $19,999
- $20,000 to $24,999
- $25,000 to $29,999
- $30,000 to $34,999
- $35,000 to $39,999
- $40,000 to $49,999
- $50,000 to $59,999
- $60,000 to $74,999
- $75,000 to $84,999
- $85,000 to $99,999
- $100,000 to $124,999
- $125,000 to $149,999
- $150,000 to $174,999
- $175,000 or more

What is your state of residence? *Drop-down menu with fifty states and the District of Columbia*

Please describe your current employment status:

- Working: as a paid employee
- Working: self-employed
- Not working: on a temporary layoff from a job
- Not working: looking for work
- Not working: retired
- Not working: disabled
- Not working: other

Please describe your political party affiliation:

- Strong Republican
- Not Strong Republican
- Leans Republican
- Undecided/Independent/Other
- Leans Democrat
- Not Strong Democrat
- Strong Democrat

Please describe your political ideology:

- Extremely liberal
- Liberal
- Slightly liberal
- Moderate, middle of the road
- Slightly conservative
- Conservative
- Extremely conservative

Consumer vs. Political Decisions
Survey Questions

Consumer Decisions
Over the past week, have you done any of the following? Check all that apply.

- Purchased food and beverages, such as breakfast cereal, milk, coffee, chicken, wine, full-service meals, and snacks.
- Purchased housing, such as rent of primary residence, owners' equivalent rent, fuel oil, and bedroom furniture.
- Purchased apparel, such as men's shirts and sweaters, women's dresses, and jewelry.
- Purchased transportation, such as new vehicles, airline fares, gasoline, and motor vehicle insurance.
- Purchased medical care, such as prescription drugs and medical supplies, physicians' services, eyeglasses and eye care, and hospital services.
- Purchased recreation, such as televisions, toys, pets and pet products, sports equipment, and admissions.
- Purchased education and communications, such as college tuition, postage, telephone services, computer software and accessories.
- Purchased other goods and services, such as tobacco and smoking products, haircuts and other personal services, and funeral expenses.

Political Decisions

Over the past week, have you done any of the following? Check all that apply.

- Talked to other people about which political candidate or party they should support. (1)
- Attended a political meeting, rally, or dinner. (2)
- Worked for a political party, candidate, or organization. (3)
- Wore a campaign button, put a political sticker on my car, or put a sign in my yard or window. (4)
- Gave money to help a political candidate or political party. (5)
- Commented on Facebook, Twitter, Instagram, or another social media website about a political issue. (6)
- Wrote a letter to the editor of a newspaper about a political issue. (7)
- Signed a petition, either in person or over the Internet, about a political issue. (8)

Table A.2 **Homo Emptor Demographics**

Characteristic	Homo Emptor	Homo Civicus
Party ID	5.06***	2.42
Ideology	3.91***	2.26
Trust in Government Spending	1.14***	1.36
Education	3.43***	3.89
Age	57.39***	51.53
Female	0.47***	0.55
White	0.833***	0.74
Income	6.36	6.27
Trump Vote	0.734***	0.09
Political Interest	1.54***	1.44
Church Attendance	3.77***	4.63
Participation	1.65***	2.36

Note: $*p<0.1; **p<0.05; ***p<0.01$

The second column of Table A.2 reports the mean responses by characteristic of subjects who agreed with the proposition that "Government should be run like a business." Third column reports mean responses of those who disagreed.

"Don't know" responses have been imputed with mean response. *Age* was calculated by subtracting subjects' birth year from 2018. *Female* and *Trump Vote* are binary. *Income* was measured on a 1–16 interval scale and *Education* was measured on a 1–6 scale. *Party ID* and *Ideology* were the standard 7-point scale, with lower numbers indicating Democratic identification. *Political Interest* is 1–4, with higher numbers indicating less interest. *Church Attendance* is 1–6, with lower numbers indicating more frequent attendance.

Table A.3 **2012 Taxpayer Receipt ANES Trust Battery Results**

	Dependent Variable	
	ANES Trust in Government Battery	
	(1)	*(2)*
Benefits	2.651*	2.397
	(1.585)	(1.572)
Tax Receipt	2.339	2.318
	(1.581)	(1.571)
Tax Receipt and Benefits Number	2.332	2.315
	(1.579)	(1.564)
Constant	33.932***	35.257***
	(1.103)	(1.920)
Observations	733	733
Covariates?	No	Yes
R^2	0.005	0.032
Adjusted R^2	0.001	0.022
Residual Std. Error	15.239 (df = 729)	15.075 (df = 725)
F Statistic	1.224 (df = 3; 729)	3.384*** (df = 7; 725)

Note: $^*p < 0.1$; $^{**}p < 0.05$; $^{***}p < 0.01$

Table A.3 relays aggregate responses to the three-question ANES Trust in Government battery, rescaled so that larger numbers indicate more trust in government. Following ANES, the scale runs from 0 to 100, with responses to each item recoded to fit this scale (e.g., responses of 0 are assigned a 0, and responses evincing the greatest possible trust for that question are assigned a 100).

Table A.4 **2012 Taxpayer Receipt Descriptive Statistics**

Variable	Control	Tax Receipt	Benefits Number	Receipt and Benefits Number
Female	91	102	112	102
Age (Mean)	Between 18 and 29	Between 18 and 29	Between 18 and 29	Between 18 and 29
Income (Mean)	Below $50,000	Below $50,000	Below $50,000	Below $50,000
Democrats	178	187	189	173
Personal Military Disability	4	3	1	2
Military Death Benefits	4	1	3	2

Note: No significant differences at p < .05

In Table A.4, *Personal Military Disability* and *Military Death Benefits* show counts, by condition, of subjects who claimed military death benefits or personal military disability benefits; imbalance on these would have been substantively worrisome. For construction of other variables, consult the "Mechanical Turk Demographic Questions" subsection. For ease of interpretation, I have collapsed sex and party ID into the binary variables displayed above. P-values reported are with associated chi-square tests of independence.

Table A.5 **2014 Alignability Tax Study Results**

	Dependent Variable	
	Trust in Government Spending	
	(1)	(2)
Costs	−0.027	−0.046
	(0.082)	(0.086)
Benefits	−0.033	−0.007
	(0.085)	(0.086)
Alignability	0.157*	0.126
	(0.083)	(0.085)
Constant	1.440***	0.878**
	(0.042)	(0.407)
Observations	366	366
Covariates?	No	Yes
R^2	0.013	0.223
Adjusted R^2	0.005	0.082
Residual Std. Error	0.564 (df = 362)	0.542 (df = 309)
F Statistic	1.611 (df = 3; 362)	1.584*** (df = 56; 309)

Note: *p < 0.1; **p < 0.05; ***p < 0.01

Table A.5 reports results from a 2014 study of the effect of alignability messages on attitudes toward government spending, with larger numbers indicating greater trust in government spending on a 3-point scale.

Table A.6 **2016 Alignability Tax Experiment Descriptive Statistics**

Variable	Aligned	Costs	Benefits
Age (Mean)	25 to 34	25 to 34	25 to 34
Education	Associate degree	Associate degree	Associate degree
Race (White)	257	253	240
Female	150	143	138
Income (Mean)	$35,000 to $39,999	$35,000 to $39,999	$35,000 to $39,999
Democrats	153	157	155
Liberals	171	157	173

Note: No significant differences at p < .05

Consult the "Mechanical Turk Demographic Questions" subsection for details on variable construction. For ease of interpretation, I have collapsed sex, race, ideology, and party ID into the binary variables displayed above.

Table A.7 **Chicago Bus Study Results**

	Dependent Variable		
	Tax Feeling Thermometer		
	(1)	*(2)*	*(3)*
Alignability	11.462*	13.769*	19.341**
	(6.593)	(6.976)	(7.936)
Benefit		6.713	12.285
		(6.641)	(7.647)
Control			11.143
			(7.735)
Constant	54.117***	51.810***	46.238***
	(3.154)	(3.893)	(5.470)
Observations	83	83	83
R^2	0.036	0.048	0.072
Adjusted R^2	0.024	0.024	0.037
Residual Std. Error	25.236 (df = 81)	25.233 (df = 80)	25.065 (df = 79)
F Statistic	3.022*	2.022	2.058
	(df = 1; 81)	(df = 2; 80)	(df = 3; 79)

Note: *p < 0.1; **p < 0.05; ***p < 0.01

Feeling thermometer results for taxes measured on a 0–100 scale from the study conducted at Chicago bus stops.

Table A.8 **Chicago Bus Study Descriptive Statistics**

Variable	Aligned	Benefit	Cost	Control
Age (mean)	35.5	34.6	38.1	36.25
Income (mean)	$89,973.37	$87,186.84	$83,579.50	$84,550.95
Female	10	14	9	11
White	14	14	15	15

Note: No significant differences at p < .05

Age was self-reported by subjects. *Female* and *White* were assessed by enumerators. *Income* was computed by a process described in Chapter 2.

Table A.9 **"You Get What You Pay For" Feeling Thermometer Results**

	Dependent Variable	
	Feeling Thermometer	
	(1)	(2)
Aligned	10.483***	10.619***
	(1.374)	(1.365)
Misaligned	6.510***	6.585***
	(1.368)	(1.361)
Constant	28.714***	45.245***
	(0.961)	(6.657)
Observations	2,693	2,693
Covariates?	No	Yes
R^2	0.022	0.072
Adjusted R^2	0.021	0.050
Residual Std. Error	29.121 (df = 2690)	28.680 (df = 2632)
F Statistic	29.769*** (df = 2; 2690)	3.379*** (df = 60; 2632)

Note: *$p < 0.1$; **$p < 0.05$; ***$p < 0.01$

Feeling thermometer results on a 0–100 scale from hypothetical earmarked taxes on either gas used in automobiles or fuel used for jets, with aligned uses as highway construction and airport construction, respectively. Misaligned uses were the inverse.

Table A.10 **"You Get What You Pay For" Descriptive Statistics**

	You Pay For (Misaligned)	You Pay For (Aligned)	You Pay For (No Use)
Race (White)	655	661	694
Sex (Female)	462	459	486
Party ID (Democrat)	334	323	330
Income (Mean)	$35,000 to $39,999	$35,000 to $39,999	$35,000 to $39,999
Age (Mean)	35 to 44 years old	35 to 44 years old	35 to 44 years old

Note: No significant differences at p < .05

Consult the "Mechanical Turk Demographic Questions" subsection for details on variable construction. For ease of interpretation, I have collapsed race, sex, and Party ID into binary variables.

Table A.11 **"You Break It, You Buy It" Feeling Thermometer Results**

	Dependent Variable	
	Feeling Thermometer	
	(1)	(2)
Aligned	4.587***	4.808***
	(1.681)	(1.669)
Misaligned	2.141	2.259
	(1.693)	(1.678)
Constant	32.824***	19.610**
	(1.208)	(8.085)
Observations	2,687	2,687
Covariates?	No	Yes
R^2	0.003	0.059
Adjusted R^2	0.002	0.037
Residual Std. Error	35.539 (df = 2684)	34.902 (df = 2626)
F Statistic	3.734** (df = 2; 2684)	2.744*** (df = 60; 2626)

Note: *p < 0.1; **p < 0.05; ***p < 0.01

Feeling thermometer results on a 0–100 scale from hypothetical earmarked taxes on either alcohol or plastic bags, with aligned uses as anti–drunk driving and antilittering efforts, respectively. Misaligned uses were the inverse.

Table A.12 **"You Break It, You Buy It" Descriptive Statistics**

	You Break (Misaligned)	You Break (Aligned)	You Break (No Use)
Race (White)	666	700	639
Sex (Female)	434	507	467
Party ID (Democrat)	335	339	310
Income (Mean)	$35,000 to $39,999	$35,000 to $39,999	$35,000 to $39,999
Age (Mean)	35 to 44 years old	35 to 44 years old	35 to 44 years old

Note: No significant differences at p < .05

Consult the "Mechanical Turk Demographic Questions" subsection for details on variable construction. For ease of interpretation, I have collapsed race, sex, and Party ID into binary variables.

Table A.13 **"You Get What You Pay For" Rate Results**

	Dependent Variable	
	Tax Rate	
	(1)	(2)
Aligned	5.155***	5.177***
	(1.181)	(1.172)
Misaligned	3.151***	2.792**
	(1.176)	(1.168)
Constant	16.733***	36.569***
	(0.827)	(5.715)
Observations	2,689	2,689
Covariates?	No	Yes
R^2	0.007	0.061
Adjusted R^2	0.006	0.039
Residual Std. Error	25.015 (df = 2686)	24.598 (df = 2628)
F Statistic	9.705*** (df = 2; 2686)	2.835*** (df = 60; 2628)

Note: *p < 0.1; **p < 0.05; ***p < 0.01

Preferred tax rate results, on a 0–100 or $0.00–$1.00 scale, from hypothetical earmarked taxes on either gas used in automobiles or fuel used for jets, with aligned uses as highway construction and airport construction, respectively. Misaligned uses were the inverse.

Table A.14 **"You Break It, You Buy It" Rate Results**

	Dependent Variable	
	Tax Rate	
	(1)	(2)
Aligned	2.350*	2.327*
	(1.360)	(1.365)
Misaligned	1.819	1.680
	(1.366)	(1.371)
Constant	19.456***	25.340***
	(0.975)	(6.603)
Observations	2,674	2,674
Covariates?	No	Yes
R^2	0.001	0.035
Adjusted R^2	0.0005	0.013
Residual Std. Error	28.659 (df = 2671)	28.476 (df = 2613)
F Statistic	1.629 (df = 2; 2671)	1.596*** (df = 60; 2613)

Note: *$p < 0.1$; **$p < 0.05$; ***$p < 0.01$

Preferred tax rate results, on a 0–100 or $0.00–$1.00 scale, from hypothetical earmarked taxes on either alcohol or plastic bags, with aligned uses as anti–drunk driving and antilittering efforts, respectively. Misaligned uses were the inverse.

Consult the "Mechanical Turk Demographic Questions" subsection for details on variable construction. For ease of interpretation, I have collapsed race, sex, ideology, and Party ID into binary variables.

Table A.15 **Trump Support and the Consumer Scale**

	Dependent Variable	
	2016 Trump Vote	Trump Approval
	(1)	*(2)*
Age	0.055***	0.088***
	(0.006)	(0.016)
Racial_Deservingness	0.096***	0.295***
	(0.008)	(0.019)
Gender_Female	−0.021***	−0.075***
	(0.006)	(0.015)
Income	0.010	−0.023
	(0.007)	(0.017)
Education	−0.011*	−0.054***
	(0.007)	(0.017)
ConsumerScale	0.062***	0.260***
	(0.007)	(0.018)
PartyID	0.247***	0.655***
	(0.008)	(0.019)
Race_White	0.017***	−0.015
	(0.007)	(0.016)
Constant	0.386***	2.233***
	(0.006)	(0.015)
Observations	2,686	2,686
R^2	0.568	0.640
Adjusted R^2	0.566	0.639
Residual Std. Error (df = 2677)	0.321	0.781
F Statistic (df = 8; 2677)	439.472***	595.415***

Note: $^*p < 0.1$; $^{**}p < 0.05$; $^{***}p < 0.01$

The survey was conducted by YouGov in July and August 2018 as part of an ongoing panel study. Subjects were included in the sampling frame by matching on the 2016 CPS Voting and Registration Supplement Sample, then weighted by propensity score. *Age* was calculated by subtracting subjects' birth year from 2018. *Gender* is either male or female. *Household Income* was measured on a 1–16 interval scale, and *Education* was measured on a 1–6 scale. *Party ID* was the standard 7-point scale, with lower numbers indicating Democratic identification.

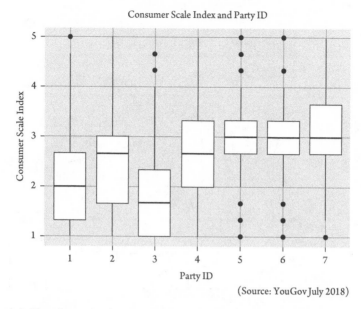

Figure A.1 The relationship between Party ID and the Consumer Scale. Party ID is the standard ANES measure, with 1 standing for Strong Democrats and 7 standing for Strong Republicans.

Table A.16 **Elites and Consumer Rhetoric Descriptive Statistics**

	Treatment	*Placebo*
Age (Mean)	36.4	37
Education (Mean)	Associate Degree	Associate Degree
Race (White) (Count)	417	424
Sex (Female) (Count)	172	167
Income (Mean)	$40,000 to $49,999	$40,000 to $49,999
Party ID (Democrat) (Count)	241	252
Ideology (Liberal) (Count)	233	230

Note: No significant differences at p < .05

Trump Vote is a binary measure of subjects' self-reported 2016 vote, while *Trump Approval* runs from 1 to 4, with higher numbers indicating greater levels of approval. All models are ordinary least squares (OLS) regressions. For missing values, the mean response was imputed. All variables have been standardized to ease comparisons across models.

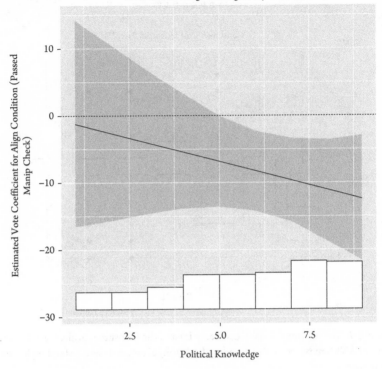

Figure A.2 Political knowledge and *Alignability* candidate.

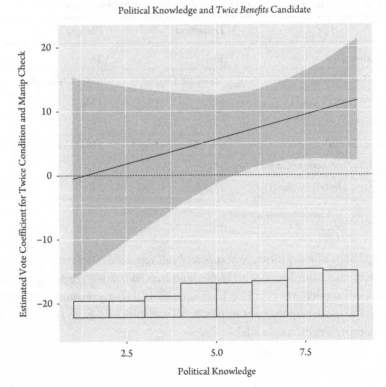

Figure A.3 Political knowledge and *Twice* candidate.

Replication Results of Alignability
Candidate Experiment

Interaction plots of assignment to the *Alignability* candidate and *Twice* candidate, respectively, from the 2018 replication of the candidate experiment.

The x-axis indicates political knowledge from the 0–9 scale, while the y-axis displays the predicted coefficient on probability of voting for the candidate. Consult Chapter 3 for the text of the political knowledge battery. These plots remove subjects who failed the manipulation check.

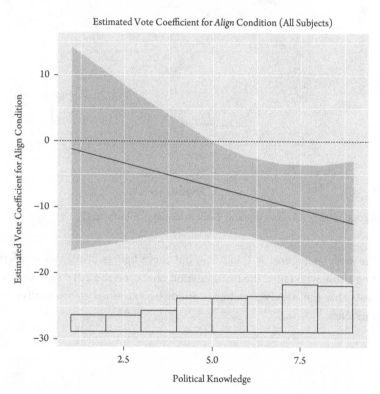

Figure A.4 Political knowledge and *Alignability* candidate (All subjects) .

Estimated Vote Coefficient for *Twice* Condition (All Subjects)

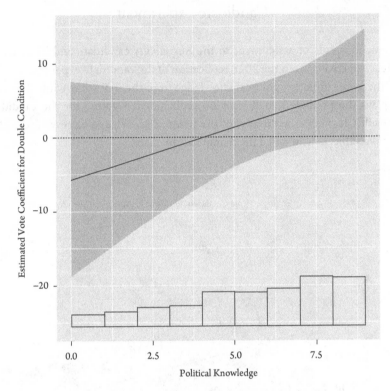

Figure A.5 Political knowledge and *Twice* candidate (All subjects).

The same as Figures A.2 and A.3, but these figures display all subjects, including those who failed the manipulation check, on the 2018 replication. This suggests that the observed pattern cannot be explained by inattentive survey respondents.

Table A.17 **2016 Alignability Candidate Experiment Results**

	Dependent Variable		
	Affect Average		
	(1)	*(2)*	*(3)*
Align	25.985**		
	(11.145)		
2xbenefits		−20.995*	
		(10.851)	
3xbenefits		−6.049	
		(10.604)	
Political Knowledge	0.813	−1.933**	−1.653*
	(0.949)	(0.922)	(0.993)
Align X Knowledge	−4.904***		
	(1.648)		
2xbenefits X Knowledge		3.246*	
		(1.678)	
3xbenefits X Knowledge			1.956
			(1.630)
Observations	237	237	237
R^2	0.076	0.042	0.049
Adjusted R^2	0.026	−0.010	−0.002
Residual Std. Error (df = 224)	21.576	21.974	21.891
F Statistic (df = 12; 224)	1.535	0.809	0.956

Note: $^*p < 0.1$; $^{**}p < 0.05$; $^{***}p < 0.01$

Not displayed, but included in the estimates, are measures of subjects' race, age, gender, party ID, ideology, household income, employment status, and education level, as described in the "Mechanical Turk Demographic Questions" subsection. The political knowledge battery used can be found in Chapter 3.

Table A.18 **2016 Alignability Candidate Experiment Descriptive Statistics**

	Align	*Twice*	*Three*
Income (Mean)	$35,000 to $39,999	$35,000 to $39,999	$35,000 to $39,999
Female	39	37	42
Democrats	41	36	40
Liberals	50	40	43
Race (White)	57	63	59
Age (Mean)	Between 25 and 34	Between 25 and 34	Between 25 and 34
Education	Associate degree	Associate degree	Associate degree

Note: No significant differences at p < .05

Obamacare Online Pretrial Treatment Messages

Fairness Message 1

To Whom It May Concern:

We are writing to tell you about our company, [NAME WITHHELD]. Our plans aren't free—that's the cost of providing good services. We are convinced that you will find that our plans will give you the best bang for your buck.

We believe that everyone in your state deserves access to affordable, high-quality health care. Our plans offer generous benefits and high-quality coverage.

By purchasing our health insurance, you are signing up for great, affordable health care. We provide two types of plans that offer low out-of-pocket expenses, allow you to choose your doctors, and provide the security of knowing you have coverage nationwide.

Enrollment in [NAME WITHHELD] for this year will close on February 15th. If you sign up by then, you will have coverage starting on March 1st.

To sign up for one of our plans, call us at [NUMBER WITHHELD]. You can also visit our website, at [WEBSITE WITHHELD].

—Your Friends at [NAME WITHHELD]

Fairness Message 2

To Whom It May Concern:

We are writing to tell you about our company, [NAME WITHHELD]. We're a nonprofit, and our costs only reflect the services provided. We are convinced that you will find our plans give you the best bang for your buck.

We believe that everyone in your state deserves access to affordable, high-quality health care. Our plans offer generous benefits and high-quality coverage.

By purchasing our health insurance, you are signing up for great, affordable health care. We provide two types of plans that offer low out-of-pocket expenses, allow you to choose your doctors, and provide the security of knowing you have coverage nationwide.

Enrollment in [NAME WITHHELD] this year will close on February 15th. If you sign up by then, you will have coverage starting on March 1st.

To sign up for one of our plans, call us at [NUMBER WITHHELD]. You can also visit our website, at [WEBSITE WITHHELD].

—Your Friends at [NAME WITHHELD]

Fairness Message 3

To Whom It May Concern:

We are writing to tell you about our company, [NAME WITHHELD]. Our costs only reflect the services provided. We are convinced that you will find they give you the best bang for your buck.

We believe that everyone in your state deserves access to affordable, high-quality health care. Our plans offer generous benefits and high-quality coverage.

By purchasing our health insurance, you are signing up for great, affordable health care. We provide two types of plans that offer low out-of-pocket expenses, allow you to choose your doctors, and provide the security of knowing you have coverage nationwide.

Enrollment in [NAME WITHHELD] for this year will close on February 15th. If you sign up by then, you will have coverage starting on March 1st.

To sign up for one of our plans, call us at [NUMBER WITHHELD]. You can also visit our website, at [NAME WITHHELD].

—Your Friends at [NAME WITHHELD]

Placebo Message

To [NAME IN FILE]:

We are writing to tell you about our company [NAME WITHHELD]. We were founded in 2010. We serve all residents in your state.

We believe that everyone in your state deserves access to affordable, high-quality health care. Our plans offer generous benefits and high-quality coverage.

By purchasing our health insurance, you are signing up for great, affordable health care. We provide two types of plans that offer low out-of-pocket expenses, allow you to choose your doctors, and provide the security of knowing you have coverage nationwide.

Enrollment in [NAME WITHHELD] for this year will close on February 15th. If you sign up by then, you will have coverage starting on March 1st.

To sign up for one of our plans, call us at [NUMBER WITHHELD]. You can also visit our website, at [WEBSITE WITHHELD].

—Your Friends at [NAME WITHHELD]

Affordable Care Act Message

To Whom It May Concern:

We are writing to tell you about our company, [NAME WITHHELD]. Our company was founded after the passage of the Affordable Care Act, or "Obamacare," in 2010. We exist to make Obamacare a success.

We believe that everyone in your state deserves access to affordable, high-quality health care. Our plans offer generous benefits and high-quality coverage.

By purchasing our health insurance, you are signing up for great, affordable health care. We provide two types of plans that offer low out-of-pocket expenses, allow you to choose your doctors, and provide the security of knowing you have coverage nationwide.

Enrollment in [NAME WITHHELD] for this year will close on February 15th. If you sign up by then, you will have coverage starting on March 1st.

To sign up for one of our plans, call us at [NUMBER WITHHELD]. You can also visit our website, at [WEBSITE WITHHELD].

—Your Friends at [NAME WITHHELD]

Pilot Tests for Obamacare Experiment Messages

In Stage 1, administered in December 2014, 406 subjects were randomly assigned to see one of three consumer fairness messages emphasizing an anonymous health insurance company's cost-benefit alignability; a placebo message recounting an anonymous health insurance company's organizational history; and a message specifically explaining that the health insurance company in question was an outgrowth of the Affordable Care Act, or Obamacare, as the message referred to it. (Full text of all online treatments are in the appendix subsection "Obamacare Online Pretrial Treatment Messages.") After seeing one of the messages, subjects were asked, "If you received this letter in the mail, how interested would you be in purchasing the health-care plan it describes?" Subjects could provide responses on a 1–5 scale, with 1 indicating they would be extremely unlikely to make such a purchase and 5 indicating that they would be extremely likely to make such a purchase.

The most popular messages were *Fairness Message 2* and *Fairness Message 3*. The Obamacare message was the least popular. To differentiate between Fairness Messages 1 and 2, we fielded Stage 2, also on Mechanical Turk, in December 2014. Subjects who had completed Stage 1 were barred from participating in Stage 2. Stage 2 participants (n = 184) were randomly assigned to see either *Fairness Message 2*, *Fairness Message 3*, or the control message, and then were asked the same question as in Stage 1. In this stage, subjects to Fairness Message 2 indicated that they would be significantly more willing to purchase the advertised health care than recipients of the treatment (t = –2.12). The mean response of those who saw the control message was 2.5—exactly in the middle of the scale. The mean response of those who saw *Fairness Message 2* was 2.875. In other words, exposure to the fairness message made subjects 15% more likely to say they would purchase health care.

Table A.19 **ACA Follow-Up Experiment Results**

	Dependent Variable			
	Willingness to Buy		Feeling Thermometer	
	(1)	(2)	(3)	(4)
Reflective Value	0.876***	0.787***	11.938***	10.872***
	(0.208)	(0.221)	(3.116)	(3.362)
Fairness	1.521***	1.484***	23.822***	23.557***
	(0.203)	(0.217)	(3.053)	(3.314)
Nonprofit	1.212***	1.174***	22.725***	21.936***
	(0.204)	(0.213)	(3.060)	(3.247)
Constant	3.809***	3.899***	46.638***	49.201***
	(0.146)	(0.787)	(2.192)	(11.990)
Observations	385	385	385	385
Covariates?	No	Yes	No	Yes
State-Fixed Effects?	No	Yes	No	Yes
R^2	0.140	0.288	0.172	0.292
Adjusted R^2	0.133	0.179	0.165	0.184
Residual Std. Error	1.417 (df = 381)	1.378 (df = 333)	21.248 (df = 381)	21.008 (df = 333)
F Statistic	20.655*** (df = 3; 381)	2.643*** (df = 51; 333)	26.356*** (df = 3; 381)	2.699*** (df = 51; 333)

Note: *p < 0.1; **p < 0.05; ***p < 0.01

The first two columns report effects on a willingness to buy health insurance from a hypothetical company, matching the descriptions described in the "Obamacare Online Pretrial Treatment Messages" subsection. Willingness to buy was measured by asking subjects, "How likely would you be to buy health insurance from a company that says it is . . . ?" and then filling in with the descriptions. Subjects could answer on a 1–7 scale, with 1 standing for

"Extremely unlikely" and 7 standing for "Extremely likely." Feeling thermometer responses were gathered by presenting subjects with a standard 0–100 feeling thermometer.

Examples of U.S. Receipts in 2016 Study

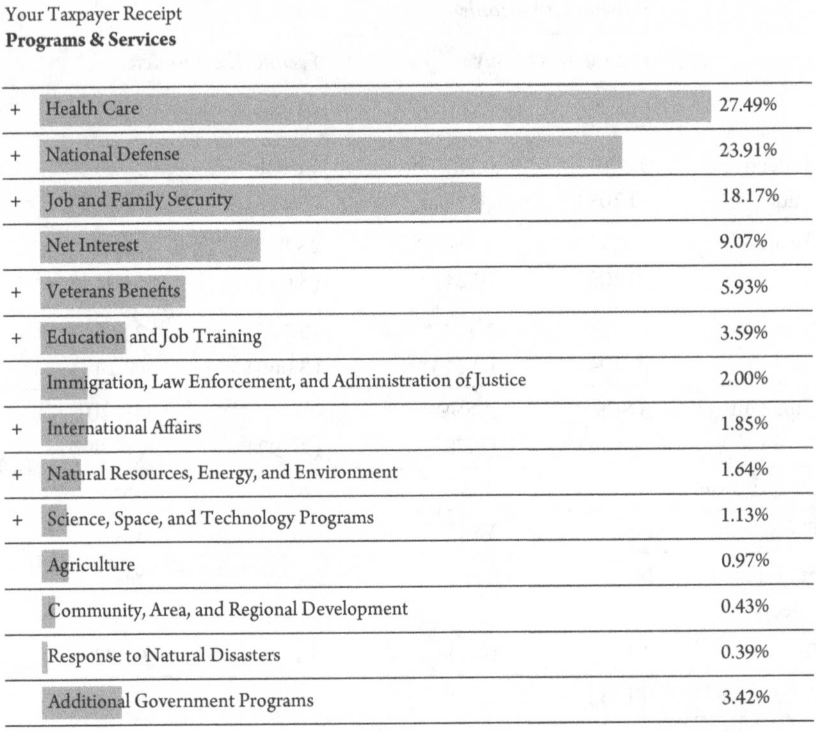

Your Taxpayer Receipt
Programs & Services

+	Health Care	27.49%
+	National Defense	23.91%
+	Job and Family Security	18.17%
	Net Interest	9.07%
+	Veterans Benefits	5.93%
+	Education and Job Training	3.59%
	Immigration, Law Enforcement, and Administration of Justice	2.00%
+	International Affairs	1.85%
+	Natural Resources, Energy, and Environment	1.64%
+	Science, Space, and Technology Programs	1.13%
	Agriculture	0.97%
	Community, Area, and Regional Development	0.43%
	Response to Natural Disasters	0.39%
	Additional Government Programs	3.42%

Figure A.6 Percentages-Only Taxpayer Receipt.

Your taxpayer receipt

Programs & Services		Your Tax Payment
Income Tax		$2,313.75
+ Health Care	27.49%	$636.05
+ National Defense	23.91%	$553.22
+ Job and Family Security	18.17%	$420.41
Net Interest	9.07%	$209.86
+ Veterans Benefits	5.93%	$137.21
+ Education and Job Training	3.59%	$83.06
Immigration, Law Enforcement, and Administration of Justice	2.00%	$46.28
+ International Affairs	1.85%	$42.80
+ Natural Resources, Energy, and Environment	1.64%	$37.95
+ Science, Space, and Technology Programs	1.13%	$26.15
Agriculture	0.97%	$22.44
Community, Area, and Regional Development	0.43%	$9.95
Response to Natural Disasters	0.39%	$9.02
Additional Government Programs	3.42%	$79.13
Total Income and Payroll Taxes You Paid		$2,313.75

Figure A.7 Standard Taxpayer Receipt.

Your Environmental Receipt:

Service	Your tax payment
Natural Resources, Energy, and Environment	$37.95

Figure A.8 Environment-Only Taxpayer Receipt.

Table A.20 **U.S. Taxpayer Receipt Effects on Environmental Knowledge Only**

	Dependent Variable	
	Correct Environmental Response	
	(1)	(2)
Tax Receipt	0.087**	0.103***
	(0.039)	(0.038)
Environment-Only Receipt	0.006	0.035
	(0.039)	(0.038)
Percentages Receipt	0.137***	0.148***
	(0.039)	(0.038)
Constant	0.471***	0.108
	(0.028)	(0.165)
Observations	1,332	1,332
Covariates?	No	Yes
R^2	0.013	0.125
Adjusted R^2	0.011	0.081
Residual Std. Error	0.497 (df = 1328)	0.479 (df = 1268)
F Statistic	5.956*** (df = 3; 1328)	2.873*** (df = 63; 1268)

Note: *p < 0.1; **p < 0.05; ***p < 0.01

The model with covariates includes variables for age, education, race, sex, household income, party ID, ideology, and U.S. state. Further variable details can be found in Appendix subsection "Mechanical Turk Demographic Questions."

Table A.21 **2016 U.S. Taxpayer Receipt Descriptive Statistics**

	Tax Receipt	Environmental Receipt	Percentages Receipt	Control
Sex (Female)	171	172	156	167
Race (White)	247	268	264	241
Age (Mean)	Between 25 and 34	Between 25 and 34	Between 25 and 34	Between 25 and 34
Democrat	163	162	166	154
Liberal	172	180	181	168
Income (Mean)	$40,000 to $49,999	$40,000 to $49,999	$40,000 to $49,999	$40,000 to $49,999
Education (Mean)	Associate degree	Associate degree	Associate degree	Associate degree

Note: No significant differences at p < .05

Consult the "Mechanical Turk Demographic Questions" subsection for details on variable construction. For ease of interpretation, I have collapsed race, sex, ideology, and Party ID into binary variables.

Table A.22 **U.K. Taxpayer Receipt Knowledge Results**

	Wave 2 Knowledge Index		
	Model 1	Model 2	Model 3
Treatment	0.097**	0.074**	0.080**
	(0.042)	(0.035)	(0.037)
Age	0.033*	0.007	0.007
	(0.018)	(0.015)	(0.015)
Female	−0.394***	−0.180***	−0.182***
	(0.043)	(0.037)	(0.037)
White	0.112*	0.124**	0.151***
	(0.062)	(0.053)	(0.052)
Conservative	0.084	0.070	0.062
	(0.056)	(0.047)	(0.047)
Labour	−0.014	−0.008	−0.042
	(0.052)	(0.044)	(0.044)
Liberal Democrat	0.139*	−0.013	−0.030
	(0.083)	(0.071)	(0.069)
Working Full-Time	0.004	0.013	−0.004
	(0.061)	(0.052)	(0.049)
Education Scale	0.131***	0.057***	0.061***
	(0.016)	(0.014)	(0.014)
Wave 1 Knowledge		0.547***	0.551***
		(0.019)	(0.019)
Constant	0.168	0.091	0.067
	(0.137)	(0.116)	(0.118)
N	2072	2072	2072
R^2	0.120	0.367	0.372
Adj. R^2	0.108	0.358	0.362
Residual Std. Error	0.941	0.798	2.050
	(df = 2042)	(df = 2041)	(df = 2041)
F Statistic	9.618***	39.447***	40.239***
	(df = 29; 2042)	(df = 30; 2041)	(df = 30; 2041)

Note: ***p < .01; **p < .05; *p < .1

This table reports the same models displayed in Table 4.2, but with covariates displayed as well. A descriptive statistics table can be found in Appendix Table A.23.

Table A.23 **U.K. Taxpayer Receipt Experiment Descriptive Statistics**

Variable Name	Control	Treatment
Age (Mean)	3.03	2.94
Female (Mean)	0.52	0.52
Conservative (Mean)	0.22	0.21
White (Mean)	0.87	0.86
Labour (Mean)	0.27	0.27
Lib Dem (Mean)	0.07	0.08
Full-Time (Mean)	0.84	0.84
Education (Mean)	4.11	4.15
Region 1 (Mean)	0.15	0.16
Region 2 (Mean)	0.32	0.32
Region 3 (Mean)	0.19	0.18
Region 4 (Mean)	0.22	0.20
Region 5 (Mean)	0.10	0.12
Region 6 (Mean)	0.01	0.02

Note: No significant differences at $p < .05$

Regions 1–6 are binary variables indicating the geographic region of the respondent; *Conservative, Labour,* and *Lib Dem* are binary variables for party membership; *Full-time* is a binary variable that reflects whether respondents are employed full-time; *Education* is a 6-point scale, ranging from "no qualifications" to "graduate degree"; *Female* is a binary variable for sex; *Age* ranges from 1 to 5, from twenty-five to thirty-four years old to over fifty-five years. All data were provided by YouGov.

U.K. Taxpayer Receipt Experiment Messages to Subjects

Below are the full texts received by the different experimental groups in each wave of the U.K. taxpayer receipt study.

Wave 1

Individuals in the control group received the following message:

You have been selected to be part of a research study. This was part one of two parts. It is important that you take this study seriously. Please pay attention to the questions asked as well as the answers you provide.

Within the next two months, we will send you a follow-up survey. The questions will concern important political and social matters. If you answer all of the questions asked, you will be entered in a lottery to win a brand-new iPad. The winner will receive his or her iPad within a month after completing the survey.

By contrast, individuals randomly assigned to the treatment group received the following:

As you may know, over the next six weeks or so, taxpayers throughout the nation will receive "tax statements" that summarise how their taxes are spent. You have been selected to be part of a research study about the statements. It is important that you read these statements.

The statements will be arriving in the post from Her Majesty's Revenue and Customs. Please read and keep them. After you receive your statement, we will send you a follow-up survey in which we will ask you several factual questions about the information in your tax statement. If you answer these factual questions correctly, you will be entered in a lottery to win a brand-new iPad. The winner will receive his or her iPad within a month after completing the survey.

Interstitial Messages

Subjects in treatment were also reminded midway through the distribution of the statements about their status. They received a message that read,

We are writing to remind you that you have been selected to be part of a research study about the "tax statements" that the government is sending out. These statements summarize how your taxes are spent, and they will be arriving in the post from Her Majesty's Revenue and Customs. Please read and keep your statement.

After you receive your statement, we will send you a follow-up survey in which we will ask you several factual questions about the information in your statement. If you answer these questions correctly, you will be entered in a lottery to win a brand-new iPad. The winner will receive his or her iPad within a month after completing the survey.

Simultaneously, subjects in control received a message that read,

We are writing to remind you that you have been selected to be part of a research study. You have already completed one of two parts of the study. It is important that you take this study seriously.

You will be receiving a follow-up study in the next few weeks. The questions will concern important political and social matters. If you answers all the questions asked, you will be entered in a lottery to win a brand-new iPad. The winner will receive his or her iPad within a month after completing the survey.

Wave 2 Treatments

Before Wave 2, subjects in treatment were shown the following:

This survey is about the "tax statements" that the government has sent out. The statements should have arrived in the post by Her Majesty's Revenue and Customs. The survey contains several fact-based questions about your tax statement. If you answer them correctly, you will be entered in a lottery to win a brand-new iPad.

In contrast, before Wave 2, subjects in control were shown the following:

This survey is about important social and political matters. It is important that you take this study seriously. If you answer all the questions asked, you will be entered in a lottery to win a brand-new iPad.

The U.K. Receipt and Interest in Writing to Political Representatives

We identified some evidence suggesting that the receipts may be able to increase people's willingness to communicate with their politically representatives. The encouragement group was more likely to express a willingness to communicate with their elected officials. Of those in the encouragement group, 44.5% responded affirmatively to the query, while only 40.8% of those in the control group did. While this 3.7% effect size approached but did not meet the standard threshold of statistical significance, we view it as providing suggestive evidence that viewing statements induced people to seek out more meaningful participation in politics than they would have otherwise. The p-value for this difference was .092. Our confidence in this effect is somewhat compounded if we compare those who recalled receiving their statements to those did not recall. Among those who recalled receiving their statement—which we didn't ask until the end of the survey—47.7% responded that they would write to their representatives. Only 41.9% who did not recall said they would do the same. The 5.8% difference between treatment and control clears the bar of statistical significance. The p-value for this difference was below .05.

While we looked into whether the content of messages sent by those who received the treatment were substantively different from the content of messages sent by the control group, a team of human coders could not find any meaningful differences. Our human coders read through the text of each message, scoring each message against a set of binary indicators about the content. For example, if a message included the word "immigrant" or "immigration," as many did, that message would be scored a "1" for including a reference to immigration. We created the categories after reading through each message in detail. In total, we provided our team of human coders with twenty-two categories. The categories included references to taxes—whether subjects wanted taxes raised or lowered; references to a particular political party, whether in support or in opposition; and references to the programs itemized in the receipt. For all twenty-two categories, there were no statistically significant differences between those in treatment and those in control.

Scarcity Study Primes

In the parentheses, the "hard" prime numbers come first, the "easy" prime numbers second:

Prime 1

"The economy is going through difficult times. Suppose your employer needs to make substantial budget cuts. Imagine a scenario in which you received a [15% / 5%] cut in your salary. Given your situation, would you be able to maintain roughly your same lifestyle under those new circumstances? If not, what changes would you need to make? Would it impact your leisure, housing, or travel plans?"

Prime 2

"Imagine that an unforeseen event requires of you an immediate [$2,000 / $200] expense. Are there ways in which you may be able to come up with that amount of money on a very short notice? How would you go about it? Would it cause you long-lasting financial hardship? Would it require you to make sacrifices that have long-term consequences? If so, what kind of sacrifices?"

Prime 3

"Imagine that your car is having some trouble, and requires a [$1,500 / $150] service. Unfortunately, your auto insurance will cover only 10% of this cost. You now need to decide the following:

(1) Pay the full amount in cash. Would this require liquidating savings? How would you go about it?
(2) Take out a loan, which you can pay back in monthly installments. A typical such loan may require monthly payments of roughly [$150 / $15] a month for 12 months, which would amount to about [$1,800 / $180] total.
(3) Take a chance, forgo the service, and hope that the car lasts for a while longer. Of course, this leaves open the possibility of breakdown, or even greater expenses in the long run.

How would you go about making this decision? Would it be an easy or a difficult decision for you to make?

Prime 4

"Suppose you have reached the point where you must replace your old refrigerator. The model you plan to buy offers two alternative financing options: (1) You can pay the full amount in cash, which will cost you [$999 / $399]. (2) You can pay in 12 monthly payments, of [$100 / $40] each, which would amount to a total of [$1,200 / $480]. Which financing option would you opt for? Would you have the necessary cash on hand? Would the interest be worth paying in this case?

Table A.24 **Scarcity Study Descriptive Statistics**

	Hard Primes	*Easy Primes*
Age (Mean)	46.7	45.34
Female (Count)	196	187
Employment Status (Mean)	Part-time	Part-time
Race (White) (Count)	270	261
Education (Mean)	Completed some college	Completed some college
Income (Mean)	$50,000–$59,999	$40,000–$49,999

Note: No significant differences at $p < .05$

Employment status was provided by SSI and ranged from unemployed to part-time employed to fully employed. *Age* was also provided by SSI. *Education*, collected apart from SSI, ranged on a 1–7 scale from "did not complete high school" to "graduate degree." *Income*, provided by SSI, ranged from 1–9, from below $20,000 to $150,000.

Scarcity Study and Household Income

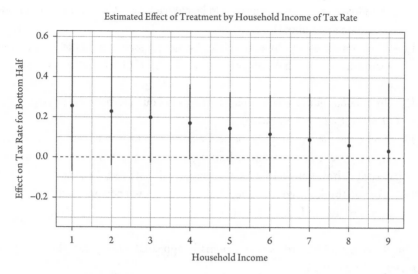

Estimated Effect of Treatment by Household Income of Tax Rate

Figure A.9 Scarcity and household income.

Pew Trust in Government Questions

These are the Pew trust questions used for the studies described in Chapter 5.

1. "All in all, how well or how badly do you think the system of democracy in this country works these days?" (1 = works well—3 = does not work well)
2. "Most civil servants can be trusted to do what is best for the country." (1 = strongly agree—5 = strongly disagree)
3. "People like me don't have any say about what the government does." (1 = strongly agree—6 = strongly disagree)
4. "Elections are a good way of making the government pay attention to the important political issues facing our country." (1 = strongly agree—5 = strongly disagree)
5. "All in all, would you say the government is having a positive or negative effect on the way things are going in this country today?" (1 = negative, 2 = positive)
6. "Which would you rather have?" (Bigger government, more services / Smaller government, fewer services)
7. "Overall, would you say the agencies and departments of the government are doing an excellent, good, only fair, or a poor job?" (1 = excellent—5 = poor)
8. "How much of the time do you think you can trust the government to do what is right?" (1 = just about always—4 = never)

9. "Which comes closer to your view?" (1 = Criticism of government is often justified / 2 = Government often does better job than given credit for)
10. "Where on the following scale of 1 to 6 would you place yourself?" (1 = Government programs should be cut back / 6 = Government programs should be maintained)
11. "How much effect do you think the government's activities—the laws passed and so on—have on your day-to-day life?" (1 = Great effect—3 = No effect)
12. "In general, is the government's effect on your life positive or negative?" (1 = Positive / 2 = Negative)
13. "Some people say they are basically content with the government, others say they are frustrated, and others say they are angry. Which of these best describes how you feel?" (1 = Content, 2 = Frustrated, 3 = Angry)
14. "Do you think the government threatens your own personal rights and freedoms, or not?" (1 = No, 2 = Yes)

The above questions are as they originally appeared, along with their original scales, before recoding.

Anytown Script

Scene 1

Visuals: Slow pull-out from Anytown welcome sign.

Voice-Over (VO): Welcome to Anytown, USA. Anytown is just like any other town in America. Over the next few minutes, we're going to tell you about the history of Anytown—how it started, how it developed, and how it got to where it is today.

Scene 2

Visuals: The scene pulls out to reveal a large piece of land with a river/lake. Sewer/water pipes, roads, town hall, houses, stores, a school, a fire department, and a police station are all built in rapid succession timing with the voice-over.

VO (begin during :26): In its early days, the people of Anytown came together to form a government. This government built the pipes and sewers, so that people would have clean water to use and to drink. This government built a town hall, to give people a place to voice their opinion and take an active role in governing. It built roads, so that people could get easily from place to place. A bridge was built to make it easier to get around. Slowly but surely, more people—families and individuals—moved into Anytown. Businesses came too; the government also built a school. It built a fire station and a police station, to protect and help out the people who lived in Anytown. The government worked to serve the people of Anytown.

Scene 3

Visuals: The scene pulls out farther as more land is added around Anytown. Pipes, underground electrical/power station, and roads are built in the new sections. New houses, business, and a new fire department and police station are all built. A fire truck puts out a fire. A library, hospital, and parks are then built.

VO: As time went on, Anytown grew, and the government worked to accommodate the town's growing needs. This meant that more roads had to be built and that more connections to surrounding towns had to be made. More and more people moved into Anytown, as did more businesses. The government organized Anytown's electrical grid and expanded the town plumbing and sewage systems. When problems arose, the government had tools to fix them. The fire department put out fires; the police department reduced crime. Schools and parks were built as well. A hospital was constructed to care for the sick and the elderly.

Scene 4

Visuals: The scene pulls out farther as more land is added to Anytown. Even more roads, houses, businesses, a fire department, a police station, and a factory are built. The lake becomes polluted, and smog covers the downtown area. A document with a recycle icon pops out of town hall. Recycle icons appear above many businesses. A recycling truck picks up recyclable materials. The water and smog clear up.

VO: While Anytown continued to grow, not everything was perfect. Pollution from factories filled the air with smog, and the lake became polluted as well. In response, Anytown's government made businesses adopt practices that were more friendly to the environment. Recycling became the rule, and both businesses and individuals abided by it. Gradually, Anytown's environment became less polluted.

Scene 5

Visuals: The scene pulls out farther as a small amount of land is added to Anytown. More houses and apartments are built on the new land and in older parts of town, making Anytown denser. A large university is then built.

VO: Anytown's growth meant that more residents wanted to live in houses. Those who couldn't afford to purchase houses turned to the government, who helped them buy the homes they wanted by reducing the taxes of new homeowners. As a result, more people who wanted to buy homes could buy homes. Eventually, the increasing number of children caused the government to help finance a local university, so that more residents could receive higher education. The university was used not only by young people but by older residents who wanted to acquire new skills.

Scene 6

Visuals: The scene pulls out farther as a small amount of land is added to Anytown. A large highway with on and off ramps is built alongside the city, exiting either side. A document with a food icon pops out of town hall followed by a documents with a social services / health icon.

VO: People all over wanted to live and work in Anytown. It was a desirable destination, and to account for the booming interest in their town, the government worked to build a highway to adjacent towns. This meant that people could get back and forth as fast as possible. The government also worked to make sure that the food that residents were eating was safe. They evaluated the town restaurants, making sure they kept to standards of hygiene and cleanliness. To be sure, not everything was perfect. There were homeless people and elderly residents who needed assistance. When and where it could, the government stepped in and offered aid.

Consider how far it had come: In the beginning, Anytown was small and populated by only a few people. These people came together and formed a government. Over time, the government worked to provide services that people needed. Clean drinking water. Roads. Schools. Fire and police stations. And a small town became a larger, bustling town.

Scene 7

Visuals: The scene slowly pulls out.

VO: Thank you for learning about Anytown. We hope you've found the experience interesting. We now have a few questions.

Table A.25 **Anytown Pew Trust in Government Results (No Covariates)**

	Dependent Variable				
	Gov Performance	Increase Gov Programs	Gov Daily Life	Gov Positive Role	CompTrust
	(1)	(2)	(3)	(4)	(5)
Anytown	0.274***	0.212**	0.184**	0.189**	0.212**
	(0.084)	(0.085)	(0.085)	(0.085)	(0.085)
Constant	−0.139**	−0.108*	−0.094	−0.096	−0.108*
	(0.060)	(0.060)	(0.060)	(0.060)	(0.061)
Observations	552	554	554	553	547
R^2	0.019	0.011	0.009	0.009	0.011
Adjusted R^2	0.017	0.009	0.007	0.007	0.009
Residual Std. Error	0.991 (df = 550)	0.995 (df = 552)	0.997 (df = 552)	0.996 (df = 551)	0.995 (df = 545)
F Statistic	10.531*** (df = 1; 550)	6.259** (df = 1; 552)	4.736** (df = 1; 552)	4.965** (df = 1; 551)	6.173** (df = 1; 545)

Note: *p < 0.1; **p < 0.05; ***p < 0.01

The complete text of the dependent variable trust questions can be found in the "Pew Trust in Government Questions" subsection.

Table A.26 **Anytown Attitudes toward Government Spending Results (All Subjects)**

	Dependent Variable			
	Trust in Government Spending		*Support for Tax Increases*	
	(1)	*(2)*	*(3)*	*(4)*
Anytown	0.596***	0.641***	0.240***	0.350***
	(0.068)	(0.070)	(0.071)	(0.068)
Constant	−0.300***	−1.081***	−0.121**	−0.151
	(0.049)	(0.399)	(0.051)	(0.394)
Observations	778	763	778	763
Covariates?	No	Yes	No	Yes
R^2	0.089	0.194	0.014	0.253
Adjusted R^2	0.088	0.125	0.013	0.184
Residual Std. Error	0.955 (df = 776)	0.938 (df = 702)	0.993 (df = 776)	0.901 (df = 697)
F Statistic	75.762***	2.809***	11.367***	3.636***
	(df = 1; 776)	(df = 60; 702)	(df = 1; 776)	(df = 65; 697)

Note: *p < 0.1; **p < 0.05; ***p < 0.01

Covariate details: Covariate models include age, income, sex, race (white), education, ideology, party ID, and U.S. state.

Covariate details: Further independent variable details can be found in Appendix subsection "Mechanical Turk Demographic Questions."

"Trust in Government Spending" captures responses to the ANES question "Do you think that people in the government waste a lot of money we pay in taxes, waste some of it, or don't waste very much of it?" Responses range from 1 to 3, with higher numbers indicating greater trust in government spending. "Support for Tax Increases" captures responses to Hansen's (1998) question: "'Do you favor increases in the taxes paid by ordinary Americans in order to increase spending on domestic programs like Medicare, education, and highways?" Responses range from 1 to 5, with higher numbers indicating greater support for tax increases to finance increased spending.

Table A.27 **Anytown Pew Trust in Government Results (with Covariates and All Subjects)**

	Dependent Variable				
	Gov Performance	Increase Gov Programs	Gov in Daily Life	Gov Positive Role	CompTrust
	(1)	(2)	(3)	(4)	(5)
Anytown	0.260***	0.337***	0.150**	0.234***	0.258***
	(0.073)	(0.064)	(0.074)	(0.071)	(0.070)
Constant	−0.037	−0.211	0.240	−0.492	−0.227
	(0.421)	(0.372)	(0.430)	(0.412)	(0.406)
Observations	761	763	763	762	754
R^2	0.151	0.340	0.119	0.188	0.218
Adjusted R^2	0.072	0.278	0.037	0.113	0.144
Residual Std. Error	0.962 (df = 695)	0.850 (df = 697)	0.985 (df = 697)	0.943 (df = 696)	0.926 (df = 688)
F Statistic	1.906*** (df = 65; 695)	5.523*** (df = 65; 697)	1.447** (df = 65; 697)	2.485*** (df = 65; 696)	2.947*** (df = 65; 688)

Note: *p < 0.1; **p < 0.05; ***p < 0.01

Covariate details: Covariate models include age, income, sex, race (white), education, ideology, party ID, and U.S. state.

Covariate details: Further variable details can be found in Appendix subsection "Mechanical Turk Demographic Questions."

Complete text of dependent variables can be found in "Pew Trust in Government Questions" subsection.

Table A.28 **Anytown Pew Trust in Government Results (No Covariates and All Subjects)**

	Dependent Variable				
	Gov Performance	Increase Gov Programs	Gov in Daily Life	Gov Positive Role	CompTrust
	(1)	*(2)*	*(3)*	*(4)*	*(5)*
Anytown	0.262***	0.244***	0.127*	0.203***	0.220***
	(0.071)	(0.071)	(0.072)	(0.072)	(0.072)
Constant	−0.132***	−0.123**	−0.064	−0.102**	−0.110**
	(0.051)	(0.051)	(0.051)	(0.051)	(0.051)
Observations	775	777	777	774	765
R^2	0.017	0.015	0.004	0.010	0.012
Adjusted R^2	0.016	0.014	0.003	0.009	0.011
Residual Std. Error	0.992 (df = 773)	0.993 (df = 775)	0.999 (df = 775)	0.995 (df = 772)	0.995 (df = 763)
F Statistic	13.477*** (df = 1; 773)	11.682*** (df = 1; 775)	3.162* (df = 1; 775)	8.047*** (df = 1; 772)	9.389*** (df = 1; 763)

Note: *$p < 0.1$; **$p < 0.05$; ***$p < 0.01$

Complete text of dependent variables can be found in "Pew Trust in Government Questions" subsection.

Table A.29 **Anytown Descriptive Statistics**

	Anytown	Placebo
Female (Count)	141	136
Democrat (Count)	120	142
Liberal (Count)	144	156
Income (Mean)	$35,000 to $39,999	$35,000 to $39,999
Education (Mean)	Associate degree	Associate degree
Race (White) (Count)	207	211

Note: No significant differences at $p < .05$

Consult the "Mechanical Turk Demographic Questions" subsection for details on variable construction. For ease of interpretation, I have collapsed race, sex, ideology, and Party ID into binary variables.

Procedural Operational Transparency
Newspaper Articles

Positive Procedural Operational Transparency Article

Congress Members Abide Grueling Schedule, Documents Show (the Associated Press)
WASHINGTON, D.C.—A PowerPoint presentation obtained by the Associated Press, originally created by bipartisan Congressional leaders, details the excruciating schedule of a typical U.S. Congress member. The presentation was meant to instruct new members about what their days would be like—and it makes clear just how much Congress members work on a daily basis.

The daily schedule envisions 12-hour days while in Washington. Members are only allotted an hour of off-time each day. Otherwise, they are expected to spend 4 hours meeting constituents, 3 hours meeting with committees, 3 hours on the floor, and 2 hours conducting outreach. And on the weekends, they're expected to return to their districts and meet with the people they represent.

[Positive figure would be displayed here] Above: Model Weekday Schedule of Congress Members

"That's a pretty typical workload for members of Congress," explained Vanessa Fishbein, an expert on the U.S. Congress. "Members spend a lot of time talking to constituents, drafting and deliberating about legislation, and going to committee hearings. There's not a lot of downtime."

Since the start of 2017, members of Congress have passed 219 bills into law and passed 609 resolutions. Most members of Congress often work seven days a week.

Negative Procedural Operational Transparency Article

Congress Members Spend Hours Every Day Raising Money, Documents Show (the Associated Press)
WASHINGTON, D.C.—A PowerPoint presentation obtained by the Associated Press, originally created by bipartisan Congressional leaders, details the daily fund-raising schedule of a typical U.S. Congress member. The presentation was meant to instruct new members about what their days would be like—and it makes clear just how much time Congress members spend raising money on a daily basis.

The daily schedule envisions 12-hour days while in Washington. Members are expected to spend 4 hours every day making calls to prospective donors. Dubbed "call time," this part of the schedule is a daily routine for Congress members, as they ask wealthy supporters, Washington D.C.–based PACs and special-interest groups for donations. Members spend the rest of their time meeting with Congressional committees, meeting with constituents, and conducting outreach to press.

[Negative figure would be displayed here] Above: Model Weekday Schedule of Congress Members

"That's a pretty typical workload for members of Congress," explained Vanessa Fishbein, an expert on the U.S. Congress. "Members spend a lot of time raising money. There's not a lot of downtime."

Since the start of 2017, members of Congress have raised $831 million. Most members of Congress spend part of each day raising money.

Placebo Procedural Operational Transparency Article

Burgett Crowned 2016 Fair Queen (the Associated Press)

Savannah Burgett was crowned the 2016 Fulton County Fair Queen Monday in a pageant which offered a number of new features.

One of these was a special jumpstart for future Fair Queen candidates, with young ladies 3 to 5 years of age given a chance to come onstage and introduce themselves as an opportunity to see what it was like to be in front of an audience.

Another new feature was the Good Will Award. Resembling the Miss Congeniality award given at many pageants, the contestants themselves voted for the girl who most closely embodied the spirit of the pageant. The first winner was Elizabeth Parker, sponsored by the Astoria America Legion.

Yet another first was the People's Choice Award, which allowed members of the audience to vote by placing money in a special jar for each candidate. The winner will receive a portion of the proceeds. The first winner of the People's Choice Award was Sarah Linder, sponsored by the Kiwanis Club of Canton.

Burgett, sponsored by the Astoria American Legion Auxiliary, is the daughter of David and April Burgett of Astoria.

During her speech, Burgett spoke about having curvature of the spine and how most people were unaware of her condition. She told the audience her condition never prevented her from doing anything she wanted.

Table A.30 **Procedural Operational Transparency Descriptive Statistics**

	Positive	*Negative*	*Placebo*
Age (Mean)	36	35.4	36.6
Race (White) (Count)	246	247	256
Female (Count)	126	134	133
Democrats (Count)	143	144	155
Liberals (Count)	190	161	172
Income (Mean)	$35,000 to $39,999	$40,000 to $49,999	$35,000 to $39,999
Education (Mean)	Associate degree	Associate degree	Associate degree

Note: No significant differences at $p < .05$

Consult the "Mechanical Turk Demographic Questions" subsection for details on variable construction. For ease of interpretation, I have collapsed race, sex, ideology, and Party ID into binary variables.

NOTES

Chapter 1

1. "Overcharged" comes from Bush (2001a). "The growing surplus exists" comes from Bush (2001b)."I told the American people" comes from Bush (2001d).
2. Others have found that consumer primes, such as exposure to money and pictures of consumer goods, can cause people to focus on their own self-interest (Vohs, Meade, and Goode 2006, 2008; Bauer et al. 2012). More recent research, however, has cast skepticism upon this initial finding (Rohrer et al. 2015).
3. Sniderman, Brody, and Tetlock (1991) and Popkin (1991) helped inaugurate the study of heuristics in political contexts, bringing a vast psychology literature into conversation with public opinion and political behavior.
4. Other scholars have profitably examined whether political behaviors are habitual (e.g., Aldrich, Montgomery, and Wood 2011). I am investigating something different: how *non*-political habits can affect political behaviors and attitudes.
5. In many of the studies presented in this book, I offer results that consider party affiliation, race, and other conventional predictors of political outcomes as pretreatment covariates, giving them their say in the results reported. I also often present results without such covariates, allowing my consumer-related treatments to stand on their own.
6. For a longer conceptual discussion about the superficial structural similarities between consumer and political decisions, consult the appendix subsection, "The Structures of Consumer and Political Decisions."
7. Such a description, for example, is offered in Ellis and Stimson (2012).
8. Before proceeding, we should define some terms. By *heuristic*, I mean any informational shortcut that people use when confronting a complex decision. When I speak of *norms*, I am speaking of noninstrumental, nonformalized rules that people follow, even if there is no clear substantive justification for them doing so. (See Elster 2011 for a broader discussion and typology.) For both the consumer and political contexts, *attitudes* are the same: They are the byproduct of evaluations of a given object, no matter if the object is a policy or a politician, or a lawn mower (Petty and Cacioppo 1986). As for decisions, I define *consumer decisions* as discrete instances in which an individual elects to purchase (or not purchase) a good. And we define *political decisions* as discrete instances in which an individual elects to express a preference (or not)—by talking to friends and relatives, by speaking out in public, by responding to a survey in a particular way, by voting or behaving politically in some other way—about a political subject.
9. The appendix section "The Structures of Consumer and Political Decisions" has an extended discussion of this topic.

10. *Exit* and *voice* dynamics, as well as their *loyalty* counterpart, were first elaborated upon in Hirschman (1970). See appendix subsection "The Structures of Consumer and Political Decisions" for a longer discussion on related matters.

Chapter 2

1. http://www.people-press.org/2017/05/03/public-trust-in-government-1958-2017/.
2. The White House blog, https://www.whitehouse.gov/blog/2012/04/06/president-obama-wants-you-know-how-your-tax-dollars-are-spent.
3. The first slide read, "There has been much talk recently about where your federal tax money actually goes. Based on the answers you've provided, we've calculated a personalized 'tax-payer receipt' for you. Click here to see where your money went."
4. These categories were national defense; health care; job and family security; education and job training; veterans' benefits; natural resources, energy and the environment; international affairs; science, space, and technology programs; immigration, law enforcement, and administration of justice; agriculture; community, area, and regional development; responses to natural disasters; additional government programs; and net interest.
5. The slide read, "Recently, there has been discussion about who benefits from the federal government, and who doesn't. Based on the answers you provided above, we have calculated your approximate level of benefits. Sometimes, these benefits are written into the tax code and lower your overall tax bill. Other times, these benefits result in direct payments from the federal government to you. Finally, other benefits consist of payments from the federal government to your state and local governments."
6. The socioeconomic status questions determined which cash transfers individuals qualified for. Dollar values for each cash transfer option were assigned using common, publicly available data. To account for tax expenditures and tax deductions, people who reported incomes below $50,000 were assigned the standard deduction based on their marital status. Those who reported incomes above $50,000 were assigned the mean value of expenditures for taxpayers in their income bracket, according to Joint Committee on Taxation data. The $50,000 threshold was chosen because the majority of taxpayers who claimed below that amount take the standard deduction. One potential objection to this method of estimating benefits is that it falsely equates tax expenditures with government spending. However, as Hacker (2002, p. 34) notes, this objection does not attend to the spirit of tax expenditures, which are designed as departures from ordinary tax rates in order to accomplish specific policy objectives. Further, the Joint Committee on Taxation regularly draws the same equivalency as this experiment.
7. I did not ask subjects about the extent to which they believed either their Taxpayer Receipt or Benefits Number. The perceived credibility of both may have impacted the results, since both present unusual information in an unusual way.
8. Technically speaking, this null result was not owed to limited statistical power. Given the number of respondents in each condition, the experiment was at greater than 95% power to detect a small but significant effect.
9. Specifically, people were asked,

> The federal government provides all citizens with a wide variety of financial benefits. These can include direct payments to you, payments to your state and local governments, and various tax rebates. You also pay the federal government in various ways. These payments include income taxes, payroll taxes, and fees for things like parks and monuments. Generally, would you prefer that the value of the benefits you receive exceed the payments you make; that the value of the payments you make exceed the value of the benefits you receive; or that the payments you make and the benefits you receive be roughly equal in value?

10. Specifically, I told them, "We are academic researchers who focus on the amount of money that government costs and the value of the benefits that government provides. The costs of government include taxes, payroll taxes, sales taxes, and fees for things like parks and monuments. The benefits of government include benefits that have been written into the tax

code, to lower your overall tax bill. Government benefits also include direct payments from the federal and state government to you. Finally, some of the benefits consist of payments from the federal government to your state and local governments, to help pay for government services you receive."

11. Here and whenever possible, I present results both with and without posttreatment covariates. Formally, throughout the rest of the book, when I am estimating a linear model without covariates, I am estimating some version of

$$Outcome_i = \beta_T ... + \varepsilon \qquad (2.1)$$

where i indexes respondents, $Outcome$ stands for the outcome(s) of interest in a study, β_T are dummy variables for treatment assignment, and ε stands for stochastic error. When I include controls in a model, I am estimating some version of

$$Outcome_i = \beta_T ... + X_i + \varepsilon \qquad (2.2)$$

in which the addition of X_i stands for a vector of controls. The covariates used for each model depend on both data availability and the substantive question at stake in the related study. More details on covariates can be found in the Appendix.

12. This result also cuts against the fiscal illusion literature (Buchanan and Wagner 1977) which argues that democracy systematically encourages citizens to underestimate the true value of their taxes, so that they will support more government spending. Fiscal illusion predicts that the inclusion of taxes in the *Alignability* condition should puncture the illusion. Citizens, as a result of seeing their benefits, should become *less* supportive of government spending. I find the opposite. Provided that the value of the taxes is alignable with the benefits received in return, mentioning taxes can increase support for government spending.

13. In one important sense, however, this result is not surprising: it is the successful replication of an earlier experiment. In 2014, I recruited 366 U.S.-based respondents over Mechanical Turk and randomly assigned them to conditions in which they were told that their benefits exceeded their costs, their costs exceeded their benefits, or the two were equivalent. There was also a control condition. The only difference between studies is that, in this earlier version, I presented subjects with dollar estimates of their costs and benefits. The *Alignability* condition significantly improved people's trust in government taxing and spending, as measured by ANES3 ($\beta = 0.15$ on a 3-point scale, p = .059). Models of these results appear in the Appendix, as Table A.5.

14. There is, however, good reason to think that the prevalence of demand effects are overstated. On Mechanical Turk, Mummolo and Peterson (2019) tried and failed to identify meaningful demand effects.

15. An affluent neighborhood was preferable because riders were less likely to qualify for a reduced fare. Reduced-fare eligibility would have obviated the cost-benefit alignability that the study was investigating.

16. Participants were also asked to provide their age and the neighborhood in which they lived. The survey takers privately estimated each subject's ethnic background and gender. The neighborhood question was asked to proxy for the respondent's socioeconomic status (SES). To measure SES, after receiving subjects' self-reported neighborhoods of residence, American Community Service data from 2009 to 2013 was merged, and median income household over this time period for each neighborhood was computed.

17. It's also possible that, in these unusual experimental settings, subjects in the control condition were advantaged. Unlike their counterparts in other conditions, subjects in control were not being asked to consider any information; they were only asked to provide their evaluation. The comparative cognitive ease of their task may have affected their responses. But this is purely speculative.

18. Specifically, the language read, "Now, we need to know how much you think the tax should be. For every [gallon of gas / gallon of jet fuel / plastic bag / standard drink of alcohol], how much should be charged for taxes? Your answers can range from $0.00 to $1.00."

19. In each study, we asked participants about their party affiliation, political ideology, state of residence, household income, race, and age.

20. For validation of Lucid as a provider of low-cost but high-quality survey experimental data, see Coppock and McClellan (2017).
21. The effect of earmarking on rate preferences when the tax and use are aligned is significant at the p < 0.1 level.

Chapter 3

1. Despite the enduring influence of capitalist values on public opinion, there has been some debate about the form of this attachment, as well as its depth. For example, Feldman (1988) found that a respondent's belief in economic individualism explains a host of political and policy views, but that one's belief in free enterprise has far more limited explanatory power. And although McCloskey and Zaller (1984, p. 302) asserted that capitalism and democracy serve as the twin pillars of Americans' national ethos, they predict that the commitment to democracy will, in the long run, win out over, or at least greatly temper, the commitment to capitalism. Williamson's more recent work (2017) found people unbothered by policies that restrain capitalism. On the other hand, as of 2017, Gallup still found 60% of Americans with positive views about capitalism, and only 35% with positive views about socialism.
2. https://2012election.procon.org/sourcefiles/Sep_22_2011_republican_debate.pdf.
3. This is reason to think that, when left to their own devices, bureaucrats will do what they can to maximize what they spend, à la Niskanen (1971). This is distinct, however, from cases in which the programs are detailed by politicians seeking reelection—the kind of case I study here.
4. Participants who declined, after two requests, to identify with a political party were removed from the remainder of the experiment.
5. The Cronbach's a was .83.
6. Here, the Cronbach's a for all three questions was .69.
7. The relationship has an r of .43. A box-and-whisker plot of the relationship between party ID and scale responses can be found in Appendix Figure A.1.
8. I'd used the name "Sean Woods" in a prior study (Porter and Wood 2016); it's a combination of popular first and last names that doesn't appear overly generic.
9. Specifically, participants were asked, (a) "Do you happen to know how many times an individual can be elected president of the United States under current laws?" and then provided a text box; (b) "Is the U.S. federal budget deficit—the amount by which the government's spending exceeds the amount of money it collects—now bigger, about the same, or smaller than it was during the late 1990s?," and then asked to choose between "Bigger," "Smaller," or "About the same"; (c) "For how many years is a United States senator elected—that is, how many years are there in one full term of office for a U.S. senator?" and then provided a text box; (d) "What is Medicare?" and asked to choose between "A program run by the U.S. federal government to pay for old people's health care," "A program run by state governments to provide health care to poor people," "A program run by state governments to provide health care to poor people," "A private health insurance plan sold to individuals in all 50 states," and "A private, non-profit organization that runs free health clinics"; (e) "On which of the following does the U.S. federal government currently spend the least?" and asked to choose between "Foreign aid," "Medicare," "National defense," and "Social Security"; and (f) asked to identity then–House Speaker Paul Ryan, then–vice president Joe Biden, then–U.K. prime minister David Cameron, and then–Chief Justice John Roberts.
10. The figure reflects 1,000 bootstraps. At the bottom of the figure, in the spirit of Hainmueller, Mummolo, and Xu (forthcoming), I show "coverage" for political knowledge, to make clear how participants scored on the political knowledge scale in each condition. Readers can make their own decisions about whether there is sufficient coverage to draw the conclusions I have drawn so far. I believe that there is.
11. All effects reported are significant at < .05.
12. In the Appendix, Figures A.2, A.3, A.4 and A.5 further underscore just how sharply political knowledge affects evaluations of these hypothetical candidates.
13. Those who signed up for our partner's insurance were effectively purchasing subsidized access to a network of doctors and health providers (with higher costs for out-of-network providers). Enrollees in our partner's insurance were entitled to two forms of generous federal

cost reduction. For those who qualified, the Alternative Premium Tax Credit (APTC) capped the amount of an enrollee's monthly premium, while Cost Sharing Reduction (CSR) provided direct reimbursement for out-of-pocket expenses.

14. I preregistered the following hypothesis with the Evidence in Governance and Politics (E-GAP), a repository for specifying experimental hypotheses in advance of data collection and analysis : "Appealing to consumer fairness norms will make citizens more likely to purchase health insurance."

15. The selection of messages is described in the Appendix subsection "Pilot Tests for Obamacare Experiment Messages"; the original messages tested are available in Appendix subsection "Obamacare Online Pretrial Treatment Messages."

16. As my preregistered hypothesis was unidirectional—that is, based on our pretesting, we expected the treatment message to have a positive effect on enrollment, compared to a placebo message—the p-value for this test was one-tailed (Blalock 1979).

17. The founding date was moved up, so that the time between receipt of the message and the founding date was roughly the same in this hypothetical experiment as it was in the actual field experiment.

Chapter 4

1. Using logit and ordered probit to measure the effects has no substantive or statistical impact on the results.

2. Again, using logit and ordered probit has no substantive or statistical impact on the results.

3. For example, the taxpayer with a gross income of £60,000 pays tax on £50,560—and of this, £32,010 is taxed at the basic rate, and £18,550 at the higher rate of 40%. A lower-income taxpayer whose income does not reach the higher bracket would see only one number here, indicating one's income taxable at the 20% basic rate.

4. For the complete study, consult Barnes et al. (2018).

5. Designs similar to ours are explained at length in Sovey and Green (2011) and Gross, Porter, and Wood (2019).

6. Those who were not presently employed and were over sixty-five years old and thus not eligible to receive a taxpayer statement were excluded from the study.

7. The p-value for this difference was below .05.

8. The key assumption is that missingness is ignorable given covariates, treatment assignment, and responses in Wave 1 (i.e., Missing At Random), which seems defensible in our context given the wealth of data we observe. In practice, we estimate the probability of missingness via logistic regression.

9. We should not read too much into the differences between those who recalled their receipt and those who did not, because of concerns about posttreatment bias (Montgomery, Nyhan, and Torres 2018).

10. The question about intent to vote was phrased as follows: "As you may know, there is a UK general election scheduled for next year (2015). How likely are you to vote in the General Election, on a scale of 0 to 10, where 10 means you would be absolutely certain to vote, and 0 means that you would be absolutely certain not to vote?" To measure willingness to write elected officials, we constructed a three-part question. In the first part, we asked, "Would you like to send a message to your local councillor MP MSP Welsh Assembly Member in order to influence decisions, laws or policies?," with responses limited to yes or no. Then we asked, "If you could, what message would you give?" We provided a text box for them to answer the question. Finally we asked, "And if you could, who would you send this message to?" We then provided them a text box to answer the question.

11. We observed quite weak effects on participants' willingness to write to their elected representatives, which we discuss in the appendix section "The U.K. Receipt and Interest in Writing to Political Representatives."

12. The full wording for these questions went as follows. To measure perceptions of fair value, we asked, "Thinking about the taxes that you pay, and the benefits and services it provides, to what extent would you agree or disagree that the government provides good value for your money?" with responses on a 1–5 agreement-disagreement scale. To measure trust in

government's use of tax money, we asked, "Do you think that people who work in government waste a lot of money we pay in taxes, waste some of it, or don't waste very much of it?," with participants able to select one of the three choices contained in the question. To measure overall tax burden, we asked, "Generally, how would you describe the amount of taxes you pay overall? We mean all taxes together, including income tax, National Insurance, VAT, Council Tax etc.," with five response choices, ranging from "much too high" to "much too low." Finally, to measure tax progressivity, we asked two questions. The first read, "Assuming this remained the same, how much do you think a household in the top fifth of income (an average household income of £83,950 a year) should pay?," followed by, "And how about the bottom fifth (an average household income of £12,690 a year)?" Choices for both progressivity questions were "Less than 10% (or, much less); Between 10 and 30% (or, a little less); Between 30 and 40% (or, about the same); Between 40 and 60% (or, a little more); Over 60% (or, much more)."

13. Mullanaithan and Shafir (2013) and Shah, Mullanaithan, and Shafir (2012) both make this point.

14. Those who saw the hard primes wrote fifteen more words on average, in response to all primes, compared to those who saw the easy primes. This difference does not rise to conventional levels of significance.

Chapter 5

1. Chanley (2002) is an excellent primer on this increase.

2. In addition, the more the process is perceived to require effort, the higher the level of satisfaction reported by customers (Mohr and Bitner 1995); feelings of reciprocity and gratitude show similar increases (Morales 2005).

3. For the complete Anytown study, consult Buell, Porter, and Norton (2018).

4. The largest spender in 2013 was Procter and Gamble, with advertising expenses that amounted to $5 billion (Taube 2014).

5. You can view the video on Vimeo at https://vimeo.com/159637364 or on my personal website, http://www.ethanporter.com/.

6. The results presented here also only reflect participants who passed an attention check and a manipulation check. Results remain substantively unchanged, and statistically more precise, if we include those participants. Tables A.26, A.27, and A.28, located in the Appendix, report results for all subjects, in the same manner as the results are presented here. For this study, we reasoned that manipulation and attention checks were necessary because of the unusual nature of the treatment: On an online survey, we were asking subjects to turn on their speakers/headphones and listen to a narrated video. For this reason, subjects who could not accurately identify the sex of the narrator were removed from the analysis, as we inferred this meant they may not have been able to hear the narration. In addition, to measure attention, we heeded the advice of Berinsky, Sances, and Margolis (2014) and asked all respondents the following: "Debates about television shows are a pastime of American life. Everyone has a different favorite show. We want to know if you are paying attention to this survey. To show you are paying attention, ignore the question below and choose both 'The Sopranos' and 'Saturday Night Live.'" Then, in the following line before a menu of fifteen options, the survey stated: "What's your favorite television show? Choose only one." Those who failed this attention check have been omitted from the analysis presented in this chapter but are included in the Appendix tables.

7. On this composite trust measure, Republicans who saw the placebo registered, on average, 2.1 on the composite trust scale, while Democrats in the placebo registered a 2.4. Republicans exposed to Anytown measured, on average, a 2.2 on the composite trust scale. This scale is an index of the fourteen Pew items averaged together (but not standardized). For comparison, in the entire study, the highest measure on the scale was 3.42, while the lowest was 1.07.

8. This experiment was exceedingly well powered. Technically, it was at greater than 95% power to detect a difference between the placebo and the positive procedural operational transparency condition of the same size that was observed for the placebo and negative procedural operational transparency condition. If, in some alternative universe, the positive condition can cause people to view their government more strongly, the effect is likely entirely negligible in size.

9. The Pew battery, the redistributive questions, and the feeling thermometers toward the branches all appeared together, but I randomized the order of each question category. Some participants saw Pew questions first, then redistributive questions, then feeling thermometer questions, while others saw the opposite. And so on.

10. Recent research argues that the vagueness of these terms actually contributes to underestimation of political knowledge (Williamson 2018).

REFERENCES

Abramowitz, Alan. 2010. *The Disappearing Center*. New Haven, Connecticut: Yale University Press.

Achen, Christopher. 1975. "Mass Political Attitudes and the Survey Response." *American Political Science Review*. 69 (4): 1218–1231.

Achen, Christopher, and Larry Bartels. 2016. *Democracy for Realists*. Princeton, New Jersey: Princeton University Press.

Aldrich, John, Jacob M. Montgomery, and Wendy Wood. 2011. "Turnout as Habit." *Political Behavior*. 33 (4): 535–563.

Alesina, Alberto, Edward Glaeser, and Bruce Sacerdote. 2001. "Why Doesn't the United States Have a European-Style Welfare State?" Brookings Paper on Economics Activity: 2. 187–278.

Allcott, Hunt. 2011. "Social Norms and Energy Conservation." *Journal of Public Economics*. 95 (9–10): 1082–1095.

American Council of Trustees and Alumni. 2016. "A Crisis in Civic Education." Accessed via https://www.goacta.org/images/download/A_Crisis_in_Civic_Education.pdf.

American National Election Studies. 2012. The ANES Guide to Public Opinion and Electoral Behavior. Ann Arbor, MI: University of Michigan, Center for Political Studies [producer and distributor]. Accessed via www.electionstudies.org.

Ansolabehere, Stephen, Marc Meredith, and Erik Snowberg. 2013. "Asking about Numbers: Why and How." *Political Analysis*. 21 (1): 48–69.

Aristotle. 1962. *The Politics*. Translated by T. A. Sinclair. New York, New York: Penguin Books.

Arnold, Doug. 1990. *The Logic of Congressional Action*. New Haven, Connecticut: Yale University Press.

Ashworth, Scott, and Joshua Clinton. 2007. "Does Advertising Exposure Affect Turnout?" *Quarterly Journal of Political Science*. 2 (1): 27–41.

Baldassarri, Delia, and Andrew Gelman. 2008. "Partisans without Constraint: Political Polarization and Trends in American Public Opinion." *American Journal of Sociology*. 14 (2): 408–446.

Barnes, Lucy, Avi Feller, Jake Haselswerdt, and Ethan Porter. 2018. "Information, Knowledge, and Attitudes: An Evaluation of the Taxpayer Receipt." *Journal of Politics*. 80 (2): 701–706.

Bartels, Larry. 1994. "The American Public's Defense Spending Preferences in the Post–Cold War Era." *Public Opinion Quarterly*. 58(4): 479–508.

Bartels, Larry. 2000. "Partisanship and Voting Behavior, 1952–1996." *American Journal of Political Science*. 44 (1): 35–50.

Bartels, Larry. 2008. *Unequal Democracy: The Political Economy of the New Gilded Age*. Princeton, New Jersey: Princeton University Press.

Bauer, Monika A., James E.B. Wilkie., Jung K. Kim and Galen Bodenhausen 2012. "Cuing Consumerism: Situational Materialism Undermines Personal and Social Well-Being." *Psychological Science*. 23 (5): 517–523.

Berinsky, Adam, Greg Huber, and Gabe Lenz. 2012. "Evaluating Online Labor Markets for Experimental Research: Amazon.com's Mechanical Turk." *Political Analysis*. 20 (3): 351–368.

Berinsky, Adam, Michele F. Margolis, and Michael Sances. 2014. 'Separating the Shirkers from the Workers? Making Sure Respondents Pay Attention on Self-Administered Surveys." *American Journal of Political Science*. 58 (3): 739–753.

Bertrand, Marianne, Dean Karlan, Sendhil Mullainathan, Eldar Shafir, and Jonathan Zinman. 2010. "What's Advertising Content Worth? Evidence from a Consumer Credit Marketing Field Experiment." *Quarterly Journal of Economics*. 125 (1): 263–306.

Blair, Tony. 2001, May 21. "Speech on Public Services." Accessed January 1, 2017, at https://www.theguardian.com/politics/2001/may/21/labour.tonyblair.

Blalock, Hubert. 1979. *Social Statistics*. McGraw-Hill Series in Sociology. *2nd edition*. New York, New York: McGraw-Hill.

Blank, Rebecca, and Patricia Ruggles. 1993. "When Do Women Use AFDC Food Stamps? The Dynamics of Eligibility vs. Participation." National Bureau of Economic Research. Accessed via http://www.nber.org/papers/w4429.

Bolsen, Toby, Paul J. Ferraro, and Juan Jose Miranda. 2014. "Are Voters More Likely to Contribute to Other Public Goods? Evidence from a Large-Scale Randomized Policy Experiment." *American Journal of Political Science*. 58 (1): 17–30.

Bolton, Lisa E., and Joseph W. Alba. 2006. "Price Fairness: Good and Service Differences and the Role of Vendor Costs." *Journal of Consumer Research*. 33 (2): 258–265.

Bonica, Adam, Nolan McCarty, Keith T. Poole, and Howard Rosenthal. 2013. "Why Hasn't Democracy Slowed Rising Inequality?" *Journal of Economic Perspectives*. 27 (3): 103–124.

Bowler, Shawn, and Jeffrey A. Karp. 2004. "Politicians, Scandals, and Trust in Government." *Political Behavior*. 26 (3): 271–287.

Breen, T. H. 2005. *The Marketplace of Revolution*. New York, New York: Oxford University Press.

Buchanan, James M., and Richard E. Wagner. 1977. *Democracy in Deficit*. Indianapolis, Indiana: Liberty Fund.

Buell, Ryan W., Tami Kim, and Chia-Jung Tsay. 2017. "Creating Reciprocal Value through Operational Transparency." *Management Science*. 63 (6): 1673–1695.

Buell, Ryan W., and Michael I. Norton. "The Labor Illusion: How Operational Transparency Increases Perceived Value." *Management Science* 57 (9): 1564–1579.

Buell, Ryan W., Ethan Porter, and Michael I. Norton. 2018. "Surfacing the Submerged State: Operational Transparency Increases Trust in and Engagement with Government." Harvard Business School Marketing Unit Working Paper No. 14-034. Available via https://ssrn.com/abstract=2349801.

Busby, Ethan, Jamie Druckman, and Alexandria Fredendall. 2017. "The Political Relevance of Irrelevant Events." *Journal of Politics*. 79 (1): 346–350.

Bush, George W. 2001a. "Transcript of President Bush's Message to Congress on His Budget Proposal." Accessed via https://nyti.ms/2OsuJnx.

Bush, George W. 2001b, February 27. "Address Before a Joint Session of the Congress on Administration Goals." Accessed via https://www.presidency.ucsb.edu/documents/address-before-joint-session-the-congress-administration-goals

Bush, George W. 2001c, February 24. "The President's Radio Address." Accessed January 2, 2017, via http://www.presidency.ucsb.edu/ws/index.php?pid=45883.

Bush, George W. 2001d, July 20. "Satellite Remarks from Genoa, Italy, to a Tax Relief Celebration in Kansas City, Missouri." *Public Papers of the Presidents of the United States, 2001*, Book 2: *George W. Bush*. Washington, D.C.: Government Printing Office.

Busse, M., J. Pope, D. Pope, and J. Silva Risso. 2015. "The Psychological Effect of Weather on Car Purchases." *Quarterly Journal of Economics*. 130 (1): 371–414.

Camerer, Colin F. 2003. *Behavioral Game Theory*. Princeton, New Jersey: Princeton University Press.

Campbell, Andrea Louise. 2009. "What Americans Think of Taxes." In *The New Fiscal Sociology: Taxation in Comparative and Historical Perspective*. Pages 48–67. Edited by

Isaac William Martin and Ajay K. Mehrotra. New York, New York: Cambridge University Press.

Campbell, Angus, Phillip E. Converse, Warren E. Miller, and Donald E. Stokes. 1960. *The American Voter*. Chicago, Illinois: University of Chicago Press.

Carmines, Edward, and Jim Stimson. 1989. *Issue Evolution: Race and the Transformation of American Politics*. Princeton, New Jersey: Princeton University Press.

Carnes, Nick. 2013. *White-Collar Government: The Hidden Role of Class in Economic Policy-Making*. Chicago, Illinois: University of Chicago Press.

Chaiken, Shelly. 1980. "Heuristic versus Systematic Information Processing and the Use of Source versus Message Cues in Persuasion." *Journal of Personality and Social Psychology*. 39 (5): 752–766.

Chandy, Rajesh, Gerard J. Tellis, Deborah J. MacInnis, and Pattana Thaivanich. 2001. "What to Say When: Advertising Appeals in Evolving Markets." *Journal of Marketing Research*. 38 (4): 399–414.

Chanley, Virginia A. 2002. "Trust in Government in the Aftermath of 9/11: Determinants and Consequences." *Political Psychology*. Special Issue: 9/11 and Its Aftermath: Perspectives from Political Psychology. 23 (3): 469–483.

Chinander, Karen R., and Maurice Schweitzer. 2003. "The Input Bias: The Misuse of Input Information in Judgments of Outcomes." *Organizational Behavior and Human Decision Processes*. 91: 243–253.

Dennis Chong and James Druckman. 2007. "Framing Theory." *Annual Review of Political Science*. 10: 103–126.

Citrin, Jack, and Donald P. Green. 1986. "Presidential Leadership and the Resurgence of Trust in Government." *British Journal of Political Science*. 16 (4): 431–453.

Citrin, Jack, and John Sides. 2008. "Immigration and the Imagined Community in Europe and the United States." *Political Studies*. 56 (1): 33–56.Clinton, William Jefferson, and Al Gore. 1992. *Putting People First*. New York, New York: Three Rivers Press.

Cohen, Lizabeth. 2003. *A Consumers' Republic*. Cambridge, Massachusetts: Harvard University Press.

Cole, Bruce. 2002, June 11. "Our American Amnesia." *Wall Street Journal*.

Converse. Phillip. 1964. "The Nature of Belief Systems in Mass Publics." *Critical Review*. 18 (1–3): 1–74.

Coppock, Alexander. 2017. "Generalizing from Survey Experiments Conducted on Mechanical Turk: A Replication Approach." Accessed via https://alexandercoppock. files.wordpress. com/2016/02/coppock_generalizability2.pdf.

Coppock, Alexander, and Oliver A. McClellan. 2017. "Validating the Demographic, Political, Psychological, and Experimental Results Obtained from a New Source of Online Survey Respondents." Accessed via http://alexandercoppock.com/ projectpages_CM_participant. html.

Cushman, John H., Jr. 2001. "Tax Rebate Draws a Mixed Response." *New York Times*. Accessed via https://nyti.ms/2paqSjS.

Dahl, Robert. 1961. *Who Governs? Democracy and Power in an American City*. New Haven, Connecticut: Yale University Press.

Delli Carpini, Michael X., and Scott Keeter. 1997. *What Americans Know about Politics and Why It Matters*. New Haven, Connecticut: Yale University Press.

Dewey, John. 1927. *The Public and Its Problems*. New York, New York: Henry Holt and Company.

DiJulio, Bianca, Mira Norton and Mollyann Brodi. 2016. "Americans' Views on the U.S. Role in Global Health." Kaiser Family Foundation. Accessed via https://www.kff.org/global-health-policy/poll-finding/americans-views-on-the-u-s-role-in-global-health/

Downs, Anthony. 1960. "Why the Government Budget Is Too Small in a Democracy." *World Politics*. 12 (4): 541–563.

Druckman, James. 2001. "On the Limits of Framing Effects: Who Can Frame?" *Journal of Politics.* 63 (4): 1041–1066.

Druckman, Jamie, and Thomas J. Leeper. 2012. "Learning More from Political Communication Experiments: Pretreatment and Its Effects." *American Journal of Political Science.* 56 (4): 875–896.

Druckman, James, and Arthur Lupia. 2000. "Preference Formation." *Annual Review of Political Science.* 3 (June): 1–24.

Eagly, A. H., and S. Chaiken. 1984. "Cognitive Theories of Persuasion." *Advances in Experimental Social Psychology.* 17: 267–359.

Eger, Maureen. 2010. "Even in Sweden: The effect of immigration on support for welfare state spending." *European Sociological Review.* 26(2): 203–217.

Ellis, Christopher, and Jim Stimson. 2012. *Ideology in America.* New York, New York: Cambridge University Press.

Elster, Jon. 2009. "Norms." In *The Oxford Handbook of Analytical Sociology.* Edited by Peter Bearman and Peter Hedström. Pages 195–217. New York, New York: Oxford University Press.

Emmons, William. 2012. "Don't Expect Consumer Spending to Be the Engine of Economic Growth It Once Was." Federal Reserve Bank of St. Louis. Accessed via https://www.stlouisfed.org/publications/regional-economist/january-2012/dont-expect-consumer-spending-to-be-the-engine-of-econom.

Endres, Kyle, and Costas Panagopolous. 2017. "Boycotts, Buycotts, and Political Consumerism in America." *Research and Politics.* https://doi.org/10.1177/2053168017738632

Feldman, Stanley. 1988. "Structure and Consistency in Public Opinion: The Role of Core Beliefs and Values." *American Journal of Political Science.* 32 (2): 416–440.

Feldman, Stanley, and John Zaller. 1992. "The Political Culture of Ambivalence: Ideological Responses to the Welfare State." *American Journal of Political Science.* 36 (1): 268–307.

Foner, Eric. 1984. "Why Is There No Socialism in the United States?" *History Workshop* 17: 57–80.

Forsythe, Robert, Joel Horowitz, N. E. Savin, and Martin Sefton. 1994. "Fairness in Simple Bargaining Experiments." *Games and Economic Behavior.* 6(3): 347–369.

Fowler, Anthony. 2017. "Partisan Intoxication or Policy Voting?" University of Chicago mimeo. Accessed via https://drive.google.com/file/d/1QxDrA_vzO-x_FxPmVQ1lLnPdFS3XmG7a/view.

Fowler, Anthony, and Andrew Hall. 2018. "Do Shark Attacks Influence Presidential Elections?" *Journal of Politics.* 80 (4): 1423–1437.

Fowler, Anthony, and B. Pablo Montagnes. 2015. "College Football, Elections, and False-Positive Results in Observational Research." *Proceedings of the National Academy of Sciences.* 112 (45): 13800–13804.

Fripp, Jon, Deborah Fripp and Michael Fripp. 2000. *Speaking of Science: Notable Quotes on Science, Engineering and the Environment.* Eagle Rock, VA: LLH Technology Publishing.

Galchen, Rivka. 2018, June 4th. "The Teachers' Strike and the Democratic Revival in Oklahoma." *New Yorker.* Pages 38–43.

Gallup. 2017, May 6. "Americans' Views of Socialism, Capitalism Are Little Changed." Accessed via https://bit.ly/2DZOgtm.

Galston, William. 2001. "Political Knowledge, Political Engagement, and Civic Education." *Annual Review of Political Science.* 4: 217–234.

Gentzkow, Matthew, and Stefano DellaVigna. 2009. "Persuasion: Empirical Evidence." National Bureau of Economic Research. Accessed via http://www.nber.org/papers/w15298.

Gerber, Alan, Donald P. Green, and Christopher W. Larimer. 2008. "Social Pressure and Voter Turnout: Evidence from a Large-Scale Field Experiment." *American Political Science Review.* 102 (1): 33–48.

Gerber, Alan, and Gregory Huber. 2009. "Partisanship and Economic Behavior: Do Partisan Differences in Economic Forecasts Predict Real Economic Behavior?" *American Political Science Review.* 103 (3): 407–426.

Gerber, Alan and Donald Green. 2012. *Field Experiments: Design, Analysis, and Interpretation.* New York, New York: W. W. Norton.

Gest, Justin. 2016. *The New Minority: White Working-Class Politics in an Age of Immigration and Inequality.* New York, New York: Oxford University Press.

Gibson, James L., and Gregory Caldeira. 2009. *Citizens, Courts, and Confirmations: Positivity Theory and the Judgments of the American People.* Princeton, New Jersey: Princeton University Press.

Gigerenzer, Gerd, and Peter M. Todd. 2000. *Simple Heuristics That Make Us Smart.* New York, New York: Oxford University Press.

Gilens, Martin. 2000. *Why Americans Hate Welfare: Race, Media, and the Politics of Antipoverty Policy.* Chicago, Illinois: University of Chicago Press.

Gilens, Martin. 2001. "Political Ignorance and Collective Policy Preferences." *American Political Science Review.* 95 (2): 379–396.

Glickman, Lawrence. 2009. *Buying Power: A History of Consumer Activism in America.* Chicago, Illinois: University of Chicago Press.

Gore, Al. 1993. "From Red Tape to Results: Creating a Government That Works Better and Costs Less." Washington, D.C.: Office of the Vice President.

Green, Donald, Bradley Palmquist and Eric Schickler. 2002. *Partisan Hearts and Minds: Political Parties and the Social Identities of Voters.* New Haven, Connecticut: Yale University Press.

Grim, Ryan, and Sabrina Siddiqui. January 8, 2013. "Call Time for Congress Shows How Fundraising Dominates Bleak Work Life." Huffington Post. Accessed via https:// bit.ly/ 2OpiKXF.

Gross, Kimberly, Ethan Porter, and Thomas J. Wood. 2019. "Identifying Media Effects through Low-Cost, Multiwave Field Experiments." *Political Communication.* 36 (2): 272–287.

Grynaviski, Jeff. 2010. *Partisan Bonds: A Unifying Account of Politicians, Political Parties, and Their Reputations.* New York, New York: Cambridge University Press.

Gurman, Mark, and Brad Stone. 2018, April 23. "Amazon Is Said to Be Working on Another Big Bet: Home Robots." Bloomberg. Accessed via https://www.bloomberg.com/news/articles/ 2018-04-23/amazon-is-said-to-be-working-on-another-big-bet-home-robots

Gustafson, Krystina. 2017, February 17. "Amazon Hints at One of Its Best-Kept Secrets: How Many Prime Members It Has." CNBC. Accessed via https://www.cnbc.com/2017/02/17/ amazon-hints-at-its-big-secret-how-many-prime-membershtml.

Guth, Werner, R. Schmittberger, and B. Schwarze. 1982. "An Experimental Analysis of Ultimatum Bargaining." *Journal of Economic Behavior and Organization.* 3(4): 367–388.

Guth, Werner, and Richard Teitz. 1990. "Ultimatum Bargaining Behavior: A Survey and Comparison of Experimental Results." *Journal of Economic Psychology.* 11: 417–449.

Habermas, Jurgen. 1989. *The Structural Transformation of the Public Sphere.* Cambridge, Massachusetts: MIT Press.

Hacker, Jacob. 2002. *The Divided Welfare State.* New York, New York: Cambridge University Press.

Hacker, Jacob, and Paul Pierson. 2010. "Winner-Take-All Politics: Public Policy, Political Organization, and the Precipitous Rise of Top Incomes in the United States." *Politics and Society.* 38 (2): 152–204.

Hacker, Jacob, Philipp Rehm, and Mark Schlesinger. 2013. "The Insecure American: Economic Experiences, Financial Worries, and Policy Attitudes." *Perspectives on Politics.* 11 (1): 23–49.

Hainmueller, Jens, Jonathan Mummolo, and Yiqing Xu. Forthcoming. "How Much Should We Trust Estimates from Multiplicative Interaction Models? Simple Tools to Improve Empirical Practice." *Political Analysis.*

Hamilton, Alexander, John Jay, and James Madison. 1788 [2011]. *The Federalist Papers* (Dover Thrift Editions). Mineola, New York.

Hansen, John Mark. 1998. "Individuals, Institutions, and Public Preferences over Public Finance." *American Political Science Review.* 92 (3): 513–531.

Hansen, Michael, Elizabeth Levesque, Jon Valant, and Diana Quintero. 2018. "The 2018 Brown Center Report on American Education: How Well Are American Students Learning?" Brookings Institution.

Hartz, Louis. 1955. *The Liberal Tradition in America*. New York, New York: Harcourt Books.

Haws, Kelly L., and William O. Bearden. 2006. "Dynamic Pricing and Consumer Fairness Perceptions." *Journal of Consumer Research*. 33 (3): 304–311.

Healy, Andrew, Neil Malhotra, and Cecilia Hyunjung Mo. 2010. "Irrelevant Events Affect Voters' Evaluations of Government Performance." *Proceedings of the National Academy of Sciences*. 107 (29): 12804–12809.

Herd, Pamela, and Don Moynihan. 2018. *Administrative Burden: Policymaking by Other Means*. New York, New York: Russell Sage Foundation.

Hibbing, John R., and Elizabeth Theiss-Morse. 2002. *Stealth Democracy: Americans' Beliefs about How Government Should Work*. New York, New York: Cambridge University Press.

Hirschman, Albert. 1970. *Exit, Voice, and Loyalty: Responses to Decline in Firms, Organizations, and States*. Cambridge, Massachusetts: Harvard University Press.

Ho, Catherine. 2012, June 3. "Romney Suggests Business Experience Should Be Prerequisite to Presidency." *Washington Post*. Accessed via https://wapo.st/ 2QzpmEk.

Hochschild, Jennifer. 1986. *What's Fair?* New Haven, Connecticut: Yale University Press.

Hochschild, Jennifer, and Katherine Levine Einstein. 2015. *Do Facts Matter? Information and Misinformation in American Politics*. Norman, Oklahoma: University of Oklahoma Press.Hofstadter, Richard. 1948 [1989]. *The American Political Tradition and the Men Who Made It*. Revised Edition. New York, New York: Vintage Books.

Hosek, Adrienne. 2015. "Tax Preference on the Income Roller Coaster." University of California Davis mimeo. Accessed via https://drive.google.com/file/ d/0BwLuq-FTY_ zeRTN2RlJKWEVxaGs/view.

House of Commons. 2012. "Statements of Taxation." Volume 539. Accessed via https://hansard. parliament.uk/Commons/2012-01-25/debates/12012538000001/StatementsOfTaxation.

Howard, Christopher. 1997. *The Hidden Welfare State*. Princeton, New Jersey: Princeton University Press.

Ipsos Mori. 2013. "Perceptions Are Not Reality." Accessed via https://www.ipsos.com/ipsos-mori/en-uk/perceptions-are-not-reality

James, William. 1892 [1985]. *Psychology: The Briefer Course*. Edited by Gordon Allport. Notre Dame, Indiana: Notre Dame University Press.

Kahneman, Daniel. 2011. *Thinking, Fast and Slow*. New York, New York: Farrar, Straus and Giroux.

Kahneman, Daniel, Jack L. Knetsch, and Richard H. Thaler. 1986a. "Fairness and the Assumptions of Economics." *Journal of Business* 59 (4): 285–300.

Kahneman, Daniel, Jack L. Knetsch, and Richard H. Thaler. 1986b. "Fairness as a Constraint on Profit Seeking: Entitlements in the Market." *American Economic Review* 76 (4): 728–741.

Kahneman, Daniel, Jack L. Knetsch, and Richard H. Thaler. 1991. "Anomalies: The Endowment Effect, Loss Aversion, and Status Quo Bias." *Journal of Economic Perspectives*. 5 (1): 193–206.

Kahneman, Daniel, and Amos Tversky. 1979. "Prospect Theory: An Analysis of Decision under Risk." *Econometrica*. 47 (2): 263–292.

Karl, Jonathan, and Gregory Simmons. 2010. "Signs of the Stimulus." ABC News. Accessed via https://abcnews.go.com/Politics/signs-stimulus/story? id=11163180.

Karpf, David. 2012. *The MoveOn Effect: The Unexpected Transformation of American Political Advocacy*. New York, New York: Oxford University Press.

Keele, Luke J. 2005. "The Partisan Roots of Trust in Government." *Journal of Politics*. 67 (3): 432–451.

Kendall, David, and Ethan Porter. March 11, 2011. "Want to See How the Government Spends Your Tax Money? Ask for a Receipt." *Washington Post*. Accessed via https://wapo.st/ 2NNGZ4R.

Key, V. O. 1966. *The Responsible Electorate: Rationality in Presidential Voting, 1936–1960*. Cambridge, Massachusetts: Harvard University Press.

Kim, Eunji. N.d. "Entertaining Beliefs in Economic Mobility." Vanderbilt University mimeo. Accessed via https://www.dropbox.com/s/1qlylublosas4h3/Entertaining%20Beliefs%20 in%20Economic%20Mobility_Kim.pdf? dl=0.

Kinder, Don, and Nathan Kalmoe. 2016. *Neither Liberal nor Conservative: Ideological Innocence in the American Public*. Chicago, Illinois: University of Chicago Press.

Klein, Ezra. 2013, November 7. "The Budget Myth That Just Won't Die." *Washington Post*. Accessed via https://wapo.st/2MAeGlK.

Kosar, Kevin R. 2014. "Advertising by the Federal Government: An Overview." Congressional Research Service. Accessed via https://fas.org/sgp/crs/misc/ R41681.pdf/.

Krasno, Jonathan, and Donald P. Green. 2008. "Do Televised Presidential Ads Increase Voter Turnout? Evidence from a Natural Experiment." *Journal of Politics*. 70 (1): 245–261.

Kruger, Justin, Derrick Wirtz, Leaf Van Boven, and T. William Altermatt. 2004. "The Effort Heuristic." *Journal of Experimental Social Psychology*. 40: 91–98.

Kuklinski, James, and Paul J. Quirk. 2000. "Reconsidering the Rational Public: Cognition, Heuristics, and Mass Opinion." In *Elements of Reason*. Edited by Arthur Lupia, Mathew D. McCubbins, and Samuel L. Popkin. Pages 153–182. New York, New York: Cambridge University Press.

Kuklinski, James, Paul J. Quirk, Jennifer Jerit, David Schwieder, and Robert F. Rich. 2000. "Misinformation and the Currency of Democratic Citizenship." *Journal of Politics*. 62 (3): 790–816.

Kuziemko, Ilyana, Michael I. Norton, Emmanuel Saez, and Stefanie Stantcheva. 2015. "How Elastic Are Preferences for Redistribution? Evidence from Randomized Survey Experiments." *American Economic Review*. 105 (4): 1478–1508.

Lavine, Howard G., Christopher D. Johnston, and Marco R. Steenbergen. 2012. *The Ambivalent Partisan: How Critical Loyalty Promotes Democracy*. New York, New York: Oxford University Press.

Lawrence, Eric, and John Sides. 2014. "The Consequences of Political Innumeracy." *Research and Politics*. Accessed via https://doi.org/10.1177/2053168014545414.

Lenz, Gabriel. 2012. *Follow the Leader: How Voters Respond to Politicians' Policies and Performance*. Chicago, Illinois: University of Chicago Press.

Lenz, Gabriel. 2018. "Time for a Change." *Critical Review: A Journal of Politics and Society*. 30 (8): 87–106.

Levitt, Steven D., and James Snyder. 1997. "The Impact of Federal Spending on House Election Outcomes." *Journal of Political Economy*. 105 (1): 30–53.

Lewis, Randall, and David H. Reiley. 2011. "Does Retail Advertising Work? Measuring the Effects of Advertising on Sales via a Controlled Experiment on Yahoo!" Yahoo Research. Accessed via http://www.davidreiley.com/papers/DoesRetailAdvertisin pdf.

Lippmann, Walter. 1922 [1997]. *Public Opinion*. New York, New York: Free Press.

Lipset, Seymour. 1996. *American Exceptionalism: A Double-Edged Sword*. New York, New York: W. W. Norton and Company.

List, John. 2007. "On the Interpretation of Giving in Dictator Games." *Journal of Political Economy*. 115 (3): 482–493.

Listokin, Y., and D. M. Schizer. 2013. "I Like to Pay Taxes: Taxpayer Support for Government Spending and the Efficiency of the Tax System." *Tax Law Review*. 66 (2): 179–215.

Lowenstein, Roger. 2006, March 5. "Who Needs the Mortgage-Interest Deduction?" *New York Times*.

Lupia, Arthur. 1994. "Shortcuts vs. Encyclopedias: Information and Voting Behavior in California Insurance Reform Elections." *American Political Science Review*. 88 (1): 63–76.

Lupu, Noam. 2013. "Party Brands and Partisanship: Theory with Evidence from a Survey Experiment in Argentina." *American Journal of Political Science*. 57 (1): 49–64.

Luttmer, Ezro. 2001. "Group Loyalty and the Taste for Redistribution." *Journal of Political Economy*. 109 (31): 500–528.

Lybarger, Jeremy. 2019. "The Price You Pay." *The Nation.* Accessed via https:// www.thenation. com/article/archive/josh-levin-the-queen-book-review/.

Mackuen, Michael B., Robert S. Erikson, and James A. Stimson. 1992. "Peasants or Bankers? The American Electorate and the U.S. Economy." *American Political Science Review.* 86 (3): 597–611.

Mackuen, Michael B., Robert S. Erikson, and James A. Stimson. 2001. *The Macro Polity.* New York, New York: Cambridge University Press.

Mani, Anandi, Sendhil Mullainathan, Eldar Shafir, and Jiaying Zhao. 2013. "Poverty Impedes Cognitive Function." *Science* 341: 976–980.

Martins, Marielza, and Kent B. Monroe. 1994. "Perceived Price Fairness: A New Look at an Old Construct." *Advances in Consumer Research.* Edited by Chris T. Allen and Deborah Roedder John, 75–78. Provo, UT: Association for Consumer Research.

Mason, Rowena. 2014, November 2. "Tax Statements from George Osborne to Show Government Spend." *The Guardian.* Accessed via https://www.theguardian.com/politics/ 2014/nov/02/ tax-statements-george-osborne-money.

Mayhew, David. 1974. *Congress: The Electoral Connection.* New Haven, Connecticut: Yale University Press.

McClosky, Herbert. 1964. "Consensus and Ideology in American Politics." *American Political Science Review.* 58 (2): 361–382.

McClosky, Herbert, and John Zaller. 1984. *The American Ethos.* Cambridge, Massachusetts: Harvard University Press.

Meltzer, Allan, and Scott F. Richard. 1981. "A Rational Theory of the Size of Government." *Journal of Political Economy.* 89 (5): 914–927.

Merola, Vittorio, and Matthew P. Hitt. 2016. "Numeracy and the Persuasive Effect of Policy Information and Party Cues." *Public Opinion Quarterly.* 80 (2): 554–562.

Mettler, Suzanne. 2011. *The Submerged State: How Invisible Government Policies Undermine American Democracy.* Chicago, Illinois: University of Chicago Press.

Michel, Jean-Baptiste, Yuan Kui Shen, Aviva Presser Aiden, Adrian Veres, Matthew K. Gray, William Brockman, The Google Books Team, Joseph P. Pickett, Dale Hoiberg, Dan Clancy, Peter Norvig, Jon Orwant, Steven Pinker, Martin A. Nowak, and Erez Lieberman Aiden. 2010. "Quantitative Analysis of Culture Using Millions of Digitized Books." *Science.* 331 (6014): 176–182.

Moffitt, Robert. 1983. "An Economic Model of Welfare Stigma." *American Economic Review.* 73 (5): 1023–1035.

Mohr, Lois and Mary Jo Bitner. 1995. "The role of employee effort in satisfaction with service transactions." *Journal of Business Research.* 32 (3): 239–252.

Mondak, Jeffrey J. 1993. "Public Opinion and Heuristic Processing of Source Cues." *Political Behavior.* 15 (2): 167–192.

Montgomery, Jacob M., Brendan Nyhan, and Michelle Torres. 2018. "How Conditioning on Posttreatment Variables Can Ruin Your Experiment and What to Do about It." *American Journal of Political Science.* 62 (3): 760–775.

Morales, Andrea C. 2005. "Giving Firms an "E" for Effort: Consumer Responses to High-Effort Firms." *Journal of Consumer Research.* 31 (4): 806–812.

Mullanaithan, Sendhil, and Eldar Shafir. 2013. *Scarcity: Why Having Too Little Means So Much.* New York, New York: Times Books.

Mullinix, Kevin J., Thomas J. Leeper, James N. Druckman, and Jeremy Freese. 2015. "The Generalizability of Survey Experiments." *Journal of Experimental Political Science.* 2 (2): 109–138.

Mummolo, Jonathan and Erik Peterson. 2019. "Demand Effects in Survey Experiments: An Empirical Assessment." 113 (2): 517–529.

National Transit Database. 2013. "2013 Annual Databases FFA10." Accessed via https://www. transit.dot.gov/ntd/2013-annual-databases-ffa10.

Neal, David T., Wendy Wood, and Jeffrey M. Quinn. 2006. "Habits: A Repeat Performance." *Current Directions in Psychological Science*. 15 (4): 198–202.

Neblo, Michael A., Kevin M. Esterling, and David J. Lazer. 2018. *Politics with the People: Building a Directly Representative Democracy*. New York, New York: Cambridge University Press.

Newport, Frank. 2017. Gallup. "Americans' Confidence in Institutions Edges Up." Accessed via http://news.gallup.com/poll/212840/americans-confidence-insti aspx.

Niskanen, William. 1971. *Bureaucracy and Public Economics*. New York, New York: Elgar Press.

Norpoth, Helmut, Michael S. Lewis-Beck, and William Jacoby. 2008. *The American Voter Revisited*. Ann Arbor, Michigan: University of Michigan Press.

Nyhan, Brendan, Ethan Porter, Jason Reifler, and Thomas J. Wood. 2017, June 29. "Taking Corrections Literally but Not Seriously? The Effects of Information on Factual Beliefs and Candidate Favorability." Accessed via https://ssrn.com/abstract= 2995128 or http://dx.doi.org/10.2139/ssrn.2995128.

Obama, Barack. 2011. "Remarks by the President in State of Union Address." Accessed via https://obamawhitehouse.archives.gov/the-press-office/ 2011/01/25/remarks-president-state-union-address.

Obama, Barack. 2009. "Remarks by the President to A Joint Session of Congress on Health Care." Accessed via https://obamawhitehouse.archives.gov/the-press-office/remarks-president-a-joint-session-congress-health-care

Office of the Under Secretary of Defense. 2012. "Operation and Maintenance Overview Fiscal Year 2013." Department of Defense. Accessed via https://comptroller. defense.gov/portals/45/documents/defbudget/fy2013/fy2013_ om_overview.pdf.

Oliver, Richard L. and John E. Swan. 1989. "Consumer Perceptions of Interpersonal Equity and Satisfaction in Transactions: A Field Survey Approach." *Journal of Marketing*. 53 (2): 21–35.

Oliver, Eric and Thomas J. Wood. 2018. "Enchanted America: How Intuition and Reason Divide Our Politics." Chicago, Illinois: University of Chicago Press.

Organisation for Economic Co-operation and Development (OECD). 2020. "Revenue Statistics OECD Countries: Comparative Tables." Accessed via https://stats.oecd.org/Index. aspx?DataSetCode=REV.

Pear, Robert. October 29, 2015. "Obama Administration Campaign Will Publicize Health Care Subsidies." *New York Times*.

Pesca, Mike. 2003, October 30. "The $600,000 Medicare Blimp." NPR. Accessed via https://www.npr.org/templates/story/story.php?storyId=1485039.

Petty, Richard, and John T. Cacioppo. 1986. "The Elaboration Likelihood Model of Persuasion." *Advances in Experimental Social Psychology*. 19: 123–191.

Piketty, Thomas, and Emanuel Saez. 2003. "Income Inequality in the United States, 1913–1998." *Quarterly Journal of Economics*. 118 (1): 1–39.

Piketty, Thomas, and Emanuel Saez. 2007. "The Evolution of Top Incomes: A Historical and International Perspective." *American Economic Review, Papers and Proceedings*. 96 (2): 200–205.

Piston, Spencer. 2018. *Class Attitudes in America*. New York, New York: Cambridge University Press.

Popkin, Samuel. 1991. *The Reasoning Voter: Communication and Persuasion in Presidential Campaigns*. Chicago, Illinois: University of Chicago Press.

Porter, Ethan. 2010. "Can't Wait 'til Tax Day!" *Democracy: A Journal of Ideas*. Accessed via https://democracyjournal.org/magazine/16/cant-wait-til-tax-day/.

Porter, Ethan, and Thomas J. Wood. 2016. "Race, Interracial Families, and Political Advertising in the Obama Era: Experimental Evidence." *Political Communication*. 33 (3): 481–502.

Porter, Ethan, and Thomas J. Wood. 2019. *False Alarm: The Truth about Politics Mistruths in the Trump Era*. New York, New York: Cambridge University Press.

Putnam, Robert. 1993. *Making Democracy Work*. Princeton, New Jersey: Princeton University Press.

Putnam, Robert D. 1995. " Tuning In, Tuning Out: The Strange Disappearance of Social Capital in America." *PS: Political Science & Politics* 28(4): 664–83.

Putnam, Robert. 2000. *Bowling Alone: The Collapse and Revival of American Community*. New York: Simon and Schuster.

Rahn, Wendy. 1993. "The Role of Partisan Stereotypes in Information Processing about Political Candidates." *American Journal of Political Science*. 37 (2): 472–496.

Rawls, John. 1971. *A Theory of Justice*. Cambridge, Massachusetts: Harvard University Press.

Rehm, Philipp, Jacob Hacker, and Mark Schlesinger. 2012. "Insecure Alliances: Risk, Inequality, and Support for the Welfare State." *American Political Science Review*. 106 (2): 386–406.

Rivlin, Alice. 1989. "The Continuing Search for a Popular Tax." *American Economic Review Papers and Proceedings*. 79 (2): 113–117.

Rohrer, Doug, Christine R. Harris, and Harold Pashler. 2015. "Do Subtle Reminders of Money Change People's Political Views?" *Journal of Experimental Psychology: General*. 144 (4): 73–85.

Sachdev, Ameet. 2015, October 23. "How an Insurance Startup's Slowdown Is Disrupting the Illinois Marketplace." *Chicago Tribune*.

Sances, Michael. 2017. "Attribution Errors in Federalist Systems: When Voters Punish the President for Local Tax Increases." *Journal of Politics*. 79 (4): 1286–1301.

Sandel, Michael. 2012. *What Money Can't Buy: The Moral Limits of Markets*. New York, New York: Farrar, Straus and Giroux.

Satz, Debra. 2008. "The Moral Limits of Markets: The Case of Human Kidneys." *Proceedings of the Aristotelian Society*. 108: 269–288.

Schultz, Marisa. May 1, 2018. "'I Can't Afford an Apartment': Congressmen Sleeping in Offices Cry Poverty." *New York Post*. Accessed via https://nyp.st/2rl3yk3.

Sears, David O., and Jack Citrin. 1985. *Tax Revolt: Something for Nothing in California*. Cambridge, Massachusetts: Harvard University Press.

Shah, Anuj, Sendhil Mullanaithan and Eldar Shafir. 2012. "Some Consequences of Having Too Little." *Science*. 338: 682–685.

Shapiro, Matthew D., and Joel Slemrod. 2003. "Consumer Response to Tax Rebates." *American Economic Review*. 93 (1): 381–396.

Shear, Michael D., and Tanzina Vega. 2014, March 19. "Administration Plays to Young in Health Push." *New York Times*.

Sides, John. 2011. "The Effects of a Tax Receipt." YouGov. Accessed via https://today.yougov.com/topics/politics/articles-reports/2011/06/20/effects-tax-receipt.

Sides, John, Michael Tesler, and Lynn Vavreck. 2018. *Identity Crisis: The 2016 Presidential Campaign and the Battle for the Meaning of America*. Princeton, New Jersey: Princeton University Press.

Skocpol, Theda, and Vanessa Williamson. 2012. *The Tea Party and the Remaking of Republican Conservatism*. New York, New York: Oxford University Press.

Sniderman, Paul, Richard A. Brody, and Phillip E. Tetlock. 1991. *Reasoning and Choice: Explorations in Political Psychology*. Cambridge Studies in Public Opinion and Political Psychology. New York, New York: Cambridge University Press.

Soss, Joe. 1999. "Lessons of Welfare: Policy Design, Political Learning, and Political Action." *American Political Science Review*. 93 (2): 363–380.

Sovey, Allison, and Donald P. Green. 2011. "Instrumental Variables Estimation in Political Science: A Readers' Guide." *American Journal of Political Science*. 55 (1): 188–200.

Spector, Joseph. 2016. "NY Spent $207M on Ads over 3 Years." Gannett. Accessed via https://www.wgrz.com/article/money/ny-spent-207m-on-ads-over-3-years/ 63527472.

Spenkuch, Jörg L., and David Toniatti. 2016. "Political Advertising and Election Outcomes." CESifo Working Paper No. 5780. Munich: Center for Economic Studies and Ifo Institute (CESifo).

Stouffer, Samuel, Carl Iver Hovland, Arthur A. Lumsdaine, and Fred D. Sheffield. 1949. *Studies in Social Psychology in World War II*. Princeton, New Jersey: Princeton University Press.

Taber, Charles, and Milton Lodge. 2013. *The Rationalizing Voter*. New York, New York: Cambridge University Press.

Taube, Aaron. 2014. "The 12 Companies That Spend the Most on Advertising." *Business Insider*. Accessed via https://www.businessinsider.com/12-biggest-advert proctor-and-gamble-spent-5-billion-on-ads-12.

Thaler, Richard H. 1985. "Mental Accounting and Consumer Choice." *Marketing Science* 4 (3): 199–214.

Thaler, Richard H. 1988. "Anomalies: The Ultimatum Game." *Journal of Economic Perspectives* 2 (4): 195–206.

Thaler, Richard H. 1999. "Mental Accounting Matters." *Journal of Behavioral Decision Making.* 12: 183–206.

Tiebout, Charles. 1956. "A Pure Theory of Local Expenditures." *Journal of Political Economy.* 64 (4): 416–424.

Titmuss, Richard. 1958. *Essays on the Welfare State.* London: Allen Unwin, 1958.

Tocqueville, Alexis de. 1835 [2001]. *Democracy in America.* New York, New York: Signet Classics.

Tomz, Michael, and Paul Sniderman. 2005. "Brand Names and the Organization of Mass Belief Systems." Stanford University mimeo. Accessed via https://bit.ly/2xfe14f.

Trentman, Frank. 2016. *Empire of Things: How We Became a World of Consumers, from the Fifteenth Century to the Twenty-First.* New York, New York: HarperCollins.

Trump, Donald. 2015, June 16. "Here's Donald Trump's Announcement Speech." *Time.* Accessed via https://ti.me/1GLpmYD.

U.S. Bureau of Economic Analysis. 2020, March 30. Personal Consumption Expenditures (PCE). Accessed via FRED, Federal Reserve Bank of St. Louis, https://fred.stlouisfed. org/series/ PCE.

Veblen, Thorstein. 1899 [1999]. *The Theory of the Leisure Class: An Economic Study of Institutions.* New York, New York: Oxford University Press.

Velez, Yamil Ricardo, and Benjamin J. Newman. 2019. "Tuning in, Not Turning Out: Evaluating the Impact of Ethnic Television on Political Participation." *American Journal of Political Science.* 63 (4): 808–823.

Verba, Sidney, Kay Schlozman, and Henry Brady. 2012. *The Unheavenly Chorus: Unequal Voice and the Broken Promise of American Democracy.* Princeton, New Jersey: Princeton University Press.

Vohs, Kathleen D., Nicole L. Mead, and Miranda R. Goode. 2006. "The Psychological Consequences of Money." *Science* 314 (5802): 1154–1156.

Vohs, Kathleen D., Nicole L. Mead, and Miranda R. Goode. 2008. "Merely Activating the Concept of Money Changes Personal and Interpersonal Behavior." *Current Directions in Psychological Science.* 17 (3): 208–212.

Wallace, David Foster. 2009. *This Is Water: Some Thoughts, Delivered on a Significant Occasion, about Living a Compassionate Life.* New York, New York: Little Brown and Co.

Walmart. 2013. "Walmart Launches National Advertising Campaign to Show 'The Real Walmart.'" Accessed via https://corporate.walmart.com/newsroom/2013/05/03/ walmart-launches-national-advertising-campaign-to-show-the.

Watts, Duncan. 2017. "Should Social Science Be More Solution-Oriented?" *Nature Human Behaviour.* 1 (1): 1–5.

Weber, Max. 2020. *Charisma and Disenchantment: The Vocation Lectures (New York Review Books Classics).* Edited by Paul Reitter and Chad Wellmon. New York, New York: NYRB Classics.

Williamson, Vanessa. 2017. *Read My Lips: Why Americans Are Proud to Pay Taxes.* Princeton, New Jersey: Princeton University Press.

Williamson, Vanessa. 2018. "Public Ignorance or Elitist Jargon? Reconsidering Americans' Overestimates of Government Waste and Foreign Aid." *American Politics Research.* 47 (1): 152–173.

Wood, Wendy, and David T. Neal. 2009. "The Habitual Consumer." *Journal of Consumer Psychology.* 19: 579–592.

Young, Iris Marion. 2000. *Inclusion and Democracy.* New York, New York: Oxford University Press.

Zaller, John. 1992. *The Nature and Origins of Mass Opinion.* New York, New York: Cambridge University Press.

Zeelenberg, M., and R. Pieters. 2004. "Beyond Valence in Customer Dissatisfaction: A Review and New Findings on Behavioral Responses to Regret and Disappointment in Failed Services." *Journal of Business Research.* 57 (4): 445–455.

INDEX